PROTESTANT BIBLICAL
INTERPRETATION

PROTESTANT BIBLICAL INTERPRETATION

A Textbook of Hermeneutics

BY

BERNARD RAMM

THIRD REVISED EDITION

BAKER BOOK HOUSE
Grand Rapids, Michigan

ISBN: 0-8010-7600-5

Copyright, 1970, by
Baker Book House Company

Eleventh printing, January 1979

DEDICATION

This volume is dedicated with Christian affection to Dean Earl Kalland of the Conservative Baptist Seminary of Denver, Colorado; a friend, scholar, and Christian.

ACKNOWLEDGMENTS

The author wishes to express his gratitude to the following publishing houses for permission to quote from their publications:

James Nisbet & Co.: *Types of Modern Theology*, by H. R. Mackintosh.

The Macmillan Company: *The Bible in the Church* (copyright, 1948), by R. W. Grant.

The Presbyterian Guardian: *The Infallible Word*.

Charles Scribner's Sons: *Faith and History*, by R. Niebuhr.

E. P. Dutton & Co.: *Apologia pro vita sua*, by Newman.

FOREWORD

Protestant Biblical Interpretation has set no publishing records since its first edition. But it has evidently served a need in the Church of Jesus Christ and went into a second edition and now a third edition. Both the first and second editions have been translated into Japanese.

We have not made a total rewriting of the book but added new matters that have come up in hermeneutics such as the New Hermeneutic, and we have more vigorously reorganized our basic theory by rewriting Chapters 3, 4, and 5.

A student of hermeneutics of the present faces two very cumberson problems. First, the amount of literature, directly or indirectly, bearing all topics of hermeneutics is beyond any one man's ability to read it all. The materials from Germany alone, in periodicals and books, could keep any scholar busy all the time. Second, the Barth-Bultmann controversy, and the development of the New Hermeneutic have made hermeneutics the most fundamental or at least controversial problem in theology. We are now going through a hermeneutical debate perhaps not less serious than that of the Reformation. And that issue itself is worthy of an entire book. The more traditional items of hermeneutics have been almost pushed to the edge.

Bernard Ramm

Seminary Knolls
Covina, California

AUTHOR'S PROLOGUE

The author has endeavored to present that system of hermeneutics which most generally characterizes conservative Protestantism. In pursuit of this goal we have not defended any specific school of thought within Protestantism.

The material has been, therefore, kept general, and individual instructors may make their own emphases. Some writers on hermeneutics devote considerable space to detailed exposition or illustrations. We have tried to restrict our illustrations to a minimum, leaving that part of hermeneutics to the teacher to supply. Other writers defend distinctive doctrines that a literal method leads to, e.g., hyperdispensationalism, dispensationalism, or premillennialism. In our view of hermeneutics these are different conclusions that men have come to following the same general method of interpretation.[1] They are the result of the interpreter's skill or art, or lack of the same. It is our purpose to lay bare the essential features of the literal system. If we commence defending specific doctrines, we confuse hermeneutics with exegesis.

Greek and Hebrew words have been put in italics. Those who know the languages may resort to them, and those not

---

[1] For example Graber definitely claims that dispensationalism and ultradispensationalism do *not differ in their respective hermeneutical systems*. The difference is in exegesis of various passages of Scripture. John B. Graber, *Ultradispensationalism* (unpublished doctoral dissertation, Dallas Theological Seminary, 1949), p. 1.

familiar with them will not be too confused by the presence in the script of the original languages.

The word 'literal' is offensive to some even within the conservative circle. In subsequent definitions, however, we make clear what the word means in our system of hermeneutics. The reader may turn to our citation in Chapter III in which E. R. Craven so clearly defines what is meant by 'literal.' There is no other word that can serve our purposes except possibly 'normal.' But the use of that word has its limitations and problems.

A special word of gratitude is to be extended to Dr. Gleason Archer for linguistic help; Dr. Edward Carnell for assistance in the chapter dealing with neo-orthodoxy; Dr. Wilbur Smith for many valuable suggestions throughout the book; Dr. Charles Feinberg for correcting the manuscript and giving valuable assistance in every way; Professor Walter Wessel for reading parts of the manuscript; Miss Inez McGahey for reading the manuscript for grammatical matters; Miss Barbara Pietsch for typing the manuscript; and to my wife for help on literary and grammatical matters.

We are grateful to God that this book in its first edition has been used in Christian schools literally around the entire world. Since the first edition we have rethought some problems, and read wider in hermeneutical literature. We have rewritten much of the book and changed the order of it in certain places.

The preaching and pulpit teaching in our land is not as yet sufficiently guided by a sound hermeneutics. One saying of Alexander Carson has stayed with us during most of this revision and could well be the theme of this revised edition:

"No man has a right to say, as some are in the habit of saying, The Spirit tells me that such or such is the meaning of such a passage. How is he assured that it is the Holy Spirit, and that it is not a spirit of delusion, except from the evidence that the interpretation is the legitimate meaning of the words?" (*Examination of the Principles of Biblical Interpretation,* p. 23.)

PREFACE

St. Luke, in his record of what has been called by some the most beautiful chapter in all the Bible, the account of the walk of the risen Lord with the two disciples on the way to Emmaus, tells us that Jesus, "beginning from Moses, and from all the prophets, interpreted to them in all the scriptures the things concerning himself." The word here translated *interpreted* is the Greek word *diermeneuo*. If we take away the two first letters, the prefix, and give a rough breathing to that initial letter "e" we have exactly the word from which our word *hermeneutics* is derived, meaning, then, the science of interpretation. (In the New Testament this word, in its various forms, may be found, e.g., in Matt. 1:23; Mark 5:41; 15:22,34; John 1:8,38; 9:7; Acts 4:36; 9:36; 13:8; I Cor. 12:10; 14:28; Heb. 7:2.) Hardly any study in the whole vast realm of intellectual life could be more important than the science of hermeneutics as applied to the Word of God, that which gives us an understanding of the eternal revelation of God to men. When such is absent not only have men misinterpreted the word, but they have taken falsehood out of the truth, and thus have deceived many when they should have led them out of darkness into light.

Half a century ago the great London preacher, Dr. Joseph Parker, delivered a sermon on the phrase, "which being interpreted is," which he entitled "The Interpreter."

Perchance most of the readers of this book have not seen a copy of this sermon, I would like in this preface to confront this generation of Bible students once again with the opening and closing paragraphs, from the heart and

mind of him who did so much to awaken new interest in the
Word of God in the London of another generation:

" 'Which being interpreted,"—that is what we need: a man to
tell us the meaning of hard words and difficult things and mysteries which press too heavily upon our staggering faith. The
interpretation comes to us as a lamp, we instantly feel the com-
fort and the liberty of illumination. When we heard that word
Emmanuel we were staggered; it was a foreign word to us, it
brought with it no home associations, it did not speak to anything that was within us; but when the interpreter came, when
he placed his finger upon the word and said to us. The meaning
of this word is God with us, then we came into the liberty and
into the wealth of a new possession.

"So we need the interpreter. We shall always need him. The
great reader will always have his day, come and go who may.
We want men who can turn foreign words, difficult languages,
into our mother tongue; then how simple they are and how
beautiful, and that which was a difficulty before becomes a gate
opening upon a wide liberty. We need a man who can interpret
to us the meaning of confused and confusing and bewildering
events; some man with a key from heaven, some man with divine
insight, the vision that sees the poetry and the reality of things,
and a man with a clear, simple, strong, penetrating voice who
will tell us that all this confusion will one day be shaped into
order, and all this uproar will fall into the cadences of a celestial
and endless music. We shall know that man when we meet him;
there is no mistaking the prophet; he does not speak as other
men speak, he is not in difficulty or in trouble as other men are;
on his girdle hangs the key, the golden key, that can open the
most difficult gates in providence and in history, and in the daily
events that make up our rough life from week to week. How
distressing is the possibility that a prophet may have been amongst
us, and we may have mistaken him for a common man! How
much more we might have elicited from him if we had listened
more intently to his wonderful voice! What miracles of music he
might have wrought in our nature; but we take the prophet
sometimes as a mere matter of course: he is a man in a crowd,

his specialty we overlook, and we know not that he is talking to us from the mountain of the heavens, from the altar of the temple unseen. . . .

"It is the prophet's business to interpret things to us, to tell us that everything has been from the beginning, to assure us that there are no surprises in providence, to calm our hearts with the deep conviction that God has seen the end from the beginning, and that nothing has occurred on all this theatre of time which God did not foresee and which God cannot control. The devil is but a black servant in the kitchen of God; the devil has limited chains; he counts the links, he would like to make seven eight, he strives to strain the links into greater length, he cannot do it, he was chained at the first, he has been chained ever since, he will be chained for ever—hallelujah! the Lord reigneth! There is but one throne, and all hell is subject to the governance and the authority of that throne . . .

" 'Which being interpreted.' We need the interpreter every day. We say, Affliction, and he says, I will interpret that word to you; it needs interpretation, it is a very bitter word, but affliction being interpreted is chastening, refining, sanctifying, making meet for the Master's use. The Cross being interpreted is law, righteousness, pardon, redemption, atonement, salvation. Being misinterpreted, it is to one class a sneer, to another an offence, to another foolishness; but to believe its interpretation at its best, it is the power of God and the salvation of God. Man being interpreted is child of God, son of the Eternal, a creature made in the image and likeness of God, and meant to live with God and to glorify Him for ever. The Church being interpreted is the most vital centre of the most blessed influence, an association of souls that love the Cross, that live in Christ, that are saved by Christ, and that have no joy that is not consonant with the purposes of God. God being interpreted is Love."

Probably in no department of Biblical and theological study has there been such a lack of worthwhile literature in the twentieth century as in the field of Biblical hermeneutics. The nineteenth century witnessed the appearance of

the best hermeneutical works the Church has ever known:
the twentieth century has seen practically none that are
important—trivial, wretchedly written, fragmentary works,
without exact scholarship and incapable of making real contributions to this study. The older works are now all out of
print, and some of them would prove too bulky, too exhaustive for present needs. Moreover, so much has occurred
in the last sixty years bearing directly upon Biblical interpretation that a new volume on hermeneutics has long
been overdue. Vast discoveries in the ancient lands of the
Bible, great strides in linguistics, in the understanding of
ancient Hebrew, and Ugaritic, and the earlier Semitic
languages, new emphases on certain portions of the Word
of God, and the sudden appearance in history of a resur-
rected Israel, along with the crazy interpretations of certain
parts of the Word of God by cults that are now winning
converts by the thousands—all these call for a new work in
the field of Biblical interpretation. I have taught hermeneutics from time to time, and unless I have missed something more important than anything I have been able to discover for use in classroom work, it is my opinion that this
volume by Dr. Ramm is the only work covering the entire
field of hermeneutics that has been published in the last
forty years suitable and satisfactory for seminary work.

The author of this volume, from whom I believe many
notable works will yet be forthcoming, if the Lord wills, Dr.
Bernard Ramm, received his B.A. degree from the Univer-
sity of Washington in 1938, followed by a B.D. degree from
Eastern Baptist Seminary in Philadelphia. In 1947 Mr.
Ramm received his M.A. degree from the University of
Southern California, and in the spring of 1950 had conferred
upon him by the same institution the degree of Doctor of
Philosophy, in the preparation for which he specialized in
the field of the philosophy of science. While at Eastern
Baptist Theological Seminary, he earned the Middler's
Scholarship Award, and the Church History prize. After a

short period as pastor of the Lake Street Baptist Church of Glendale, California, Mr. Ramm for one year, 1943–1944, was Professor of Biblical Languages in the Los Angeles Baptist Theological Seminary; from 1944 to the spring of 1950, he was the head of the Department of Philosophy and Apologetics at the Bible Institute of Los Angeles. During this time he was a Mid-Term Lecturer at Western Baptist Theological Seminary, the lectures later appearing in his first work, *Problems in Christian Apologetics*. As this book comes from the press, Dr. Ramm begins his new work as Associate Professor of Philosophy in Bethel College and Seminary in St. Paul, Minnesota.

Personally, it amazes me that one as young as Dr. Ramm has been able to produce such a mature work as this volume will immediately appear to be to those who know something of the problems and the literature of hermeneutics. Teachers in Bible institutes and professors in theological seminaries will unite in gratitude to this young man for making available for them a greatly needed textbook. I predict that in the next two years it will be the accepted text for hermeneutical studies in the majority of conservative schools in this country, where men are being trained in that holiest of all work, the interpretation of the Word of God, the group which Dr. Alexander Whyte called "that elect and honorable and enviable class of men that we call students of New Testament exegesis . . . the happiest and the most enviable of all men who have been set apart to nothing else but to the understanding and the opening up of the hid treasures of God's Word and God's Son."

Wilbur M. Smith

Pasadena, California

Note: Dr. Parker's sermon, '"The Interpreter," appears in his *City Temple Pulpit*, London, 1899, pp. 40–47.
The words quoted from Dr. Whyte are to be found in his inimitable work, *The Walk, Conversation, and Character of Jesus Christ Our Lord*, p. 53.

TABLE OF CONTENTS

CHAPTER   PAGE

  I. Introduction   1

 II. Historical Schools   23

III. The Protestant System of Hermeneutics . .   93

 IV. The Protestant System of Hermeneutics
     (Continued)   128

  V. The Protestant System of Hermeneutics
     (Continued)   149

 VI. The Doctrinal Use of the Bible   163

VII. The Devotional and Practical Use of the Bible . 185

VIII. The Problem of Inerrancy and Secular Science
     in Relation to Hermeneutics   201

 IX. The Interpretation of Types   215

  X. The Interpretation of Prophecy   241

 XI. The Interpretation of Parables   276

     Epilogue   289

     Index of Names   291

     Index of Scripture   293

     Index of Topics   295

CHAPTER I

INTRODUCTION

A. THE NEED FOR HERMENEUTICS

HERMENEUTICS is the science and art of Biblical interpretation. It is a science because it is guided by rules within a system; and it is an art because the application of the rules is by skill, and not by mechanical imitation. As such it forms one of the most important members of the theological sciences. This is especially true for conservative Protestantism which looks on the Bible as *sola fidei regula* and not as just *prima fidei regula*. *Sola fidei regula* is the Reformation position that the Bible is the only authoritative voice of God to man. The Roman Catholic Church and the Eastern Oriental Church accept the Bible as the first or primary authority among other authorities, *e.g.*, the moral unanimity of the Fathers, the ancient Creeds, the decisions of the ecumenical councils, and oral tradition.

These additional authorities function to help interpret the Scriptures. In that conservative Protestantism takes *only* the Bible as authoritative, there is no secondary means of making clear the meaning of the Bible. Therefore we know what God has said by the faithful and accurate interpretation of the Scriptures. The authorities of the Roman Catholic and Eastern Oriental Churches will not be ignored by a careful exegete, but he will consider them as helps and assistants, human and fallible, not as divine authorities.

1. *The Primary Need*

That God has spoken in Holy Scripture is the very heart of our faith and without this certainty we should be left to

1

the relativity and dubiousness of *human* knowledge. God has spoken! But what has He said?

This is the primary and basic need of hermeneutics: *to ascertain what God has said in Sacred Scripture; to determine the meaning of the Word of God.* There is no profit to us if God has spoken and we do not know what He has said. Therefore it is our responsibility to determine the meaning of what God has given to us in Sacred Scripture.

To determine what God has said is a high and holy task. With fear and trembling each should be ever so careful of that which he has adopted as his method of Biblical interpretation. Upon the correct interpretation of the Bible rests our doctrine of salvation, of sanctification, of eschatology, and of Christian living. It is our solemn responsibility to know what God has said with reference to each of these. This can be done only if we have carefully, thoroughly, and systematically formulated that system of Biblical interpretation which will yield most readily the native meaning of the Bible.

Further, we need to know the correct method of Biblical interpretation so that we do not confuse the voice of God with the voice of man. In every one of those places where our interpretation is at fault, we have made substitution of the voice of man for the voice of God. We need to know hermeneutics thoroughly if for no other reason than to preserve us from the folly and errors of faulty principles of understanding God's Word.

Because Scripture has not been properly interpreted the following has been urged as the *voice of God:* in that the patriarchs practiced polygamy we may practice it; in that the Old Testament sanctioned the divine right of the king of Israel, we may sanction the divine right of kings everywhere; because the Old Testament sanctioned the death of witches, we too may put them to death; because the Old Testament declared that some plagues were from God, we may not use methods of sanitation, for that would be thwarting the purposes of God; because the Old Testament forbade usury in the agrarian commonwealth of Israel we may not employ it in our economic system; because the Scripture makes certain remarks about the suffering of women in childbirth we may not approve any method of easing the pain; because tithing was a law (*de jure*) in Israel, it is a law to the Church—and, incidentally, when it was so considered the people were tithed to such a point of penury that the Church had to check it before complete economic exhaustion prevailed.

A sound hermeneutics would have prevented all of this. It would prevent an uncritical and unrealistic application of the Old Testament to Christian morality. It would prevent an expositor from using some mere phrase as an eternal principle of morality. It would prevent the effort of trying to force some binding principle upon contemporary life from an obscure Old Testament incident. It would prevent the justification of ritualism and priestcraft from an improper extension of the Tabernacle worship and sacrificial system.

The result of an erratic hermeneutics is that the Bible has been made the source of confusion rather than light. "There is no folly, no God-dishonouring theology, no iniquity, no sacerdotal puerility," writes Edward White, "for which chapter and verse may not be cited by an enslaved intelligence. And under these circumstances it is impossible to express in adequate terms the importance of a correct estimate and exposition of 'The Bible' " (*Inspiration*, p. 153). In Bassanio's mouth Shakespeare puts these words: "In religion, what damned error but some sober brow will bless it, and approve it with a text, hiding the grossness with fair ornament" (*The Merchant of Venice*, Act III, scene 2).

Certainly many of the doctrinal variations in Christendom are due to differences in interpretation. As our subsequent historical study will reveal there are major differences in approach to the interpretation of the Bible among the Roman Catholics, Eastern Oriental Church, and Protestantism. The hermeneutical systems of orthodoxy, neo-orthodoxy, and religious liberalism have very important divergences. Even a cursory reading of the literature of Christian Science will bring to light the fact that a different system of Biblical interpretation is being employed than that which is characteristic of historic Protestantism. Cults and sects employ one or more specialized principle of Biblical interpretation which makes their basic hermeneutics a different species from that of the Reformers and historic Protestantism. Differences in eschatology arise from the adoption of different principles of prophetic interpretation.

The only way to clear the atmosphere and to determine what is right and wrong, proper and improper, orthodox and heretical, is to give one's self to a careful study of the science of Biblical hermeneutics. Otherwise we deal with symptoms, not with causes; we debate about superstructure when we should be debating about foundations.

It is important, therefore, to determine how God's Word is to be understood that we may know what God has said. This is the chief and foremost need for hermeneutics.

2. *The Secondary Need*

The second great need for a science of hermeneutics is *to bridge the gap between our minds and the minds of the Biblical writers.* People of the same culture, same age, and same geographical location understand each other with facility. Patterns of meaning and interpretation commence with childhood and early speech behaviour, and by the time adulthood is reached the principles of interpretation are so axiomatic that we are not aware of them.

But when the interpreter is separated culturally, historically, and geographically from the writer he seeks to interpret, the task of interpretation is no longer facile. The greater the cultural, historical, and geographical divergences are, the more difficult is the task of interpretation. In reading the Bible we find ourselves with a volume that has great divergences from us.

The most obvious divergence is that of *language*. The

Bible was written in Hebrew, Aramaic, and Greek. To formulate rules to bridge this gap is one of the most important tasks of Biblical hermeneutics. The basic problem at this point is that languages are structurally different. The English language is analytic in structure. The *sense* of a sentence depends largely on word order. "The rat ate the cheese" does not have the same meaning as "the cheese ate the rat" although the same words are used in both sentences. Greek is an agglutinative language, and so declines nouns and adjectives, and conjugates verbs. Hence one can alter the order of a Greek sentence two or three different ways and still get the same meaning, for meaning is not basically dependent on *word order*, but on *word endings*.

To translate from Greek to English is not the simple task of finding an English word for each Greek word. The translator has to tack back and forth between languages that are structurally different. He has the tricky job of trying to find equivalents in the English verb system of forms in the Greek verb system.

Nor is it easy to find words in English that closely match the word in the Hebrew or Greek text. Each word is a little pool of meanings. Here again it taxes the learning and judgment of the wisest scholars to decide out of the pool of meanings which is the meaning intended in a given sentence, and then to try to match it with some word in the English language which is itself a pool of meanings.

There is also the *culture-gap* between our times and Biblical times which the translator and interpreter must bridge. Culture, in the anthropological sense, is all the ways and means, material and social, whereby a given people carry on their existence. Until we can recreate and understand the cultural patterns of the various Biblical periods we will be handicapped in our understanding of the fuller meaning of Scripture. For example, the web of relationships among husband, wife, concubines and children that existed in Abraham's time, has now been recovered from clay tablets. Abraham's treatment of Hagar is now seen as protocol in terms of these relationships. Joseph's shaving before he saw Pharaoh, his receiving Pharaoh's ring, and his wearing the gold chain about his neck, are now understood as Egyptian practices. Many of the features in the parables of our Lord are drawn from the manners and customs of the people of his day, and the better understanding of the parables is dependent upon a knowledge of the Jewish culture of that century.

A knowledge of marriage customs, economic practices, military systems, legal systems, agricultural methods, etc., is all very helpful in the interpretation of Scripture.

The *geography* of the various Bible lands is very instrumental for understanding the Sacred Text. The geography of Egypt is apparent in many of the features of the Ten Plagues as recorded in Exodus. Some light is shed on the life of Christ and the travels of Paul by a knowledge of Palestinian and near-East geography. References to towns, places, rivers, mountains, plains, lakes, and seas all lend a flicker of light to the meaning of the Bible if we will study them with the help of geographical science.

The understanding of most passages of Scripture is dependent on some understanding of *history*. If geography is the scenery of Scripture, history is the plot of Scripture. Each incident is dependent on a larger historical context for its better understanding. To understand the life of Christ it is necessary to know what occurred during the inter-Biblical period. We must know something of the Roman rule of the entire ancient world; Roman practices with reference to local governments; and the history of Roman rule in Palestine.

To understand Paul's travels, it is necessary to know the history of the various provinces of Asia Minor. Sir William Ramsay has demonstrated how much such historical knowledge helps to interpret the book of Acts. And what may be said of the life of Paul and of the life of our Lord, pertains to the entire Bible.

In summary, the two great needs for the science of hermeneutics are: (i) that we may know what God has said, and (ii) that we may span the linguistical, cultural, geographical, and historical gaps which separate our minds from those of the Biblical writers. Speaking of the fact that in modern times a host of data have come to light with reference to the geography, culture, and history of the Bible, Barrows correctly says:

The extended investigations of modern times in these departments of knowledge have shed a great light over the pages of inspiration, *which no expositor who is worthy of the name will venture to neglect.*[1]

B. GENERAL INTRODUCTION

1. *Assumptions*

The conservative Protestant interpreter comes to his text believing in its divine inspiration. This is not an assumption but the demonstration of the theologian and the apologist. Exegesis itself is involved in demonstrating the divine inspiration of Scripture, to be sure. But exegetical work is carried on within a circle of theological conviction, and the conservative Protestant works within a circle which affirms the divine inspiration of the Holy Bible. This also involves the demonstration of the true canon of Scripture. Theological considerations and historical criticism unite to settle the problem of the canon. The Jewish faith accepts its Hebrew Old Testament as the only inspired Scripture. The Roman Catholic faith adds to these books the Apocryphal books and the New Testament. The Protestants accept the Jewish canon for the Old Testament rejecting the Apocryphal books, and have the same canon in the New Testament as the Catholics.

When an interpreter sets out to interpret *Scripture*, the

---

[1] *Companion to the Bible*, p. 525. Italics are ours.

boundary of Scripture must be determined. It is the study
of the Sacred Canon which determines the boundary of Scripture. The interpreter presumes that the Protestant canon
has been demonstrated to be the true content of Sacred Scripture.

After the Sacred Canon has been settled, the next task is
to determine its truest text. There is no single manuscript
of the Old or New Testament which is *the official manuscript.*
There are *manuscripts.* A study of these manuscripts reveals
many differences. The first task is to collect all the manuscripts and other materials which will help to determine the
true text. The second task is to work out *basic theory* concerning how the true text is to be determined. The third task is to
determine how the basic theory determines the text of any
given verse.

The publication of the Revised Standard Version and the
discussion it provoked revealed how improperly many ministers understood the problems of textual criticism. The dele-
tion of a phrase or verse was judged as tampering with the
Bible. But if some previous copyist added to the Scripture,
the only sane thing to do is to delete his addition. The
textual critic is not trying to add to nor take away from the
Word of God, *but to determine what was the original wording
of the Word of God.*

Textual criticism is complicated and difficult. Enormous
labors have been spent on collecting, collating, and interpreting the readings. This material is presented in critical
editions of the Hebrew and Greek Testaments. Textual criticism is absolutely necessary. The careful and faithful interpreter will avail himself of the findings of textual criticism
and will endeavor to determine his text before he commences
his actual exegesis.

After the most careful scrutiny by scholars of the Old and
New Testament texts, it is now evident that the Old and New
Testaments are the best preserved texts from antiquity. The
number of really important textual variations of the New

Testament that cannot be settled with our present information is very small, and the new manuscripts available from the various caves around the Dead Sea show the remarkable purity of our present Old Testament text.

After the canon and text have been settled, the matters of *historical criticism* must be discussed. Lower criticism is the Biblical science which determines the text of Scripture. Historical criticism deals with the literary and documentary character of the books of the Bible. Historical criticism deals with such matters as authorship of the book, date of its composition, historical circumstances, the authenticity of its contents, and its literary unity. Historical criticism is a necessary Biblical science if we wish a faith that is neither gullible nor obscurantistic.

Because men with little regard for traditional views of historical criticism and some with no respect for the divine inspiration of Scripture have written much in this field, historical criticism is sometimes known as *radical* criticism or *German rationalism*. It was called *radical* because of the novelty and extremeness of many of the positions defended in contrast to traditional views. It was called *German rational-ism* because many of the leaders in the radical movement were Germans. Sometimes it is called *higher criticism*. "Higher" in contrast to "lower" meant no more than historical or literary criticism in contrast to lower or textual criticism. But unfortunately the term *higher criticism* became synonymous with *radical* criticism, and so the expression is now ambiguous. Because these radical critics engaged in many innovations they were also called *neologists* and their views, *neologism*.

Unfortunately, due to the heated controversy of radical criticism with conservative and traditional [2] scholarship, the

---

[2] By traditional in this sentence we mean referring to those opinions about dates and authorships of Biblical books as held from great antiquity by the Jews and by the early Christian Church, which though not infallible, are held as reliable until proven otherwise. The *conserva-*

entire task of historical criticism has not been given the attention by conservative scholarship that it deserves. Literary and historical criticism of the Bible is not an evil but a necessity, and no man can do full justice to a book of the Bible till he has done the best he can to determine who wrote the book, when it was written, if its contents are authentic, and if the book is a literary unit or not.[3]

These three things hermeneutics assumes as having been accomplished. It is at this point that exegesis begins. The study of the canon determines the inspired books; the study of the text determines the wording of the books; the study of historical criticism gives us the framework of the books; hermeneutics gives us the rules for the interpretation of the books; exegesis is the application of these rules to the books; and Biblical theology is the result.

2. *Definitions*

The word *interpretation* occurs in both Testaments. The Hebrew word *pathar* means "to interpret," and *pithron* means an interpretation. Most of the usages in the Old Testament refer to the interpretation of dreams for they were usually symbolic in form and their meaning therefore was not obvious.

The word occurs many times in many forms in the New Testament (*hermēneia*, interpretation; *hermēneuō*, to interpret; *diermēneuō*, to interpret, to explain; *methermēneuomai*, to interpret, to translate; *dysermēneutos*, difficult to interpret; *diermēneutes*, interpreter; *epilusis*, interpretation).

---

tive position is frequently the *traditional* position, but not uniformly so. The belief in the authenticity and genuineness of Scripture involves *ex hypothesi* that many of the traditional views are the correct ones.

[3] "Exegesis proper presupposes textual and literary criticism of the document. The exegete of the New Testament has to know, for instance, whether the text upon which he works represents the original text of the autographs, or the textual form of the fourth century. His work also presupposes knowledge of the historical background of the author, the document, and its subject matter." Otto A. Piper, "Principles of New Testament Interpretation," *Theology Today*, 3:192, July, 1946.

Most of the references are to translations from Hebrew or Aramaic into Greek.

The word *hermeneutics* is ultimately derived from Hermes the Greek god who brought the messages of the gods to the mortals, and was the god of science, invention, eloquence, speech, writing, and art.

As a theological discipline hermeneutics is the science of the correct interpretation of the Bible. It is a special application of the general science of linguistics and meaning. It seeks to formulate those particular rules which pertain to the special factors connected with the Bible. It stands in the same relationship to exegesis that a rule-book stands to a game. The rule-book is written in terms of reflection, analysis, and experience. The game is played by concrete actualization of the rules. The rules are not the game, and the game is meaningless without the rules. Hermeneutics proper is not exegesis, but exegesis is applied hermeneutics.

Hermeneutics is a *science* in that it can determine certain principles for discovering the meaning of a document, and in that these principles are not a mere list of rules but bear *organic* connection to each other. It is also an *art* as we previously indicated because principles or rules can never be applied mechanically but involve the skill (*technē*) of the interpreter.

3. *Divisions*

There is no set number of divisions to the study of hermeneutics. Some writers make *psychological hermeneutics* (the requisite spiritual qualifications of the interpreter) a basic division. Others do not. Most books follow at least the two-fold division of *general* and *special* hermeneutics. General hermeneutics refers to those rules which pertain to the interpretation of the entire Bible. Special hermeneutics refers to those rules which are developed with reference to special parts of Scripture, e.g., parables, prophecy, apocalypse, and poetry.

4. *Limitations of a Mere Knowledge of Hermeneutics*

Learning the rules of hermeneutics does not make a student a good interpreter. A person with a good memory may memorize the rules of chess and yet be a mediocre player. A person may be limited in his native mental endowment, and although able to memorize the rules of hermeneutics unable to apply them with skill. A person with a good mind may go astray due to the pressure of very strong biases. Equally great scholars are to be found among Jewish, Catholic, and Protestant interpreters. It can hardly be denied that bias in this regard will prevent one scholar from seeing an opposing position sympathetically, and will in turn see his own position glow with invulnerability. Millennial and eschatological biases are the source of many over-statements, under-statements, and unguarded statements found in the literature of this subject.

A good knowledge of hermeneutics may aid a poor education but it cannot supply what is lacking from an inadequate education. To know that a man should resort to the original languages for the best interpretation does not give the interpreter the knowledge of the languages. An interpreter unfamiliar with the history of interpretation may fall into some error of long standing.

5. *Qualifications of an Interpreter*

That spiritual qualifications have an important place in the list of qualifications cannot be debated. If spiritual things are spiritually discerned only the spiritual man can discern them. If the natural or carnal mind is at enmity with God, only a regenerate mind will be at home in Scripture. That an interpreter must have the same Spirit who inspired the Bible as the *sine qua non* for interpreting the Bible has been well stated by Marcus Dods:

In order to appreciate and use the Bible, the reader of it must himself have the same spirit which enabled its writers to understand their revelation of God and to record it. The Bible is a record, but it is not a dead record of dead persons and events, but a record inspired by the living Spirit who uses it to speak to men now. . . . It is the medium through which the living God now makes himself known. But to find in it the Spirit of God the reader must himself have that Spirit.[4]

The first spiritual qualification of the interpreter is *that he be born again*. Angus and Green write: "This first principle of Bible interpretation is taken from the Bible itself. It occupies the same place, too, in the teaching of our Lord, who, in His first recorded discourse, assured Nicodemus that 'except a man be born again, he cannot see'—can neither understand the nature nor share the blessedness—of the kingdom of God." [5]

The second spiritual qualification is that a man have *a passion to know God's word*. He must have the zeal that consumes; and the enthusiasm that breeds both reverence and industry.

The third spiritual qualification is this: *let the interpreter have always a deep reverence for God*. Meekness, humility, and patience are prime virtues for understanding Holy Scripture, and these virtues are a reflection of our reverence for God. The devout and scholarly Dean Alford has said: "Approach the Holy Gospels from the side of trust and love, and not from that of distrust and unchristian doubt. . . . Depend upon it, FAITH is the great primary requisite for the right use of the Gospels." [6]

The final spiritual qualification is that of *utter dependence on the Holy Spirit to guide and direct*. A good proverb for a student of Scriptures is: *Bene orasse est bene studuisse.*[7] "To pray well is to study well." Aquinas used to pray and fast

[4] *The Nature and Origin of the Bible*, p. 102. Cf. Cellérier, *Biblical Hermeneutics*, "Psychological Hermeneutics." Pp. 56–72.
[5] Angus and Green, *Cyclopedic Handbook to the Bible*, p. 179.
[6] H. Alford, *How to Study the New Testament*, p. 13. Caps are his.
[7] Angus and Green, *op. cit.*, p. 179.

when he came to a difficult passage of Scripture. Most of the scholars whose Biblical studies have blessed the church have mixed prayers generously with their studies. The heart must be kept sensitive to the indwelling Spirit who in turn has inspired the Word.

This leading of the Holy Spirit will never be as crystal clear as the original inspiration of the Scriptures. This would be a confusion of inspiration and illumination. Inspiration is infallible, but not illumination. No man can say he has had *infallible* illumination from the Holy Spirit. The illumination of the Spirit is not the conveyance of truth for that is the function of inspiration. The Holy Spirit influences our attitudes and spiritual perception. Devout expositors who do not understand the distinction between illumination and inspiration should weigh well the words of Angus and Green:

It is necessary to complete this truth by adding that the Spirit of God does not communicate to the mind of even a teachable, obedient, and devout Christian, any doctrine or meaning of Scripture which is not *contained already in Scripture itself.* He makes men wise *up to* what is written, not beyond it.[8]

Matters of fact cannot be settled solely by spiritual means. One cannot pray to God for information about the authorship of Hebrews and expect a distinct reply. Nor is it proper to pray for information with reference to other matters of Biblical introduction expecting *a revelation* about *the revelation.*

An interpreter should have the proper educational requirements. No man in the history of the Christian church has possessed *all* such requirements. The person with an average measure of intelligence can with industry and adequate guidance from teachers and books discover the central meaning of the majority of the passages of the Bible. The requirements for understanding the principal truths of the Bible are not so strict as to shut the Bible up to the *literati.*

[8] *Loc. cit.* Italics are theirs.

Rowley has very adequately stated this truth when he wrote:

Not every interpreter can have the ideal equipment. Indeed, nor can attain to the ideal, and all that any can hope to do is to attain a reasonable balance of the qualities and varieties of equipment his task demands. To ask that every interpreter of the Bible should possess a wide linguistic equipment would be to deny the task of its interpretation to all but a handful of specialists, who might lack other equally essential qualities even though they possessed the linguistic knowledge. It does not seem unreasonable to ask, however, that all who would interpret the Bible to others should have some acquaintance with Hebrew and Greek. We should be astonished at one who claimed to be a specialist in the interpretation of Greek tragedy but who could not read Greek, or who offered to expound the Confucian classics without any knowledge of Chinese. But too often the biblical interpreter has little or no access to the original texts that he so confidently handles.[9]

In the Middle Ages theology was the queen of the sciences and therefore a student was not prepared for theology until he had been through the arts. The wisdom of a liberal arts education prior to a theological training has been justified by centuries of theological education. A short-cutting to theological education without a study of the liberal arts almost uniformly results in a cutting-short of the true dimensions of Christian theology. A good liberal arts education is the basis for good interpretation, especially a course that has been rich with studies in literature, history, and philosophy.

This should be followed by a standard theological education which should include studies in Hebrew, Greek, and theology. To be a competent Biblical interpreter a knowledge of the original languages is indispensable. It is true that not all ministers have ability in languages. However, it is also true that all our language experts should not be theological professors but as Barrows observes: "It is a principle of

[9] H. H. Rowley, "The Relevance of Biblical Interpretation," *Interpretation*, 1:10–11, January, 1947.

Protestantism, the soundness of which has been confirmed
by the experience of centuries, that there should always be
in the churches a body of men able to go behind the current
versions of the Scripture to the original tongues from which
these versions were executed." [10] These men complement the
men in the seminaries for they are in turn able to judge the
worth of the commentaries written by the professional
scholar.

The specialists must know various cognate languages. Old
Testament scholars must now delve into Aramaic, Arabic,
Ugaritic, Akkadian, and Latin. New Testament scholars can
profit from a knowledge of Aramaic and Latin. Ancient tablets and inscriptions are important in the study of the alphabet, ancient culture, and in the understanding of Hebrew
words and grammar. A knowledge of the Aramaic and Latin
enables the scholar to study ancient, valuable versions of the
Hebrew and Greek Testaments.

Finally, there are intellectual requirements for good interpretation. Hermeneutics is not only a science but an *art*.
The rules must be applied with skill and this requires intellectual ability. There must be an *openmindedness* to all
sources of knowledge. The standards of the finest scholarship must be employed with insight. A judicious use of
intellectual abilities reflects itself in a high quality of exegesis.
Such men as Lightfoot, Ellicott, Calvin, Maclaren, and
G. Campbell Morgan exhibited remarkable skill and taste
in their expositions of Scripture.

C. The Equipment of the Interpreter

An interpreter must work with tools. Certainly he ought
to work with the latest critical editions of the Hebrew, Greek,
and Septuagint texts. He must have those works which deal
with the inspiration, canon, and criticism of Scripture. He
should have standard grammars, lexicons, and concordances
of the Hebrew and Greek languages. He should consult the

[10] Barrows, *op. cit.*, p. 525.

learned commentaries of the past and present. For those students who need some guide through the labyrinth of books we suggest: Wilbur Smith, *Profitable Bible Study* (revised edition); John R. Sampey, *Syllabus for Old Testament Study;* A. T. Robertson, *Syllabus for New Testament Study; A Bibliography of Bible Study,* and, *A Bibliography of Systematic Theology* (published by The Theological Seminary Library, Princeton, New Jersey); and the list we shall submit in the next section.

Supplementary material of importance is to be had from Bible dictionaries, Bible encyclopedias, Bible atlases, and specialized books on such subjects as Bible history, archaeology, manners and customs, and Bible backgrounds.

Exegetical and expository material of worth will be found in such journals as: *Interpretation, The Expository Times, The Evangelical Quarterly, Bibliotheca Sacra, The Journal of the Society of Biblical Literature, New Testament Studies,* and *Theological Studies.*

It is often asserted by devout people that they can know the Bible competently without helps. They preface their interpretations with a remark like this: "Dear friends, I have read no man's book. I have consulted no man-made commentaries. I have gone right to the Bible to see what it had to say for itself." This sounds very spiritual, and usually is seconded with *amens* from the audience.

But is this the pathway of wisdom? Does any man have either the right or the learning to by-pass all the godly learning of the Church? We think not.

First, although the claim to by-pass mere human books and go right to the Bible itself sounds devout and spiritual *it is a veiled egotism.* It is a subtle affirmation that a man can adequately know the Bible apart from the untiring, godly, consecrated scholarship of men like Calvin, Bengel, Alford, Lange, Ellicott, or Moule. In contrast to the claim that a man had best by-pass the learned works of godly expositors, is a man like Henderson, author of *The Minor*

Prophets. He spared no mental or intellectual pains to equip himself with the necessary linguistic ability to understand the Bible, and then he read patiently and thoroughly in all the literature that might help him in his interpretation of the Scriptures. He consecrated his *entire mind* and all that that involved to the understanding of Sacred Scripture. This is truly the higher consecration.

Secondly, such a claim is the old confusion of the inspiration of the Spirit with the illumination of the Spirit. The function of the Spirit is not to communicate *new* truth or to instruct in *matters unknown,* but to illuminate what is revealed in Scripture. Suppose we select a list of words from Isaiah and ask a man who claims he can by-pass the godly learning of Christian scholarship if he can out of his own soul or prayers give their meaning or significance: Tyre, Zidon, Chittim, Sihor, Moab, Mahershalahashbas, Calno, Carchemish, Hamath, Aiath, Migron, Michmash, Geba, Anathoth, Laish, Nob, and Gallim. He will find the only light he can get on these words is from a commentary or a Bible dictionary.

It is true that commentaries can come between a man and his Bible. It is true that too much reliance on commentaries may make a man bookish, and dry up the sources of his own creativity. But the abuse of commentaries is by no means adequate grounds to forsake the great, godly, and conservative commentaries which have been to our blessing and profit.

Thomas Horne has given us some excellent advice on the use of commentaries.[11] The advantages of good commentaries are: (i) they present us with good models for our interpretation; (ii) they give us help with difficult passages. But he also warns us that: (i) they are not to take the place of Bible study itself; (ii) we are not to slavishly bind ourselves to them as to authorities; (iii) we are to use only the best ones; (iv) where their interpretations are conjectures

[11] Thomas Horne, *An Introduction to the Critical Study and Knowledge of the Holy Scriptures* (eighth edition), I:353–354.

they are to be used with utmost care; and (v) we should use original commentaries rather than those that are mere compilations of previous works.[12]

D. A SUGGESTED MINIMUM BIBLIOGRAPHY FOR EXEGETICAL WORK

(1). *Biblical Texts.* Hebrew: R. Kittel, *Biblia Hebraica* (fourth edition). Greek: Nestles, *Greek New Testament* (nineteenth edition). Septuagint: Editions of Rahlfs or Sweet.

(2). *Biblical Grammars.* Hebrew: Any of the standard introductory grammars, e.g., Yates, A. B. Davidson, or Gesenius-Kautzsch. Greek: Any of the standard introductory grammars as Machen, *New Testament Greek for Beginners,* and one or two of the intermediate and advanced grammars such as: H. Dana and J. Mantey, *A Manual Grammar of the Greek New Testament.* A. T. Robertson and W. Davis, *A New Short Grammar of the Greek New Testament.* W. D. Chamberlain, *An Exegetical Grammar of the Greek New Testament.* A. T. Robertson, *A Grammar of the Greek New Testament in the Light of Historical Research.*

(3). *Lexicons.* Hebrew: Translations and revisions of Gesenius, *Hebrew and Chaldee Lexicon to the Old Testament Scriptures* by Tregelles; or Robinson; or Brown, Driver and Briggs. L. Koehler and W. Baumgartner, *Lexicon in Veteris Testamenti Libros* (in German and English). Greek: J. H. Thayer, *A Greek Lexicon of the New Testament.* J. H. Moulton and G. Milligan, *The Vocabulary of the Greek New Testament.* H. Cremer, *Biblical Theological Lexicon of New Testament Greek.* Bauer's *Deutsches Wörterbuch zu den Schriften des Neuen Testaments* (fourth edition) will appear in English translation as a cooperative effort of the Concordia Theological Seminary and the University of Chicago Press. De-

---

[12] Further bibliographical data on commentaries will be found in: Wilbur Smith, *Profitable Bible Study* (revised edition), pp. 94–202; James Orr, "Commentaries," *The International Standard Bible Encyclopedia,* II, 680–85; C. H. Spurgeon, *Commenting and Commentaries;* R. M. Grant, "Commentaries," *Interpretation,* 2:454–64, October, 1948.

tails of this venture will be found in *Concordia Theological Monthly*, 26:33–37, January, 1955. Since 1927 under the direction of G. Kittel, German scholars have been working on a lexicon like Cremer's only on a much larger scale. It is called the *Theologisches Wörterbuch zum Neuen Testament.* Four of these masterful studies of words of the New Testament have appeared in English translation in a work edited by J. R. Coates (*Bible Key Words:* "Love," "The Church," "Sin," "Righteousness"). Some monographs on individual words have been published in English, and more translations like Coates' are sure to appear.

(4). *Concordances.* Hebrew: *Englishman's Hebrew and Chaldee Concordance.* A. B. Davidson, *Concordance of the Hebrew and Chaldee Scriptures.* Wigram, *A Handy Hebrew Concordance.* Septuagint: Hatch and Redpath, *A Concordance to the Septuagint.* Greek: W. Greenfield, *A Concordance to the Greek New Testament* (abridgment of Schmidt). *Englishman's Greek Concordance.* Hudson, *A Critical Greek and English Concordance.* Moulton and Geden, *A Concordance of the Greek New Testament.*

(5). *Dictionaries. The International Standard Bible Encyclopedia.* W. Smith, *Dictionary of the Bible.* Hastings, *Dictionary of the Bible. Dictionary of Christ and the Gospels. Dictionary of the Apostolic Church.*

(6). *Atlases.* G. A. Smith, *Historical Geography of the Holy Land.* G. A. Smith, *Historical Atlas of the Holy Land.* G. Wright and F. Filson, *The Westminster Historical Atlas of the Bible.* G. Dalman, *Sacred Sites and Ways.* J. M. Adams, *Biblical Backgrounds.* B. Maisler, *The Graphic Historical Atlas of Palestine.* Various articles in the journal, *The Biblical Archeologist.*

(7). *Archeology, History, and Culture.* W. Thomson, *The Land and the Book.* H. Dana, *The New Testament World.* S. Angus, *The Environment of Early Christianity.* C. Cobern, *The New Archeological Discoveries and their Bearing on the New Testament.* A. Deissmann, *Light from the Ancient East.*

S. Caiger, *Bible and Spade.* J. Muir, *How Firm a Foundation.*
M. Burrows, *What Mean These Stones.* M. Unger, *Archaeology and the Old Testament.* W. Albright, *From the Stone Age to Christianity.* W. Albright, *Archaeology and the Religion of Israel.* W. Albright, *The Archaeology of Palestine.* J. Finegan, *Light from the Ancient Past.* G. Barton, *Archeology and the Bible* (seventh edition). M. Muir, *His Truth Endureth.* J. Adams, *Ancient Records and the Bible.* A. Olmstead, *The History of Palestine and Syria to the Mohammedan Conquest* (somewhat outdated by archeology). W. Blaikie, *A Manual of Bible History* (with C. Mathews, revised, 1940). S. Caiger, *Archaeology of the New Testament. The Biblical Archeologist.*
    (8). *Biblical Introduction.* H. Miller, *General Biblical Introduction.* Willoughby (editor), *Study of the Bible Today and Tomorrow.* C. Manley (editor), *The New Bible Handbook.* Woolley and Stonehouse (editors), *The Infallible Word.* J. Young, *Introduction to the Old Testament.* J. Raven, *Old Testament Introduction.* M. Unger, *Introductory Guide to the Old Testament.* J. Bewer, *Literature of the Old Testament.* R. Pfeiffer, *Introduction to the Old Testament.* R. Pfeiffer, *History of New Testament Times with an Introduction to the Apocrypha.* H. Thiessen, *Introduction to the New Testament.* E. Scott, *Literature of the New Testament.* J. Moffatt, *An Introduction to the Literature of the New Testament.* F. Kenyon, *Our Bible and the Ancient Manuscripts.* W. Green, *Introduction to the Old Testament: Text.* A. T. Robertson, *Introduction to the Textual Criticism of the New Testament.*
    (9). *Commentaries. The International Critical Commentary.* J. Lange, *Commentary on the Holy Scriptures. Cambridge Bible for Schools and Colleges. The Westminster Commentaries.* J. Ellicott (editor), *The Bible Commentary for English Readers.* Jamieson, Faussett, and Brown, *Critical and Experimental Commentary. The Interpreter's Bible.* C. Cooke (editor), *The Bible Commentary.* J. Calvin, *Commentaries.* Keil and Delitzsch, *Commentaries on the Old Testament.* W. Nicoll (editor), *The Expositor's Greek Testament.*

C. Wordsworth, *Greek Testament with Notes. Cambridge Greek Testament for Schools and Colleges.* H. Alford, *The Greek Testament.* M. Vincent, *Word Studies in the New Testament.* A. T. Robertson, *Word Pictures in the New Testament.* H. Meyer, *Critical and Exegetical Commentary on the New Testament* (kept up to date in German but not English). *The Moffatt New Testament Commentary.* R. Lenski, *The Interpretation of the New Testament.*

There are several single volume commentaries on the entire Bible, e.g., *The New Bible Commentary.* They are better than no help at all, but satisfactory exegesis requires more space than a one volume commentary can afford. The famous Strack-Billerbeck, *Kommentar zum Neuen Testament aus Talmud und Midrasch,* with its wide learning in rabbinical materials yet awaits translation.

For further elaboration and evaluation of such materials see Wilbur Smith, *Profitable Bible Study* (revised edition), p. 94 ff. Also see the following articles in *Interpretation.* John Bright, "Biblical Geographies and Atlases," 2:324–36, July, 1948. James L. Kelso, "Archaeology," 2:66–73, January, 1948. Bruce M. Metzger, "Grammars of the Greek New Testament," 1:471–85, October, 1947. Balmer H. Kelley, "Hebrew Grammars and Lexicons," 2:186–98, April, 1948. Howard Tillman Kuist, "New Testament Lexicons," 1:226–37, April, 1947. Charles T. Fritsch, "Bible Dictionaries and Encyclopedias," 1:363–71, July, 1947. Robert M. Grant, "Commentaries," 2:454–64, October, 1948. Donald G. Miller, "Concordances," 1:52–62, January, 1947. John Wick Bowman, "The Rabbinic Writings," 3:437–449, October, 1949.

CHAPTER II

HISTORICAL SCHOOLS

FEW studies are so rewarding in granting insight and perspective into problems as historical studies. This is true of the history of hermeneutics.

Terry has well said:

A knowledge of the history of biblical interpretation is of inestimable value to the student of the Holy Scriptures. It serves to guard against errors and exhibits the activity and efforts of the human mind in its search after truth and in relation to noblest themes. It shows what influences have led to the misunderstanding of God's word, and how acute minds, carried away by a misconception of the nature of the Bible, have sought mystic and manifold meanings in its content.[1]

One of the cardinal mistakes in interpretation is provincialism, i.e., believing that the system in which one has been trained is the *only* system. Another mistake is to assume that certain traditional or familiar interpretations are the only adequate interpretations. Certainly hermeneutics ought to be purged of subjectivism and provincialism, and fewer studies are more capable of doing this than historical studies in interpretation.

Rather than trace the long history of interpretation from Ezra until today, the typical schools of interpretation will be presented, and this will preserve much of the historical element.

---

[1] M. S. Terry, *Biblical Hermeneutics* (revised edition), p. 31.

A. ALLEGORICAL SCHOOLS

1. *Greek Allegorism*

Allegorical interpretation believes that beneath the letter (*rhētē*) or the obvious (*phanera*) is the real meaning (*hyponoia*) of the passage.[2] Allegory is defined by some as an extended metaphor. There is the literary allegory which is intentionally constructed by the author to tell a message under historical form. Bunyan's *Pilgrim's Progress* is such a one and such allegories occur in Scripture too.[3] If the writer states that he is writing an allegory and gives us the cue, or if the cue is very obvious (as in an allegorical political satire), the problem of interpretation is not too difficult. But if we presume that the document has a secret meaning (*hyponoia*) and there are no cues concerning the hidden meaning interpretation is difficult. In fact, the basic problem is to determine if the passage has such a meaning at all. The further problem arises whether the secret meaning was in the mind of the original writer or something found there by the interpreter. If there are no cues, hints, connections, or other associations which indicate that the record is an allegory, and what the allegory intends to teach, we are on very uncertain grounds.

It may seem strange to list as our first school of interpretation the Greek school, but this is necessary to understand the historical origins of allegorical interpretation. The Greeks were not concerned with Sacred Scripture but with their own writings, and in this sense it is improper to classify them within the context of Biblical interpretation. But in that their allegorical method was adopted by both Jew and Christian they deserve this special attention.

[2] H. A. Wolfson, *Philo*, I, 115. For Greek allegorical interpretation see: *Wolfson*, ibid., I, 131–133. J. Geffcken, "Allegory," *Hastings Encyclopedia of Religion and Ethics*, I, 327–331. F. W. Farrar, *History of Interpretation*, pp. 131–136. H. P. Smith, *Essays in Biblical Interpretation*, Chapter III, "The Triumph of Allegory." K. Fullerton, *Prophecy and Authority*, p. 59 ff.

[3] Terry, *op. cit.*, Part Second, Chapter VII.

The Greeks had two noble traditions. (i) They had a religious heritage in Homer and Hesiod. Homer's influence seemed to increase with the extension of time rather than diminish. The "Bible" of the Greek was the writings of Homer and Hesiod. To question or to doubt them was an irreligious or atheistic act. (ii) They had an astute philosophical (Thales, *et al.*) and historical tradition (Thucydides and Herodotus), which developed principles of logic, criticism, ethics, religion, and science.

The *religious tradition* had many elements which were fanciful, grotesque, absurd, or immoral. The philosophical and historical tradition could not accept much of the religious tradition as it lay in the written documents. Yet, the hold of Homer and Hesiod was so great, popularly and with the thinkers, that Homer and Hesiod could not be declared worthless and forsaken. How was the tension of the two traditions to be resolved? The problem is at once *apologetic* and *hermeneutical*. It is interesting that the religious apology and the allegorical method of hermeneutics have the same historical root. The tension was relieved by *allegorizing* the religious heritage. The stories of the gods, and the writings of the poets, were not to be taken *literally*. Rather underneath is the secret or real meaning (*hyponoia*). Wolfson, Farrar, Geffcken and Smith have demonstrated how widespread this allegorical method became in Greek thought.

The important item to notice here is that this Greek tradition of allegorizing spread to Alexandria where there was a great Jewish population and eventually a large Christian population.

2. *Jewish Allegorism*

The Alexandrian Jew faced a problem similar to his fellow Greek. He was a child of Moses instructed in the law and the rest of a divine revelation. But as he mingled with the cosmopolitan population of Alexandria he soon learned of the Greek literature with its philosophical heritage. Some of

these Jews were so impressed that they accepted the teachings of Greek philosophy.

The Greek faced the tension of a religious-poetic-myth
tradition and a historical-philosophical tradition. The Jew
faced the tension of his own national Sacred Scriptures and
the Greek philosophical tradition (especially Plato). How
could a Jew cling to both? The solution was identical to the
Greek's solution to his problem. In fact, the Jew even got it
from the Greek for Farrar writes, "The Alexandrian Jews
were not, however, driven to invent this allegorical method
for themselves. They found it ready to their hands." [4]

Here is one of the strange fates of history. The allegorical
method arose to save the reputation of ancient Greek religious poets. This method of interpretation was adopted by
the Alexandrian Greeks for the reasons stated above. Then
it was bequeathed to the Christian Church. "By a singular
concurrence of circumstances," continues Farrar, "the
Homeric studies of pagan philosophers suggested first to the
Jews and then, through them, to Christians, a method of
Scriptural interpretation before unheard of which remained
unshaken for more than fifteen hundred years." [5]

The first writer who seems to have written in this Jewish
tradition of allegorism was Aristobulus (160 B.C.). His
works exist only through fragments and quotations by other
writers. Wolfson,[6] a leading Philonian scholar, believes that
Philo actually cites from Aristobulus, thus aligning himself
with those who believe that the writings (or oral teachings)
of Aristobulus antedate Philo. Aristobulus asserted (i) that

[4] Farrar, *op. cit.*, p. 134.
[5] *Ibid.*, p. 135. Wolfson (*op. cit.*) qualifies this by noting that the
rabbis themselves had commenced to do some allegorizing to make
ancient laws relevant to contemporary situations. Feldman (*The Parables and Similes of the Rabbis*) has some important material about
the use of allegorical interpretation among the rabbis. P. 3 ff. Philo
was not influenced at this point only by the Greeks but by his own
rabbinic traditions.
[6] *Op. cit.*, I, 95.

Greek philosophy borrowed from the Old Testament, especially from the Law of Moses; and (ii) that by employing the
allegorical method the teachings of Greek philosophy could
be found in Moses and the prophets.

The outstanding Jewish allegorist was Philo (born about
20 B.C.; died about A.D. 54). He was a thoroughly convinced
Jew. To him the Scriptures (primarily in the Septuagint
version) were superior to Plato and Greek philosophy. He
teaches practically a dictation-theory of inspiration he so
emphasizes the passivity of the prophet. Yet, he had a great
fondness for Greek philosophy, especially Plato and Pythag-
oras. By a most elaborate system of allegorizing he was
able to reconcile for himself his loyalty to his Hebrew faith
and his love for Greek philosophy.

One scholar notes that Philo actually had about twenty
rules which indicated that a given Scripture was to be treated
allegorically. Most of his rules however, can be classed under
general headings.[7] Philo did not think that the literal meaning was useless, but it represented the immature level of
understanding. The literal sense was the body of Scripture,
and the allegorical sense its soul. Accordingly the literal was
for the immature, and the allegorical for the mature. Nor
did Philo believe that the allegorical method denied the reality of the historical events.

There were three canons which dictated to the interpreter
that a passage of Scripture was to be allegorically interpreted: (i) If a statement says anything unworthy of God;
(ii) if a statement is contradictory with some other statement
or in any other way presents us with a difficulty; and (iii) if
the record itself is allegorical in nature.

However, these three canons spill over into many sub-

---

[7] Special attention to Philo's allegorical system is given by Gilbert,
Interpretation of the Bible, Chapter II.   Farrar, *op. cit.*, pp. 136–157.
Briggs, *Biblical Study*, p. 305 ff.   Wolfson, *op. cit.*, p. 115 ff.   Jean
Daniélou (*Origen*) sets forth the data showing how much Origen was
influenced by Philo. Pp. 178–191.

canons. (i) *Grammatical* peculiarities are hints that underneath the record is a deeper spiritual truth. (ii) *Stylistic*
elements of the passage (synonyms, repetition, etc.) indicate
that deeper truth is present. (iii) *Manipulation* of punctua-
tion, words, meaning of words, and new combinations of
words can be so done as to extract new and deeper truth from
the passage. (iv) Whenever *symbols* are present, we are to
understand them figuratively not literally. (v) Spiritual truth
may be obtained from *etymologies* of names. (vi) Finally, we
have the law of *double-application.* Many natural objects
signify spiritual things (heaven means the mind; earth means
sensation; a field, revolt, etc.).

Actual examples of this method may be found in the literature. Some of this is sound (major canon iii, and sub-canon
iv) for there are allegorical and figurative elements in Scripture. But most of it led to the fantastic and the absurd.
For example, Abraham's trek to Palestine is *really* the story
of a Stoic philosopher who leaves Chaldea (sensual understanding) and stops at Haran, which means "holes," and
signifies the emptiness of knowing things by the holes, that
is the senses. When he becomes Abraham he becomes a truly
enlightened philosopher. To marry Sarah is to marry abstract wisdom.[8]

3. *Christian and Patristic Allegorism*

The allegorical system that arose among the pagan Greeks,
copied by the Alexandrian Jews, was next adopted by the
Christian church and largely dominated exegesis until the
Reformation, with such notable exceptions as the Syrian
school of Antioch and the Victorines of the Middle Ages.

The early Christian Fathers had as their Bible the Old
Testament in Greek translation. This had been the Bible of
Christ and the Apostles judging from their citations of the
Old Testament in the New. One of the most basic convictions

[8] The validity of allegorical and typological interpretation will be
discussed in the chapter on prophecy.

of the early church was that the Old Testament was a Christian document. C. H. Dodd's work, *According to the Scripture*, is an effort to isolate out these *testimonia* of the New Testament wherein Old Testament Scriptures are used to show the Messianic witness of the Old Testament to Christianity. The New Testament itself is replete with Old Testament citations, allusions, and references. The apologetic of Matthew and Hebrews is directly a proof of the fulfilment of the Old in the New. The allegorical method of interpretation sprang from a proper motive, in spite of the fact that it was usually improper in practice.

The proper motive was the firm belief that the Old Testament was a Christian document. This ground the Church can never surrender without retreating to Marcionism in some revived form. The allegorical method was its primary means of making the Old Testament a Christian document.

It must also be kept in mind that although these writers used the allegorical method to excess, they did unconsciously use the literal method. If we underscore everything they interpret literally (even though they might not spend too much time defending the literal sense of Scripture), we discover how much the literal approach was used in actual practice. In some cases the historical (approximating the literal) is actually made part of their hermeneutical system.

Two things may be said for the allegorizing of the Fathers: (i) They were seeking to make the Old Testament a Christian document. With this judgment the Christian Church has universally agreed. (ii) They did emphasize the truths of the Gospel in their fancies. If they had not done this, they would have become sectarian.

The difficulties with the method are many. (i) There was a lack of a genuine historical sense in exegesis. The historical connections of a passage of Scripture were usually completely ignored. (ii) Their method of citing the Old Testament revealed that they had a very infantile understanding of the progress of revelation. They had the basic understanding that a great shift had taken place from the Old to the New Testament. But citing verses in the Old Testament, in themselves frequently very obscure, as if superior to verses in the New, revealed no understanding of the significance of historical and progressive revelation for hermeneutics. (iii) They considered the Old (especially) and the New Testaments filled with parables, enigmas, and riddles. The allegorical method alone sufficed to bring out the meaning of these parables, enigmas, and riddles. (iv) They confused the allegorical with the typical, and thus blurred the distinction between the legitimate and the improper interpretation of the Old Testament. The "allegorical," the "mystical," the "pneumatic," and the "spiritual," are practically synonymous. (v) They believed that Greek philosophy was in the Old Testament and it was the allegorical method which discovered it. (vi) In that the method is highly arbitrary, it eventually fostered dogmatic interpretation of the Scripture. Fullerton's judgment against the allegorical method at this point is very sharp:

Instead of adopting a scientific principle of exegesis they introduce Church authority under the guise of Tradition as the norm of interpretation. The movement of thought which we have been following now becomes associated with the great dogmatic consolidations of the second and third centuries that led directly to ecclesiastical absolutism.[9]

The curse of the allegorical method is that it obscures the true meaning of the Word of God and had it not kept the Gospel truth central it would have become cultic and heretical. In fact, this is exactly what happened when the gnostics allegorized the New Testament. The Bible treated allegorically becomes putty in the hand of the exegete. Different doctrinal systems could emerge within the framework of allegorical hermeneutics and no way would exist to determine

[9] K. Fullerton, *Prophecy and Authority*, p. 81. Italics have been omitted.

which were the true. This was precisely one of the problems in refuting the gnostics. The orthodox wished to allegorize the Old Testament, but not the New. The gnostics accused them of inconsistency. The only method of breaking an exegetical stalemate created by the use of the allegorical method is to return to the sober, proper and literal interpretation of the Scriptures. The allegorical method puts a premium on the subjective and the doleful result is the obscuration of the Word of God. To cite Fullerton again:

When the historical sense of a passage is once abandoned there is wanting any sound regulative principle to govern exegesis. . . . The mystical [allegorical] method of exegesis, is an unscientific and arbitrary method, reduces the Bible to obscure enigmas, undermines the authority of all interpretation, and therefore, when taken by itself, failed to meet the apologetic necessities of the time.[10]

To present a clearer picture of some of the patristic hermeneutical theory we shall briefly study Clement, Origen, Jerome, and Augustine.

(1). *Clement.* Clement of Alexandria found five possible meanings to a passage of Scripture.[11] (i) The *historical* sense of Scripture, i.e., taking a story in the Old Testament as an actual event in history; (ii) the *doctrinal* sense of Scripture, i.e., the obvious moral, religious, and theological teachings of the Bible; (iii) the *prophetic* sense of Scripture including predictive prophecy and typology; (iv) the *philosophical* sense which follows the Stoics with their cosmic and psychological meaning (which sees meanings in natural objects and historical persons); and (v) a *mystical* sense (deeper moral, spiritual and religious truth symbolized by events or persons).

(2). *Origen.* Patristic scholarship is indebted to Jean Daniélou for a thorough study of Origen in his book entitled *Origen.* Part II of this work is devoted to "Origen and the Bible."

[10] *Ibid.,* p. 75. Italics are his.
[11] R. M. Grant, *The Bible in the Church,* p. 64, in which he summarizes the findings of C. Mondésert, *Clément d'Alexandrie.*

Origen is in the Aristobulus-Philo-Pantaenus-Clement tradition. Daniélou shows how deeply Origen's system was marked by Philo. Origen had an apologetic motivation to be sure. He wanted to escape the crudities of lay people who were literalists to the point of taking everything symbolic or metaphorical or poetic literally. He was motivated to show that the New Testament does have its roots in the Old and so reply to the Jews. He wished to eliminate what were absurdities or contradictions in Scripture and make Scripture acceptable to the philosophically minded. His approach can be summed up as follows: [12]

(i). The *literal meaning* of the Scripture is the preliminary level of Scripture. It is the "body," not the "soul" (moral sense) nor the "spirit" (allegorical sense) of the Bible. The literal sense is the meaning of Scripture for the layman. Actually we perhaps should say "letterism" rather than literalism for reasons we pointed out in the previous paragraph.

Further, the literal sense would leave us in Judaism. If we were to take the Old Testament in a strict literal sense we would believe and practice exactly as the Jews. We escape Judaism by spiritualizing the Old Testament.

Again, the literal in Scripture is the sign of the mysteries and images of things divine. It is to provoke us to a deeper and more spiritual study of the Bible. History, for example, is to be taken symbolically. Origen has a Platonic view of history which he reinterprets by means of Christian theology. The symbolization of history does not deny the actual historicity of the story.

(ii). To understand the Bible *we must have grace given to us by Christ*. Christ is the inner principle of Scripture and only those with the Spirit of Christ can understand Scripture.

(iii). The true exegesis is *the spiritual exegesis of the Bible*. "The Bible is one vast allegory, a tremendous sacrament in which every detail is symbolic," writes Daniélou of Origen's

---

[12] Origen's hermeneutics is treated in *De Principiis*, Book IV.

fundamental thesis.[13] The Bible is a spiritual book, and its meaning is found only by spiritualizing it. Even the New Testament has elements in it which cannot be taken literally, and so must be spiritualized. In many cases this means nothing more than that a figure of speech has no literal meaning.

Origen's *spiritual* exegesis is a mixture of the typological and the allegorical. Daniélou knows that the allegorical method was greatly abused, and is not in high regard among scholars. He seeks to rescue Origen from the charge of being an allegorist by insisting that he has basically a typological exegesis. That Origen allegorized Daniélou does not deny. That his theory was much better than his practice he strongly affirms. But he does object to classifying Origen as an allegorist, pure and simple, and then condemning him because he is an allegorist. Daniélou believes that Origen has the correct Christian principle of interpretation, but that Origen poorly practiced it, and that subsequent scholarship misrepresents him.

(iv). Origen believed that *the Old is the preparation for the New*. This implies two further assertions: (a) If the Old is the preparation of the New, the New is in the Old in a concealed manner, and it is the function of the Christian exegete to bring it to the surface. This is *typological exegesis* and is based on the fundamental harmony of the Old and New Testaments. (b) If the New fulfils the Old, the Old is now superseded. There is continuity and divergence in the relationship between the New and the Old. Continuity means that the New is like the Old and therefore the Old is capable of typological interpretation. There is divergence between the New and the Old, and this means the Old is now out of date.

(3). *Jerome.* Jerome was a great Bible scholar in terms of the scholarship of antiquity. He translated the Bible into

[13] *Origen*, p. 184. Cf. Grant (*op. cit.*, p. 65 ff.) for a less sympathetic treatment of Origen.

Latin (*Latin Vulgate*) which required him to become proficient in Greek and Hebrew. He noticed that the Hebrew Bible did not contain the Apocrypha and suggested its secondary nature and that it ought to be put between the Testaments. This suggestion was not carried out until Luther. Jerome placed great emphasis on the historical and the literal.

Jerome is similar to Augustine. In theory he developed some sound principles, especially because he was influenced by the literal school of Antioch. In practice he was an allegorist. He started out as an extreme allegorist, but influenced by the school of Antioch, he retreated from the allegorical tradition in theory or principle and emphasized the historical and literal.

He insisted that the literal is not contradictory to the allegorical as the extremists in the Alexandrian school asserted. On the other hand he evaded the *letterism* of the Jews. But in practice he was a typical allegorist even to allegorizing the New Testament.

(4). *Augustine.* Augustine developed a handbook of hermeneutics and homiletics called *De Doctrina Christiana.*[14] One very interesting aspect of this treatment is that *Augustine endeavors to develop a theory of signs.* This is missed by practically all the hermeneutical studies, yet in the light of contemporary philosophy it is most important. Here is a Father of the church that in so many words indicates that a theory of signs is basic to any theory of hermeneutics. Or, Biblical hermeneutics is but a special case of semantics (or semiotic). Augustine speaks of natural objects which are percepts but not signs, e.g., a piece of wood or metal. Next he speaks of things which signify other things. A tree may signify forestry service, a shoe a shoemaker, and an anvil

---

[14] A new translation of this is: *The Fathers of the Church.* Vol. IV: *The Writings of Saint Augustine.* "Christian Instruction" translated by John J. Gavigan. Besides treatments of Augustine in standard histories of hermeneutics cf. David S. Schaff, "St. Augustine as an Exegete." *Nicene and Post-Nicene Fathers* (first series), VI, vii–xii.

the blacksmith guild. Then there are things whose sole function is to signify other things, i.e., words.

He defines a sign as: "A thing which apart from the impression that it presents to the senses, causes of itself some other thing to enter our thoughts." [15] These signs are conventional or natural. Smoke is a natural sign of fire. Conventional signs "are those which living creatures give to one another." [16] From this he proceeds to discuss sounds and speech; God's method of communication to man through speech; and speech incarnate in the written Scripture. This is typical of the genius of Augustine to have put his finger on a critical point in a discussion which sometimes took a millennium or more to realize. It is regrettable that: (i) he did not follow through with complete consistency from his theory of signs to hermeneutics; (ii) that others did not catch any glimmer of light in his remarks about signs; and (iii) that historians of hermeneutics for the most part ignore Augustine's treatment of signs.

Augustine was driven to the allegorical interpretation of Scripture by his own spiritual plight. It was the allegorical interpretation of Scripture by Ambrose which illuminated much of the Old Testament to him when he was struggling with the crass literalism of the Manicheans. He justified allegorical interpretation by a gross misinterpretation of 2 Cor. 3:6. He made it mean that the *spiritual* or *allegorical* interpretation was the real meaning of the Bible; the *literal* interpretation kills.[17] For this experimental reason Augustine could hardly part with the allegorical method.

[15] *Christian Instruction*, Bk. II, Ch. 1, paragraph 1.

[16] *Ibid.*, II, 2, 3.

[17] This abuse of this Scripture has continued throughout history and to this hour. Orthodoxy uses it to put criticism in its place ("A spiritual understanding of the Bible gives life but an academic, critical and scholarly study of the Bible kills"). Neo-orthodoxy uses it to rout the orthodox ("Existential interpretation gives life; literal interpretation is the wooden, lifeless letter"). Religious modernism also so used it against orthodoxy. Cults use it to justify their fanciful impositions on Scripture. Cf. *Confessions*, VI, 4, 6 for Augustine's statement.

Summing up Augustine's hermeneutics we would say his controlling principles were:

(i) A genuine Christian faith was necessary for the understanding of the Scriptures. The inner spirit of the exegete was as important as his technical equipment. (ii) Although the literal and historical are not the end of Scripture we must hold them in high regard. Not all of the Bible is allegorical by any means, and much of it is both literal and allegorical. Augustine's great theological works indicate that the literal method was employed far more than he admitted on paper. (iii) Scripture has more than one meaning and therefore the allegorical method is proper. The supreme test to see whether a passage was allegorical was that of love. If the literal made for dissension, then the passage was to be allegorized. Besides this he had seven other somewhat farfetched rules for allegorizing the Scriptures. He did work on the principle that the Bible had a hidden meaning, and so in his allegorical interpretations he was frequently as fanciful as the rest of the Fathers. However, whatever was allegorized was in theory to be built upon the literal and historical meaning of the text. (iv) There is significance in Biblical numbers. Augustine regarded the entire world of logic and numbers as eternal truths, and therefore numbers played a special role in human knowledge. If this is so then we can get much truth by an allegorical or symbolic interpretation of numbers in Scripture. (v) The Old Testament is a Christian document because it is a Christological document. In finding Christ in too many places however he obscured the genuine Christology of the Old Testament. (vi) The task of the expositor is to get the meaning out of the Bible, not to bring a meaning to it. The expositor is to express accurately the thoughts of the writer. (vii) We must consult the *analogy of faith*, the true orthodox creed, when we interpret. If orthodoxy represents Scripture, then no expositor can make Scripture go contrary to orthodoxy. To this must be added *love*. No man understands Scripture if he is not built up in love to God and man. Love and analogy of faith are apparently the two major controlling principles in his hermeneutics. In truth, love may be a form of spiritual intuition necessary for the deeper apprehension of Scripture. (viii) No verse is to be studied as a unit in itself. The Bible is not a string of verses like a string of beads, but a web of meaning. Therefore we must note *the context* of the verse; what the Bible says on the same subject somewhere else; and what the orthodox creed states. (ix) If an interpretation is insecure, nothing in the passage can be made a matter of orthodox faith. (x) We cannot make the Holy Spirit our substitute for the necessary learning to understand Scripture. The able interpreter must know Hebrew; Greek; geography; natural history; music; chronology; numbers; history; dialectics; natural science; and the ancient philosophers. (xi) The obscure passage must yield to the clear passage. That is, on a given doctrine we should take our primary guidance from those passages which are clear rather from those which are obscure. (xii) No Scripture is to be interpreted so as to conflict with any other —the harmony of revelation. But to do this we must *distinguish the times*. Augustine's statement ("Distinguish the times [*tempora* not *saeculae*] and you harmonize the Scriptures") means that we must take into account *progressive revelation*. Polygamy conflicts with monogamy only if we fail to note that revelation progresses. If we are aware of the progressive character of revelation we shall not make Scripture conflict. This is very different from the dispensational interpretation put on these words, which is only possible by taking *tempora* as if it meant *saeculae*.

As magnificent an effort as this appears, it is disheartening to realize how far short in so many instances Augustine came. There is hardly a rule he made which he did not frequently violate. What compensated for this was: (i) the actual usage of the literal understanding of Scripture even though such a principle was not fully developed in his hermeneutical theory; and (ii) his great theological genius which could not help but see the theological grandeur of the Scriptures.

4. *Catholic Allegorism*

It would be over-simplification to assert that the only method of exegesis during the Middle Ages was the allegorical. It would not, however, be an exaggeration to assert that the preponderance of exegetical work was allegorical.[18] To clarify terminology we should note that the scholastics divided the meaning of the Bible into the literal and the spiritual (i.e., the *spirit* is more central to human personality than the body, so the spiritual meaning of the Bible is the more important one) or the mystical (i.e., it is more refined, subtle, less obvious). Under the spiritual or mystical are the three divisions of (i) allegorical or what passes as a combination of typology and allegorism, (ii) tropological or moral interpretation, and (iii) anagogical or how the church *now* anticipates the church glorified, the eschatological sense.

The Catholic Church in imitation of the Fathers has maintained the validity of the allegorical method or the spiritual method of interpretation. We shall not try to survey the history of interpretation during the Middle Ages but will present the Catholic theory which eventually emerged from it.

In studying Catholic pronouncements on hermeneutics it is very clear that the advancement of Biblical studies by Protestants has had its telling influence on the very spirit of the Catholic approach. (i) Catholic scholars admit the extremes that allegorism was carried to by some of the Fathers and some of the Scholastics. There is no stout defense of these exaggerations in Catholic hermeneutical literature except from real patristic sentimentalists. (ii) The importance and primacy of the literal meaning of Scripture is extolled.

---

[18] Besides the general histories of hermeneutics listed at the end of this chapter, material for exegesis in the Middle Ages may be found in Beryl Smalley, *The Study of Bible in the Middle Ages* (second edition, 1952). We shall note later the literalistic Victorines.

No longer is the literal declared to be for spiritual infants or to be the mere surface of the Scripture. The position of the Alexandrians at this point especially is repudiated.

(1). Catholic scholars accept the Latin Vulgate as the authentic version for *public lectures, disputations, sermons,* and *expositions.*[19] This includes the apocryphal books as listed by the Council of Trent (Fourth Session). This puts the Catholic Church in odd position because the Hebrews wrote their Bible in Hebrew and Aramaic and the Apostles in Greek. This is common information to all Biblical scholars. It thus appears rather unusual for a translation to be given authentic status when the document may be had in the original languages. If the entire dogmatic structure of Catholic theology is based on the Latin it could be disconcerting to find it at variance with Greek and Hebrew.

One Catholic scholar states very directly the implied essence of the Catholic position: "The Greek and Hebrew texts are of the greatest value, as means in order to arrive at the genuine sense and full force of many passages in the Latin Vulgate." [20] Another scholar, however, has tried to use the Greek and Hebrew as his more basic sources in translating the Bible, and has been charged with duplicity.[21] This is a surface admission of the authenticity of the Latin but a tacit admission of the priority of the Hebrew and Greek.

(2). The Catholic interpreter obediently accepts whatever the Catholic Church has *specifically* said about matters of Biblical Introduction, and authorship of the books of the Bible.

[19] So decreed by the *Council of Trent,* Session IV. Also repeated in the *Dogmatic Decrees of the Vatican Council.*

[20] Humphry (a Jesuit) quoted by Salmon, *Apocrypha,* I, xxix (*Holy Bible Commentary*). Note that this is exactly the opposite of the Protestant position. The Protestant uses the Latin to help him understand the inspired Hebrew and Greek. Humphry says the Greek and Hebrew help in understanding the authentic Latin.

[21] Cf. the scholarly review of Knox's (Roman Catholic) translation of the Bible in the *London Times* (Literary Supplement, December 23, 1949, p. 834).

(3). The Catholic interpreter accepts all verses which the Church has officially interpreted in the sense in which they have been interpreted. All told not more than twenty such verses have been officially interpreted. Further, in some instances the Church has indicated what meaning a verse cannot have. However, the number is actually much more than this because many of the official documents of the Church involve certain definite interpretations of certain verses. The official definition of the meaning of a verse is not usually made unless the verse has become controversial and the interpretation of it must be made.

(4). The literal and historical interpretation of Scripture is the foundation of the study of the Bible.[22] Maas and Fuller both make a strong point that Catholic exegesis considers itself built on the substantial ground of the literal interpretation and historical interpretation of Scripture. This is not exactly new in their tradition. Aquinas emphasized the importance of the literal and even stated that no doctrine could be erected on spiritual exegesis. But making literal and historical interpretation such virtues is certainly due to the impact of Protestant Biblical scholarship.

(5). The Scriptures do possess a spiritual or mystical meaning which is beyond the literal. Thomas Aquinas taught very clearly that Scripture may have more than one sense because the author of Scripture is God.[23] God was able to inspire men in such a way that they wrote not only literal and his-

---

[22] Cf. A. J. Maas, "Exegesis," The Catholic Encyclopedia; V, 692–706, and "Hermeneutics," Ibid., VII, 271–276. R. C. Fuller, "The Interpretation of Scripture," A Catholic Commentary on Holy Scripture, pp. 53–60. Maas calls the First Law of hermeneutics to be the grammatical, philological, contextual and historical study of a passage of Scripture.

[23] Summa Theologica, I, 1, 10, "Whether in Holy Scripture a Word may have Several Senses." Cf. "The author of Holy Scripture is God, in Whose power it is to signify His meaning, not by words only (as man also can do) but also by things themselves. . . . That signification whereby things signified by words have themselves also a signification is called the spiritual sense, which is based on the literal and presupposes it."

torical truth but spiritual and figurative truth. Therefore, Thomas concludes, it is not proper to limit the meaning of Scripture to the literal sense.

This spiritual or mystical interpretation which is an outgrowth of the allegorizing of the early church became codified during the Middle Ages under three rules. (i) A passage may have an *allegorical* meaning. This refers to its future or prophetic meaning and includes allegorical and typological interpretation. In view of the abuses of the allegorical method many contemporary Catholics prefer the word *typological* to *allegorical*. (ii) A passage may have an *anagogical* (eschatological) meaning. It may "lead up" to the Church Triumphant. Thus the Church militant has features about it which anticipate the Church in glory. (iii) A passage may have a *tropological* meaning, i.e., teach a *tropos*, a way of life. This is the moral significance of the passage.

This spiritual meaning must be built upon the literal and historical meaning. Modern Catholic scholarship is making a serious effort to take the arbitrariness out of spiritual and allegorical exegesis. It is fully aware of the sordid history of fanciful allegorical interpretation. The Protestant scholar too must face the typical and predictive in the Old Testament, and so he likewise has a problem. It is the actual *practice* which reveals a very fundamental cleavage. When the manna in the wilderness, the passover of the exodus, the bread and wine of Melchisedec, and the diet of meal and oil by Elijah are made types of the Eucharist the Protestant objects. When Newman argues that the change of the Old Testament worship system as demanded by the New does not make a profound alteration from the material to the spiritual, again the Protestant objects.[24] Reading back into the Old Testament the sacramental and clerical system of Catholicism appears as simple *eisegesis* (reading into) and not *exegesis* (reading out of). It was this necessity of making all the Bible

[24] Jaak Seynaeve, *Cardinal Newman's Doctrine of Holy Scripture*, Part II, Newman's Hermeneutics. Pp. 197–396. Cf. pp. 260–261.

sacramental and *sacerdotal* which was one of the reasons Newman wrote that "it may be almost laid down as a historical
fact, that the mystical [allegorical] interpretation and orthodoxy will stand or fall together." [25]

(6). The Catholic Church is the official interpreter of Scripture. There are several important considerations here. First,
the Church is the *custodian* of Scripture. The Bible was not
given to the world but deposited in the Church. Hence one
of the rights of the Church is to interpret the Scriptures.
Another consideration is that the Catholics believe that
Christianity is *The Deposit of Faith* deposited in the Catholic
Church in an oral and written form. The usual Protestant
notion that the Catholics have the Bible to which they add
tradition is not quite accurate. There is the Original Tradition, or Revelation, or Deposit of Faith which is transmitted
through the centuries in an oral form (tradition), and a written form (Bible). The final consideration is that the written
form is obscure and needs an official interpreter. The average
man is not competent to interpret the Scripture because it is
a task beyond his abilities. For example a Catholic writes
that "Every biblical scholar knows perfectly well that there
is no book in the world more difficult than the Bible. It is
a sheer absurdity to say that ordinary people, with no knowledge of Hebrew or Greek or archaeology or of the writings
of the Fathers of the Church, are competent to interpret it." [26]

(i). The Church which bears the true Tradition (oral and
written) is thereby the official interpreter of the Scriptures.
Only that Church which bears the mark of apostolicity can
know the real meaning of the written tradition.

(ii). No passage of Scripture can be interpreted to conflict
with the Roman Catholic doctrinal system. "Any meaning
[of a passage of Scripture] . . . not in harmony with the fact
of inspiration and the spirit of the Church's interpretation

---

[25] J. H. Newman, *An Essay on Development of Christian Doctrine.*
P. 344.
[26] M. Sheehan, *Apologetics and Catholic Doctrine*, I, 149, fn. 13.

cannot be the true sense of Scripture," writes a Catholic author.[27] This was also maintained by the Council of Trent (Fourth Session) in which not only the Church's right as interpreter was set forth, but individual interpretation condemned. Sometimes this is called interpretation by *the analogy of faith.*

Councils, commissions, and congregations do not have the virtue of infallibility, but their interpretations of Scripture enjoy a high authority.

(7). The Fathers are to be a guide in interpretation according to three principles:

(i). The interpretation must be solely about *faith and morals.* Statements about natural or scientific matters, or historical matters are not binding.

(ii). The Father must be bearing witness to the Catholic Tradition (the *Quod ubique, quod semper, quod omnibus creditum est* [what has been believed everywhere, always, by everyone] of Vincent, the classical definition of orthodoxy), and not to personal opinion.

(iii). The Fathers must have a unanimous witness to the given interpretation.

However, even when not all three canons may be applied to a given interpretation, nevertheless the opinions of the Fathers are to be held in veneration. This veneration of the Fathers resulted in much medieval exegesis being really studies in patristics and not exegesis in the proper sense.

(8). Obscure and partial teaching of the Scripture is to be explained by the fuller teaching in the unwritten tradition of the Church. The Roman Catholic believes that he has two sources of revelation which mutually interpret each other. Scripture makes clear matters of the unwritten tradition, and unwritten tradition makes clear obscure matters

[27] A. J. Maas, "Hermeneutics," *Catholic Encyclopedia*, VII, 272. He also wrote: "Since the Church is the official custodian and interpreter of the Bible, her teaching concerning the Sacred Scriptures and their genuine sense must be *the supreme guide* of the commentator." *Ibid.*, V, 698. Italics are ours in both quotes.

in Scripture.[28] Hence the Catholic scholar does not feel it necessary to find full teaching of all his doctrines in the Bible but allusions are sufficient (e.g., prayers for the dead, veneration for Mary, confession, the supremacy of Peter). The Catholic Church does not intend to limit itself entirely to the word of Scripture. Its source of revelation is the Deposit of Faith in an unwritten and written form. The unwritten tradition may then be used to fill out what is deficient in the written form (Scripture).

(9). The Bible is to be understood in terms of *the principle of development*. No one will deny that there is considerable difference between a modern cathedral and its worship services and the fellowship gatherings of the Christians as recorded in the book of Acts. The Catholic theologian believes that the doctrines of the New Testament are *seeds* which grow and develop so that what is seen in a modern Catholic cathedral was contained in seed form in the apostolic Church of the book of Acts.

(i). First, this is justified by the principle of implication. We are bound to believe all that is in the Scriptures and that which may be *properly deduced*. The Trinity is not taught in so many words in the New Testament but the Christian Church has believed it to be a *proper deduction*.

(ii). Secondly, this is justified by the principle of *epigenesis*. Seeds do not merely enlarge. New doctrines are not determined solely by construing the necessary implications of Scripture. Seeds grow, develop and change. Yet in a real sense the "truth" of the tree is identical with the "truth" of the seed. This notion of the *epigenetic growth* of seed doc-

---

[28] Cf. "Thus the knowledge of apostolic Tradition can make up for the silence of the ambiguity of the letter of the New Testament and restore the exact sense it wanted to transmit to us." A. Bubarle, "Introduction to Holy Scripture," in A. M. Henry, *Introduction to Theology*, I, 67. "What is contained by way of outline in the written Gospel has light thrown upon it by traditions which are in their own way also bearers of the mystery of Christ." A. Liégé, "The Sources of the Christian Faith," *Ibid.*, I, 12.

trines into the elaborate doctrines of the Roman Catholic
Church was classically elaborate by J. H. Newman in his
famous work, *The Development of Christian Doctrine.* The
essay is a tacit admission that the present Catholic Church
is far removed from the apostolic Church of the New Testament.[29]

(10). The attitude of the Catholic Church toward the Protestants is contained in the Encyclical, *Providentissimus Deus*
of Leo XIII.

Though the studies of non-Catholics, used with prudence, may
sometimes be of use to the Catholic student, he should, nevertheless, bear well in mind . . . that the sense of Holy Scripture
cannot be expected to be found in writers, who being without the
true faith, *only gnaw the bark of Sacred Scripture, and never attain
its pith* [italics are ours].

B. LITERAL SCHOOLS

1. *Jewish Literalism*

The literal method of interpreting the Bible is to accept
as basic the literal rendering of the sentences unless by virtue of the nature of the sentence or phrase or clause within
the sentence this is not possible. For example, figures of
speech or fables or allegories do not admit of literal interpretation. The spirit of literal interpretation is that we
should be satisfied with the literal meaning of a text unless
very substantial reasons can be given for advancing beyond
the literal meaning, and when *canons of control* are supplied.

Ezra is considered the first of the Jewish interpreters and
the ultimate founder of the Jewish, Palestinian, hyperlit-
eralist school. The Jews in the Babylonian captivity ceased

[29] Modern Catholic scholarship has approved rather than disavowed
Newman's principle claiming although not in scholastic form it still
reflects what has been Catholic teaching. Cf. A. M. Dubarle, *op. cit.*,
I, 65. G. H. Joyce, "Revelation," *The Catholic Encyclopedia*, XIII, 4.
Walter P. Burke, "The Beauty Ever Ancient," *American Essays for the
Newman Centennial*, pp. 206–207.

speaking Hebrew and spoke Aramaic. This created the language gap between themselves and their Scriptures. It was the task of Ezra to give the meaning of the Scriptures by paraphrasing the Hebrew into the Aramaic or in other ways expounding the sense of the Scriptures. This is generally admitted to be the first instance of Biblical hermeneutics.[30]

Far removed from the land of Palestine, the Jews in captivity could no longer practice their accustomed religion (Mosaism) which included the land, their capitol city, and their temple. There could be no Mosaism with no temple, no land about which there were many regulations, and no harvest. Robbed of the national character of their religion the Jews were led to emphasize that which they would take with them, their Scriptures. Out of the captivities came Judaism with its synagogues, rabbis, scribes, lawyers, and traditions.

There is no simple manner by which Jewish exegesis can be *adequately* summed up. It is a complex system contained in a voluminous corpus of literature. Through the course of the centuries many talented rabbis expressed themselves on hermeneutics and various schools emerged (e.g., Karaites and Cabbalists). The Karaites were the literalists and the Cabbalists were the allegorists.

The Palestinian Jews did develop some sound principles of exegesis which reflected a token approach to the literal understanding of the Scriptures. Hillel formulated seven rules, Ishmael thirteen, and Eliezar thirty-two. Some of these principles are still part of a valid hermeneutics.

(i). They insisted that a word must be understood in terms of its sentence, and a sentence in terms of its context.

(ii). They taught that Scriptures dealing with similar topics should be compared, and that in some instances a third Scripture would relieve the apparent contradiction between two Scriptures.

[30] See Farrar's fine tribute to Ezra. *Op. cit.*, p. 54. However Davidson (*Old Testament Prophecy*, p. 80) lists the prophets as the first interpreters. He appeals to Isaiah 43:27. However others translate the word as "ambassador." The RSV has "mediators."

(iii). A clear passage is to be given preference over an obscure one if they deal with the same subject matter.

(iv). Very close attention is to be paid to spelling, grammar, and figures of speech.

(v). By the use of logic we can determine the application of Scripture to those problems in life Scripture has not specifically treated. In this connection some of the valid forms of the logic of deduction or implication were used by the rabbis. This is still standard procedure in theological hermeneutics.

(vi). Their insistence that the God of Israel spoke in the tongues of men was their way of asserting that the God of Israel had adapted His revelation to the recipients of it. This implies a measure of accommodation and cultural conditioning of the divine revelation.

It would not be unfair to rabbinic exegesis to assert that it did not develop a profound self-conscious and critical theory of hermeneutics. Nor would it be unfair to state that they wandered far off from the good rules they did construct.

The major weakness of their system was the development of a hyperliteralism or a *letterism*. In the intense devotion to the details of the text, they missed the essential and made mountains out of the accidental. This was based on the belief that *nothing* in Scripture was superfluous and therefore all the grammatical phenomena of the text (pleonasm, ellipsis, etc.) had an import to the interpreter. Further, because the Bible was given of God the interpreter could expect numerous meanings in the text. The combination of these two principles led to the fantastic interpretations of the rabbis. The errors were then compounded by the enormous authority given to tradition.

Eventually this system developed into the system of the Cabbalists wherein *letterism* and *allegorism* form a grotesque alliance. By the use of *notarikon* all sorts of exegetical gymnastics were performed. Each letter of a word was made to stand for another word. By use of *gemetria* they endowed words with numerical values which became grounds for arbitrary and odd associations of verses. Let the modern student who wishes to play with the numbers of the Bible first read what the Jews did with *gemetria* and so learn moderation and restraint. By the use of *termura* they permutated the letters of a word and so extracted new meanings from old words.

Fortunately the Karaites and the Spanish Jews started a more intelligent procedure for the understanding of the Old Testament, and from this new inspiration has come much valuable exegetical literature.[31]

There is one major lesson to be learned from rabbinical exegesis: the evils of *letterism*. In the exaltation of the very letters of the Scripture the true meaning of the Scripture was lost. The incidental is so exaggerated as to obscure the essential.[32] Any exegesis will go astray which bogs itself down in trivialities and *letterism*.

2. *Syrian School of Antioch*

It has been said that the first Protestant school of hermeneutics flourished in the city of Antioch of Syria, and had it not been crushed by the hand of orthodoxy for its supposed heretical connections with the Nestorians, the entire course of Church history might have been different. The Christian community was influenced by the Jewish community and the result was a hermeneutical theory which avoided the *letterism* of the Jews and the *allegorism* of the Alexandrians.

---

[31] Farrar, (*op. cit.*, Lecture II, "Rabbinic Exegesis," and, "Notes to Lecture II," and, "Notes to Lecture V"), should be read for first-hand examples of Jewish exegetical fantasies. But one must bear in mind the judgment of Abrahams that Farrar is not always fair, and that buried amidst this exegesis are some very substantial contributions to exegetical science. Cf. Israel Abrahams, "Rabbinic Aids to Exegesis," *Cambridge Biblical Essays*, pp. 159–192.

[32] Gilbert (*op. cit.*, Chapter I) lists five major criticisms of Jewish exegesis but they all boil down to one, *viz.*, the failure to develop an adequate theory of hermeneutics. In process of publication is a commentary which hopes to summarize the Jewish exegetical wisdom of the ages, *viz.*, Kasher, *Encyclopedia of Biblical Interpretation* (vol. I, 1953).

It boasted of such names as Lucian, Dorotheus, Diodorus, Theodore of Mopsuestia and Chrysostom. As a school it influenced Jerome and modulated the allegorism of Alexandria in the West. It also had an influence on medieval exegesis, and found itself again in the hermeneutics of the Reformers.

The Syrian school fought Origen in particular as the inventor of the allegorical method, and maintained the primacy of the literal and historical interpretation of the Scripture. It is true that in practice some of the Antiochenes were found dipping into allegorizing, nevertheless in hermeneutical theory they took a stout stand for literal and historical exegesis. They asserted that the literal was plain-literal and figurative-literal. A plain-literal sentence is a straightforward prose sentence with no figures of speech in it. "The eye of the Lord is upon thee," would be a figurative-literal sentence. According to the Alexandrians the literal meaning of this sentence would attribute an actual eye to God. But the Syrian school denied this to be the literal meaning of the sentence. The literal meaning is about God's omniscience. In other words literalism is not the same as *letterism*.

Further, they avoided dogmatic exegesis. Dogmatic exegesis, which kept growing in the West due perhaps to so many controversies with the heretics, eventually developed into Roman Catholic authoritarian exegesis. But the Syrians insisted that the meaning of the Bible was its historical and grammatical meaning, and interpretations must so be justified.

The Syrians insisted on the reality of the Old Testament events. They accused the allegorists of doing away with the historicity of much of the Old Testament and leaving a shadowy world of symbols. The literal and historical approach guarantees to the Old Testament history its important reality.

In place of an allegorical interpretation of the Old Testament the Syrians presented a more sane typological approach. According to the allegorists, floating above the obvious historical meaning of the Old Testament events was another more spiritual or theological meaning. But according to the Syrians the historical and the Messianic were blended together like woof and warp. The Messianic did not float above the historical, but was implicit in it. This not only weeded out much of the fanciful Old Testament Christological interpretation of the allegorists, but it rested the subject on a far more satisfactory basis. The relationship of the Old and New Testaments was made typological and not allegorical.

This also enabled the Syrians to defend the unity of the Bible from a better vantage point. They admitted the development of revelation. An allegorist might find something far richer about Jesus Christ and salvation in Genesis than in Luke. But if progressive revelation is correctly understood such a maneuver by an exegete is impossible. Secondly, they admitted that the unity of the Bible was Christological. The bond between the Two Testaments is prophecy (predictive and typological) understood in terms of (i) progressive revelation and (ii) the literal and historical exegesis of Messianic passages.

The result of these principles was some of the finest exegetical literature of ancient times. As Gilbert says, "The commentary of Theodore [of Mopsuestia] on the minor epistles of Paul is the first and almost the last exegetical work produced in the ancient Church which will bear any comparison with modern commentaries." [33] Grant observes that this school had a remarkable influence in the Middle Ages and became the pillar of the Reformation, and finally became the "principal exegetical method of the Christian Church." [34]

[33] *Op. cit.*, p. 135. Commenting on the good hermeneutical taste yet oratorical ability of Chrysostom (the "golden-mouthed," or in our idiom "the silver tongued") M. B. Riddle wrote: "Great pulpit orators do not need to indulge in mystical fancies nor does their power arise from dogmatic warping of the sense of Scripture." "St. Chrysostom as an Exegete," *Nicene and Post-Nicene Fathers* (first series), X, p. xix.

[34] Grant, *op. cit.*, p. 84.

3. The Victorines

Scholars of the medieval period have established the fact that a strong historical and literal school existed in the Abbey of St. Victor in Paris.[35] Its outstanding men were Hugo of St. Victor, Richard of St. Victor, and Andrew of St. Victor. Just as the Jewish scholarship in Antioch of Syria influenced the Christian scholars there for literalism, so the Jewish scholars of the medieval period influenced the Victorines for literalism. Miss Smalley at several points in her exposition notes the friendly relations and interactions of this school with the Jewish scholars.

The Victorines insisted that liberal arts, history, and geography were basic to exegesis. History and geography especially form the natural background for literal exegesis. Literal exegesis gave rise to doctrine, and doctrine was the natural background for allegorization. A close check is hereby put on allegorization for none is permitted that does not root in doctrine established by the literal sense.

The literal, rather than a preliminary or superficial study, was the basic study of the Bible. The Victorines insisted that the mystical or spiritual sense could not be truly known until the Bible had been literally interpreted. By literalism they did not mean *letterism* but the true and proper meaning of a sentence. This emphasis on the literal carried over into an emphasis on syntax, grammar, and meaning. True interpretation of the Bible was *exegesis*, not *eisegesis*.

4. The Reformers

The tradition of the Syrian school was reflected among the Victorines and became the essential hermeneutical theory of the Reformers. Although historians admit that the West was ripe for the Reformation due to several forces at work

[35] Cf. Beryl Smalley, *The Study of the Bible in the Middle Ages* (revised edition), Chapters III and IV. The older historians of interpretation apparently were ignorant of the existence of this school.

in European culture, nevertheless there was a *hermeneutical Reformation* which preceded the ecclesiastical Reformation.

There were two main factors that prepared the way for the Reformation in terms of hermeneutics. The first of these was the philosophical system of Occam. Occam was a nominalist, and much of the training which Luther had was in the philosophy of Occam. In Occam we find a separation of revelation and human reason. Human reason had as its territory nature, philosophy, and science. Revelation which was received through faith had for its territory salvation and theology. This was a radical separation of two elements that existed on friendlier terms in the philosophy of Aquinas. In Thomism reason not only dealt with philosophy but with natural religion, and natural religion became the mediating link between philosophy and revelation.

The two realms of grace and nature were separated by Occam. Therefore, whatever we know of God we know by divine revelation, not by human reason. The authority for theological dogma rested solely on divine revelation, and therefore upon the Bible. Thus Luther was so trained as to magnify the authority of the Bible as over against philosophy. When called upon to prove his position he appealed to Scripture and reason (logical deductions from Scripture). A traditional Catholic theologian would appeal to Scripture and reason but also to Thomistic philosophy, councils, creeds, and the Fathers. (The traditional interpretation of Luther and Occamism has been challenged by B. Haegglund: "Was Luther a Nominalist?" *Theology*, 59:226–234, June, 1956.)

The second factor was the renewed study of Hebrew and Greek. Beryl Smalley (*The Study of the Bible in the Middle Ages*) had demonstrated that Hebrew studies were not as completely lacking among the scholastics as scholars formerly thought. It was Reuchlin, a humanist and a lawyer, who translated Kimchi's Hebrew grammar into Latin so that if a man had the time he could decipher some main elements of the Hebrew language.[36] With the Renaissance came a renewed interest in Greek, and Erasmus published the first Greek New Testament in modern times in 1516. The entire Bible in its original languages was now available for study, for a Hebrew Testament had been printed by 1494. Luther learned his Latin for the priesthood and could so handle the Latin Vulgate, and he also learned his Greek and Hebrew. He had a photographic memory and this did him good service in public debate for he could recall the reading of the Greek or Hebrew on a given passage. When he thought he might be shut up in prison, he selected as his two books of consolation a Hebrew and a Greek Testament.

Luther's hermeneutical principles were: [37]

(1). *The psychological principle.* Faith and illumination were the personal and spiritual requisites for an interpreter. The believer should seek the leading of the Spirit and depend on that leading. In his *Table Talk* he writes: "We ought not to criticise, or judge the Scriptures by our mere reason, but diligently, with prayer, meditate thereon, and seek their meaning" (*On God's Word*, IV). In that Scripture was inspired it demanded a spiritual approach by the interpreter for he also wrote: "The Bible should be regarded with wholly different eyes from those with which we view other productions" (*On God's Word*, IX).

(2). *The authority principle.* The Bible is the supreme and final authority in theological matters, and is therefore above all ecclesiastical authority. Its teaching cannot be countermanded nor qualified nor subordinated to ecclesiastical authorities whether of persons or documents.

[36] For the details of Hebrew learning at the time of the Reformation and for Luther's own knowledge of the language see W. H. Koenig, "Luther as a Student of Hebrew," *Concordia Theological Monthly*, 24:845–853, Nov., 1953.

[37] Besides the standard works on history of interpretation see R. F. Surburg, "The Significance of Luther's Hermeneutics for the Protestant Reformation," *Concordia Theological Monthly*, 24:241–261, April, 1953. Farrar (*op. cit.* 326 ff.) gives two different lists of Luther's hermeneutical principles.

(3). *The literal principle.* In place of the four-fold system
of the scholastics, we are to put the literal principle. The
scholastics had developed their hermeneutics into two divisions, the literal and the spiritual. The spiritual had been
divided into three divisions (allegorical, anagogical, and tropological). Luther maintained strongly the primacy of the
literal interpretation of Scripture. In the *Table Talk* he
affirms that "I have grounded my preaching upon the literal
word" (*On God's Word*, XI). Farrar cites him as writing:
"The literal sense of Scripture alone is the whole essence of
faith and of Christian theology." [38] Briggs cites him as saying: "Every word should be allowed to stand in its natural
meaning, and that should not be abandoned unless faith
forces us to it." [39]

The literal principle implies three sub-principles:

(i). Luther rejected allegory. He calls allegorical interpretation "dirt," "scum," "obsolete loose rags," and likens
allegorizing to a harlot and to a monkey game. Yet this is
not the entire story. This was his opinion of allegory as used
by the Catholics. He was not adverse to allegory if the content were Christ and not something of the papacy. In fact
students of Luther have indicated his inconsistency at this
point for Luther himself engages in some typical medieval
allegorization. But in principle he broke with it, and in much
practice he repudiated it even though he was not entirely
free from it.

(ii). Luther accepted the primacy of the original languages.
He felt that the original revelation of God could not be truly
recovered until it was recovered from the Hebrew and Greek
Testaments. His advice to preachers was: "While a preacher
may preach Christ with edification though he may be unable
to read the Scriptures in the originals, he cannot expound or
maintain their teaching against the heretics without this in-

---

[38] *Op. cit.*, p. 327.
[39] C. A. Briggs, *History of the Study of Theology*, II, 107.

dispensable knowledge." Luther did a great deal to sponsor the revival of Hebrew and Greek studies.

(iii). The historical and grammatical principle. This is inseparable from the literal principle. The interpreter must give attention to *grammar;* to the *times, circumstances, and conditions* of the writer of the Biblical book; and to the *context* of the passage.

(4). *The sufficiency principle.* The devout and competent Christian can understand the true meaning of the Bible and thereby does not need the official guides to interpretation offered by the Roman Catholic Church. The Bible is a *clear* book (the *perspicuity* of Scripture). Catholicism had maintained that the Scriptures were so obscure that only the teaching ministry of the Church could uncover their true meaning. To Luther the *perspicuity* of the Bible was coupled with the *priesthood of believers,* so that the Bible became the property of all Christians.

The competent Christian was *sufficient* to interpret the Bible, and the Bible is *sufficiently* clear in content to yield its meaning to the believer. Further, the Bible was a world of its own and so *Scripture interprets Scripture.* At points where the Bible was obscure the Catholic referred to the unwritten tradition of the Church. But Luther shut the interpreter up within the Bible and made the obscure passage yield to a clear passage. Much of Catholic exegesis was nothing more than studies in patristics. This Luther rejected:

> I ask for Scriptures and Eck offers me the Fathers. I ask for the sun, and he shows me his lanterns. I ask: "Where is your Scripture proof?" and he adduces Ambrose and Cyril . . . With all due respect to the Fathers I prefer the authority of the Scripture.[40]

A corollary at this point is: *the analogy of faith.* The scholastics interpreted by glosses and catena of citations from the Fathers. This was arbitrary and disconnected.

[40] Cited by Farrar, *op. cit.,* p. 327.

Luther insisted on *the organic, theological unity of the Bible.*
All of the relevant material on a given subject was to be
collected together so that the pattern of divine revelation
concerning that subject would be apparent.

(5). *The Christological principle.* The literal interpretation
of the Bible was not the end of interpretation. The function
of all interpretation is to find Christ. Luther's rule at this
point was: "Auch ist das der rechte Prüfstein alle Bücher
zu tadeln, wenn man siehet ob sie Christum trieben oder
nicht." [41] Smith cites Luther as saying: "If you will interpret
well and securely, take Christ with you, for he is the man
whom everything concerns." [42]

This is Luther's method of making the entire Bible a
Christian book. The Fathers did it with their allegorical
method. Luther does it with his Christological principle.

This has been one of Luther's most controversial utterances. (i) One group (especially the neo-orthodox) claims
that Luther did not hold to a narrow verbal inspiration view
of Scripture. Luther felt free to challenge anything in Scripture not Christological. (ii) The strict orthodox Lutheran
theologians claim that this is purely a hermeneutical principle, and not a principle of Biblical criticism. They adduce
numerous statements of Luther to prove that he held to an
infallible, inerrant Bible. Fortunately, the study of hermeneutics does not have to await the outcome of this debate
for it is crystal clear that this principle is first of all a hermeneutical maxim of Luther's.

(6). *The Law-Gospel principle.* Luther saw the root heresy
of the Galatian churches transposed into a different key in
the Catholic Church. The Galatians had been taught to
(i) be circumcized—the seal of the Old Testament Covenant
and (ii) to believe in Christ—the center of the New Covenant,
and they would be saved. The Catholic Church taught that

---

[41] Farrar, *op. cit.*, p. 333. "This is the correct touchstone to censure
(or test) all [biblical] books, if one sees if they urge Christ or not."
[42] H. P. Smith, *Essays in Biblical Interpretation*, p. 78.

(i) to do religious works, and (ii) believe in Christ would save them. Justification by faith alone not only repudiated the Judaizers of the Gospel, but the Roman Catholic system of salvation.

Luther taught that we must carefully distinguish Law and Gospel in the Bible, and this was one of Luther's principal hermeneutical rules. Any fusion of the Law and Gospel was wrong (Catholics and Reformed who make the Gospel a new law), and any repudiation of the Law was wrong (antinomianism). The Law was God's word about human sin, human imperfection, and whose purpose was to drive us to our knees under a burden of guilt. The Gospel is God's grace and power to save. Hence we must never in interpreting the Scriptures confuse these two different activities of God or teachings of Holy Scripture.

* * *

With reference to Calvin, Fullerton observes that "Calvin may not unfittingly be called the first scientific interpreter in the history of the Christian Church." [43] Is there any other man in the history of the Christian Church who has turned out such a scientific, able, and valuable commentary on almost the entire Scriptures and also made one of the greatest contributions to theology in his *Institutes*? It is true that to Luther we owe the honor of having broken through to a new Protestant hermeneutics, but it was Calvin who exemplified it with his touch of genius. Speaking of Calvin's commentaries Wright says: "The more one studies these commentaries, the more astonished he becomes at their scholarship, lucid profundity, and freshness of insight. Although biblical studies have moved a long way since the sixteenth century,

[43] *Prophecy and Authority*, p. 133. Cf. also P. T. Fuhrman, "Calvin, the Expositor of Scripture," *Interpretation*, 6:188–209, April, 1952. For a description of the sheer genius of Calvin see A. M. Hunter, "The Erudition of John Calvin," *The Evangelical Quarterly*, 18:199–208, July, 1946.

there is still little which can be held to be their equal." [44]

(i). Calvin insisted that the *illumination of the Spirit* was the necessary spiritual preparation for the interpreter of God's Word.

(ii). Calvin, with Luther, rejected allegorical interpretation. Calvin called it Satanic because it led men away from the truth of Scripture. He further stated that the inexhaustibility of Scripture *was not in its so-called fertility of meanings.*

(iii). "Scripture interprets Scripture" was a basic conviction of Calvin. This meant many things. It meant *literalism* (as defined in this book) in exegesis with a rejection of the medieval system of the four-fold meaning of Scripture. It meant listening to the Scripture, not reading Scripture to justify a host of dogmatic presuppositions—although scholars are not sure that Calvin escaped doing this himself. Calvin wrote: "It is the first business of an interpreter to let his author say what he does, instead of attributing to him what we think he ought to say," [45] and in the dedicatory letter to one of his commentaries he added:

We were both of this mind that the principal point of an interpreter did consist in a lucid brevity. And truly, seeing that this is in a manner his whole charge, namely, to show both the mind of the writer whom he hath taken upon himself to expound, look, by how much he leadeth the readers away from the same, by so much he is wide of the mark . . . Verily the word of God ought to be so revered by us that through a diversity of interpretation it might not be drawn asunder by us, no not so much as a hair's breadth . . . It is an audacity akin to sacrilege to use the Scriptures at our own pleasure and to play with them as with a tennis ball, which many before us have done. [46]

The "Scripture interprets Scripture" principle led Calvin to make a strong emphasis on grammatical exegesis, philol-

---

[44] G. E. Wright, "The Christian Interpreter as Biblical Critic," *Interpretation*, 1:133 ff., April, 1947.
[45] Quoted by Farrar, *op. cit.*, p. 347.
[46] Quoted by Fullerton, *op. cit.*, p. 134.

ogy, the necessity of examining the context, and the necessity of comparing Scriptures which treated common subjects.

(iv). Calvin showed a marked independence in exegesis. He not only broke with Catholic exegetical principles, but with any sort of exegesis which was shoddy, superficial, or worthless. He rejected arguments for very orthodox doctrines if the exegesis involved was unworthy.

(v). Finally, Calvin anticipated much of the modern spirit with reference to the interpretation of Messianic prophecy. He showed caution and reserve in these matters, and stated that the exegete ought to investigate the historical settings of all prophetic and Messianic Scriptures.

5. *Post-Reformation*

In general the spirit and the rules of the Reformers became the guiding principles of Protestant orthodox interpretation. To name the scholars who followed in the footsteps of Luther and Calvin would be to name most of the great exegetes from Reformation times until now. Briggs claims that the Puritans worked out the Protestant hermeneutics to a fine point.[47]

Not all post-Reformation exegesis was of the same high standard as that of Calvin, and that there were extremists no one can doubt although Farrar's judgment on these men is extreme. However, a very significant advance was made by Ernesti, who was a classical scholar. He published his *Institutio Interpretis* in 1761 and in it maintained the thesis that the skills and tools of classical studies were basic to New Testament exegesis. Ernesti stated that grammatical exegesis has priority over dogmatic exegesis, and that literal interpretation was preferred over allegorical exegesis. His principal emphasis was on the necessity of sound philology in exegesis. Of Ernesti Briggs writes: "It is the merit of Ernesti in modern times that he so insisted upon grammatical

---

[47] Cf. his discussion of the rules of the Puritans in *Biblical Study*, p. 335 ff.

exegesis that he induced exegetes of all classes to begin their work here at the foundation" [grammatical interpretation].[48]

D. Devotional Schools

The devotional interpretation of Scripture is that method of interpreting Scripture which places emphasis on the edifying aspects of Scripture, and interpreting with the intention of developing the spiritual life.

1. Medieval Mystics

The medieval period produced both scholasticism and mysticism. The mystics read the Scriptures as means of promoting the mystical experience. Such representative men were the Victorines (Hugo but more especially, Richard) and Bernard of Clairvaux. The principal book of the mystics was the *Song of Songs* which they readily interpreted as the love relationship between God and the mystic resulting in spiritual delights told in terms of physical delights.

2. Spener and Francke—Pietism

The post-Reformation period was a period of theological dogmatism. It was a period of heresy hunting and rigid, creedal Protestantism. Farrar's account of it although perhaps extreme is nevertheless depressing.[49] He says it was characterized by a three-fold curse: "The curse of tyrannous confessionalism; the curse of exorbitant systems; the curse of contentious bitterness." [50] Speaking of bitterness among theologians, he writes: *"They read the Bible by the unnatural glare of theological hatred."* [51]

It was in reaction to this situation that *pietism* developed.

[48] *Op. cit.*, p. 352. However, there are some items in Ernesti's system which are not acceptable to historic Christianity. These principles are stated and challenged in Carson, *Examination of the Principles of Biblical Interpretation.*
[49] *Op. cit.*, p. 357 ff.
[50] *Ibid.*, p. 359.
[51] *Ibid.*, p. 363. Italics are ours.

Pietism was the effort to recover the Bible as spiritual food and nourishment to be read for personal edification. It was a distinct reaction against dogmatic and fanciful exegesis. Spener, who was influenced by Richard Baxter, published his *Pia Desidera* in 1675 and maintained that the Bible was the instrument in God's hands for effecting true spirituality. Spener organized his *Collegia pietatis* wherein believers met together for Bible study, devotions, and prayer.

The second great pietist was A. H. Francke who was much more the scholar, linguist and exegete. Francke organized with Anton and Schade a *Collegium Philobiblicum* for the study of the Scriptures with an emphasis on philology and the practical bearing of Scripture on life. Later he went to the University at Halle which became the center of pietism. Francke insisted that the entire Bible be read through frequently; that commentaries were to be used but with discretion so as not to take the place of the study of Scripture itself; and that only the regenerate could understand the Bible.

Farrar says that Bengel was the "heir and continuator of all that was best in Pietism." [52] Bengel studied under the pietists and was impressed by their spirituality, their wonderful Christian fellowship, their emphasis on grammatical and historical interpretation, and their emphasis on the application of Scripture to spiritual life. Bengel eventually wrote his famous *Gnomon* which is concise, grammatical, penetrating, and which emphasizes the unity of the Scriptural revelation. His work in textual criticism represents one of the great landmarks in the development of New Testament textual criticism.

The influence of pietism was great. It influenced the Moravians and Zinzendorf. Others in the pietistic tradition

[52] *Op. cit.*, p. 392. Cf. J. Pelikan, "In Memoriam: Joh. Albrecht Bengel," *Concordia Theological Monthly*, 23:785–796, November, 1952. Charles T. Fritsch, "Bengel, Student of Scripture," *Interpretation*, 5:203–215, April, 1951.

(or at least emphasizing the devotional, practical, and edifying study of the Bible) are the Puritans, Wesley, Edwards, Matthew Henry, and the Quakers.[53]

3. *Modern Emphasis*

The insights of the pietists have not been lost. It would not be amiss to say that the average Christian reads his Bible in the devotional tradition, i.e., for his own blessing and spiritual food. The devotional material on our book shelves is imposing and the preacher is expected to have a devotional emphasis in every sermon above and beyond whatever doctrinal or exegetical remarks he may have to make.

The devotional and practical emphasis in Bible teaching is *absolutely* necessary. The purpose of preaching is more than doctrinal communication or exposition of the meaning of Scripture. It must reach over into life and experience, and this is the function of the devotional teaching of Scripture. The vital, personal, and spiritual *must be present in all the ministries of the Word.*

There are two weaknesses of devotional interpretation:

(i). It falls prey to allegorization especially in the use of the Old Testament. In the effort to find a spiritual truth or application of a passage of Scripture the literal and therefore primary meaning of the passage is obscured. If it is not a case of bald allegorizing it may be excessive typology. Given enough allegorical and typological rope one may prove a variety of contradictory propositions from the Old Testament. One may prove Calvinistic security (the central board in the wall of the Tabernacle) or Arminian probationalism (the failure of faith at Kadesh-Barnea). A Reformed expositor may prove that the soul feeds on Christ while discuss-

---

[53] Cf. Dana's discussion. *Searching the Scriptures*, p. 81 ff. Immer claims that the chief error of the pietists was that "the Scriptures were not so much explained as overwhelmed with pious reflections." Cited by Terry, *op. cit.*, p. 62 fn.

ing the sacrificial system, and a Catholic prove his doctrine of the mass.

All sorts of distortions have been made of the historical records of the Old Testament (and occasionally the New) in order to derive a spiritual blessing or to make a devotional point.

(ii). Devotional interpretation may be a substitute for the requisite exegetical and doctrinal studies of the Bible. Strong doctrinal sinews and solid exegetical bones are necessary for spiritual health. If the emphasis is completely devotional the requisite doctrinal and expository truth of Scripture are denied God's people.

D. LIBERAL INTERPRETATION

As early as Hobbes and Spinoza rationalistic views were held about the Bible. The debate over the Bible in modern times is a debate of rationalism versus authoritarianism. Rationalism in Biblical studies boils down to the fundamental assertion that whatever is not in harmony with *educated* mentality is to be rejected. The critic defines *educated* in a very special way. The authoritarian position asserts that if God has spoken, the human mind must be obedient to the voice of God. That there is a blind or credulous authoritarianism cannot be denied, but it is not true that authoritarianism is anti-intellectual.[54] The rationalistic premise has led to radical criticism of the Scriptures.

This radical treatment of Scriptures reached its full tide in the nineteenth century. Suffice it·to say that by the middle of the twentieth century most theological seminaries have accepted the basic theses of radical criticism, and many of its conclusions. The Barthian reaction will be discussed later. In broad perspective the following rules have governed the

[54] Protestants accept authority when underwritten by the criteria of truthfulness. Cf. E. Carnell, *An Introduction to Christian Apologetics.* P. 71.

religious liberals as they approached the study of the Bible: [55]
(i). *Religious liberals believe that "modern mentality" is to govern our approach to Scripture.* This "modern mentality" is made up of a complex of presuppositions, e.g., standards of scholarship as practiced in higher education, the validity of the scientific *outlook* as well as *method*, and the ethical standards of educated people. Whatever in the Scriptural account does not measure up to these criteria is rejected. Scholarship claims that all books are to be treated as human documents and by the same methods and the Bible is no exception.[56] Science presumes the regularity of nature so miracles are not accepted. The doctrines of sin, depravity, and hell offend the liberals' moral sensitivities so these doctrines are rejected. This also means a rather free use of the text of the Bible. If a book of the Bible seems "patched" the text may be re-arranged, e.g., as Moffatt does with the Gospel of John in his translation. If the text is obscure the text may be remade, e.g., as is done too frequently in the Old Testament part of the *Revised Standard Version.*[57]

(ii). *Religious liberals redefine inspiration.* All forms of genuine inspiration (verbal, plenary, dynamic) are rejected. If liberalism rejects all transcendental and miraculous activity of God, then it must reject a supernaturalistic doctrine of inspiration and revelation which it does.[58] In its place it puts Coleridge's principle that the inspiration of the Bible is its power to inspire religious experience. Revelation is redefined as human insight into religious truth, or human dis-

[55] Generally speaking radical views of the Bible have accompanied liberal views of theology. However, an atheist may hold to radical criticism and reject liberal theology. There are scholars who have accepted radical criticism and maintained orthodox theology, as is evident from W. B. Glover's *Evangelical Nonconformists and Higher Criticism in the Nineteenth Century* [in Great Britain].
[56] Cf. E. C. Colwell, *The Study of the Bible,* Chapters III, IV, and V. Also, H. E. Fosdick, *The Modern Use of the Bible.*
[57] Cf. Piper's sharp criticism of rationalism in the hermeneutics of religious liberalism. Otto A. Piper, "Principles of New Testament Interpretation," *Theology Today,* 3:202, July, 1946.
[58] Fosdick, *op. cit.,* pp. 30–31.

covery of religious truths. Or as Fosdick puts it: "The under side of the process is man's discovery; the upper side is God's revelation." [59]

The canon of criticism is "the spirit of Jesus." Whatever in the Bible is in accord with the "spirit of Jesus" is normative, and whatever is below the ethical and moral level of the "spirit of Jesus" is not binding. Bewer writes quite clearly at this point: "To the Christian the only norm and standard is the spirit of God as revealed in Jesus . . . . all those parts of the Old Testament which are contrary to the spirit of Jesus, or which have no direct spiritual meaning to us, are for us without authority." [60]

This means that the doctrinal or theological content of Scripture is not binding. It was Sabatier who argued that religious experience was fundamental and theology was the afterthought of this experience. But the religious experience could not be completely expressed in thought-form so theological expression was but symbolical of the religious experience. With this essential thesis Fosdick agrees, for to him religious experience is the heart of religion and theological forms are temporary. One of the chapters of his book has the title, "Abiding Experiences and Changing Categories." His thesis is expressed in these words: "What is permanent in Christianity is not mental frameworks but abiding experiences that phrase and rephrase themselves in successive generations' ways of thinking and that grow in assured certainty and richness of content." [61]

(iii). *The supernatural is redefined.* The supernatural may mean: that which is extraordinary, miraculous, oracular, not

[59] *Ibid.*, p. 30. This thesis is found widely in the literature of religious liberalism and no clearer expression of it has been given than in A. Sabatier's *Outlines of a Philosophy of Religion based on Psychology and History.* See p. 34 ff.

[60] Bewer, *Authority of the Old Testament* in T. Kepler's *Contemporary Religious Thought*, p. 127.

[61] Fosdick, *op. cit.*, p. 103. Cf. also his remarks in Kepler, *op. cit.*, pp. 13-20. But is not this thesis itself *a theological proposition?* Therefore, *this* theological proposition is prior to religious experience. Result: his basic position is contradictory.

attainable in knowledge or power by ordinary human nature. Or it may mean: above the material order, or beyond mere natural processes, e.g., prayer, ethics, pure thought, immortality. Historic orthodoxy has accepted supernaturalism in both these meanings. Religious liberalism accepts only the latter.

Everything in the Bible which is supernatural in the first sense is rejected. Colwell argues that the *same* methodology must be used in interpreting the Bible as is used in interpreting the classics; no special principle may be appealed to by Christians. If, therefore, we reject all reports of miracles in the classics as violating our scientific good sense, then we must reject miracles in the Scriptures.[62] When the miracle or supernatural is found in Scripture it is treated as folklore or mythology or poetic elaboration.

(iv). *The concept of evolution is applied to the religion of Israel and thereby to its documents.* Fosdick's book, *The Modern Use of the Bible*, is considered a most lucid presentation of the Wellhausenian interpretation of the Old Testament. The primitive and crude, ethically and religiously, is the earlier; and the advanced and elevated, is the later. We can thereby recreate the evolution of the religion of Israel and rearrange our documents accordingly. "We know now that every idea in the Bible started from primitive and childlike origins and, with however many setbacks and delays, grew in scope and height toward the culmination of Christ's Gospel," is Fosdick's point of view.[63]

[62] Colwell, *op. cit.*, p. 122 f. Piper's comment is: "Critics who had no experience of the supernatural concluded, for instance, that everything in the Bible which referred to the supernatural was wrong. Sound criticism would have contented itself with saying: 'My judgment as to the truthfulness of these documents has to be suspended because I know nothing of these things.' " *Op. cit.*, p. 201.

[63] *Op. cit.*, p. 11. H. P. Smith (*Essays in Biblical Interpretation*) speaking of the application of evolutionary principles to Biblical criticism says that such application is widely accepted because men see evolution in *history* as well as nature. However, a great reversal has taken place in anthropological theory and the evolutionary principle of social cultural no longer dominates anthropological theory. P. 141.

In the study of the canon this put the prophets *before* the law. The basic Wellhausen position calls for considerable rearrangement of books and materials.[64]

The same procedure has been applied to the New Testament. Harnack's *What is Christianity?* is considered the finest and clearest expression of religious liberalism. Its thesis is that Jesus, a good man in the highest prophetic order, is transmuted by theological speculation and Greek metaphysics into the strange God-man of the creeds. The critic of the New Testament must be an expert archeologist and geologist to uncover the strata of accretions imposed on the true Jesus of history.

However, archeological work, further work in criticism, and the uncovering of much papyri demonstrated that all such stratigraphy was due to fail. In *Formgeschichte* (form or historical criticism) an effort is made to develop a pre-literary theory for accounting for the New Testament. The New Testament was the creation of the Christian community out of its spiritual needs, and so the Gospels are not the life of Christ as much as they are the life of the early church.

(v). *The notion of accommodation has been applied to the Bible.* Much of the theological content of the Bible is weakened or destroyed by asserting that the theological statements are in the transitory and perishable mold of ancient terminology. For example, the only terms in which Paul could describe the death of Christ were from bloody Jewish sacrifices or the blood-baths of Mythraism. Thus Paul's doctrine of the atonement is accommodated to the expressions of his time and these are not binding on us. It is claimed that our Lord in dealing with the Jews had to accommodate his teaching to their condition, especially in matters of Bibli-

---

[64] However, this entire concept is now under severe criticism. Cf. Albright, *From the Stone Age to Christianity, and, Archeology and the Religion of Israel.* John Bright, "The Prophets Were Protestants," *Interpretation,* I:153-82, April, 1947.

cal Introduction, e.g., the historicity of Adam and Eve, of Jonah, of the Davidic authorship of the Psalms.[65]

The religious liberal feels it is his assignment to recast the essence of the New Testament doctrine in the language of his contemporaries, and in so doing must strip off the concepts and images of the Old and New Testament cultures.

(vi). *The Bible was interpreted historically—with a vengeance.*[66] The historical interpretation is used in a special leveling and reductionist sense by the religious liberal. He means more than painting the historical backdrop of the various passages of the Bible. It is a method which endeavors to break the uniqueness of the Scriptures. It makes religion a changing, shifting phenomenon so that it is impossible to "canonize" any period of its development or its literature. It believes that there are social conditions which create theological beliefs and the task of the interpreter is not to defend these theological beliefs (as in orthodoxy) but to understand the social conditions which produced them. It stresses the continuity of Biblical religion with surrounding religion, and emphasizes "borrowing," "syncretism," and "purifying."

Further, in so stressing the necessity of finding the meaning of a passage for the original hearers of it, it repudiates the prophetic or predictive element of prophecy. It rejects typology and predictive prophecy as Christian abuses (although in good faith) of the Old Testament.

(vii). *Philosophy has had an influence on religious liberalism.* Immanuel Kant made ethics or moral will the essence

[65] That our Lord did not accommodate himself in this sense is thoroughly argued by C. J. Ellicott, *Christus Comprobatur.* Horne (*An Introduction to the Critical Study and Knowledge of the Holy Scriptures,* eighth edition) has an able refutation of this type of accommodation, too, that although written more than a hundred years ago is still relevant. Gore's essay in *Lux Mundi* argued that the incarnation involved ignorance and so Christ knew only what a typical Jew would know about matters of Biblical Introduction.

[66] Cf. Colwell, (*op. cit.,* Chapter VI), for the results of a religious liberal's use of the historical principle in criticism. Also, H. P. Smith (*op. cit.*), Chapter XIII, "Historical Interpretation."

of religion. Kant shut himself up almost completely to the *moral* interpretation of Scripture. Whatever was not of this he rejected. This emphasis on the moral element of Scripture with its tacit rejection of theological interpretation has played a major role in the liberals' use of the Scripture.

Deism made ethics the essence of religion too. In a typically deistic fashion Jefferson went through the Gospels picking out the ethical and moral, and rejecting the theological and so published his *Jefferson Bible*.

Hegelianism has had its influence on Biblical interpretation. According to Hegel progress in the clarification of an idea involves three terms: the thesis, the antithesis, and the synthesis. This Hegelian waltz was applied to the totality of human culture including religion. Hegelian students were not slow in applying it to the Biblical records. Wellhausen applied it to the Old Testament, and Strauss and the Tuebingen school to the New. Thus in the Tuebingen school the strife between Pauline factions and Petrine factions is harmonized by the Lucan approach.

Ethical idealism and idealism with strong ethical and religious elements has had its influence on American religious liberalism. At the headwaters of much of our American religious philosophy were Josiah Royce and Borden Parker Bowne. Bowne's personalism through his students and their students has had a real influence on much of Methodist and liberal theology in America.

E. NEO-ORTHODOXY

Karl Barth ushered in a new era in Biblical interpretation when he published his *Römerbrief* at the end of World War I. This was a new approach to the theological interpretation of the book of Romans. This new movement has been called "crisis theology" because it so emphasized God's judgment of man; "Barthianism," because it stems from the original thought of Karl Barth; "neo-orthodoxy" because it dissevers itself from liberalism and seeks to recover the insights of the

Reformers; "neo-supernaturalism" because in contradiction
to modernism it reënstates the category of the transcendental; "logotheism" because it is a theology of the Word of
God; "neo-evangelicalism" because it seeks to recover the
Christian gospel in contrast to the social gospel of liberalism;
"neo-liberalism" because it is claimed that although differing
in many ways from liberalism it has not really broken with
it; and "Biblical realism" because it makes a new effort to
rediscover the theological interpretation of the Bible.[67]

The movement has been fractured into a series of submove-
ments rendering simple description difficult. We shall try to
set forth those hermeneutical principles which would more or
less characterize the center of this movement.

(i). *The revelation principle.* This movement makes it very
clear that the historic, orthodox position with reference to
inspiration, revelation, and Biblical criticism can no longer
be maintained.[68] The *infallibility* of the Bible is denied. The
Bible is not one harmonious whole but a series of conflicting
theological systems and ethical maxims. Some parts of the
Bible are definitely sub-Christian and perhaps it would not
be too strong to say even anti-Christian.[69] The *inerrancy* of
the Bible is denied. In matters of science, anthropology,
history, and geology, the Bible is flatly contradicted by modern science. The Hebrews had the typical Semitic cosmology
and outlook on nature. The traditional notion of *revelation*
is denied. Revelation as a communication of that truth not

[67] The literature of neo-orthodoxy has become voluminous. For discussions of hermeneutics which come right to the point see Edwin Lewis,
The Biblical Faith and Christian Freedom (especially chapter II); B. W.
Anderson, *Rediscovering the Bible* (especially chapter I); Brunner, *Dogmatic*, I & II; and Niebuhr, *Nature and Destiny of Man.* Barth discusses
hermeneutics in *Die Kirchliche Dogmatik*, I, 2, pages 513 ff., 546 ff.,
810 ff., 515 ff., 546 ff., and 812 ff.

[68] This entire story from the neo-orthodox viewpoint is told directly
and energetically by Lewis, *op. cit.*, chapter III, "The Emancipation
of the Word of God."

[69] Cf. Lewis, *op. cit.*, p. 121.

ascertainable by human powers is strongly repudiated. It is dubbed "propositional revelation" and an attack on "propositional revelation" is one of the typical themes of neo-orthodoxy. All historical and orthodox forms of *inspiration* are denied (verbal, conceptual, plenary),[70] and in more than one neo-orthodox treatise the word inspiration never even makes the index. Those who believe in verbal inspiration are guilty of a *mechanical* or *dictational* theory of inspiration and the additional charge of *bibliolatry* is made against them.

Although neo-orthodoxy has challenged some of the theses of radical criticism it has accepted in main the results of the same. Lewis puts it bluntly but he expresses the opinion of the movement when he writes: "The one certain thing about the new Biblicism is that it is not a revamped fundamentalism." [71]

However, no matter how strongly neo-orthodoxy has reacted to the orthodox view of the Bible, it has not capitulated to modernism. It finds its normative use of the Bible in terms of its doctrine of revelation. Very briefly the essence of the doctrine is this: *Only God can speak for God.* Revelation *is* when, and only when, God speaks. But God's speech is not words (orthodox view) but is *His personal presence.* "The Word of God" is God Himself present to my consciousness. The "objective" form of this speech is Jesus Christ which is God present in mercy, grace, and reconciliation. When God addresses me by Jesus Christ and I respond, then revelation

[70] Brunner's attack on verbal inspiration will be found throughout his work, *Revelation and Reason*, and also in his *Dogmatics*, I., and, *The Philosophy of Religion.* Barth rejects it in his *The Doctrine of the Word of God* (cf. pp. 126, 156, 309 f.). Niebuhr's attack on "theological literalism" will be found in *The Nature and Destiny of Man* (*in passim*) and in, *Faith and History*, pp. 33–34. Monsma accuses Barth of breaking with the literal sense of Scripture (Cf. his *Karl Barth's Idea of Revelation*). Hamer accuses Barth of being a spiritualizer (in *The Hibbert Journal*, 48:84, October, 1949). For a sharp criticism of Barth's hermeneutics cf. Behm, *Pneumatische Exegese?*

[71] Lewis, *op. cit.*, p. 46.

occurs. Revelation is thus *both* God speaking to me of grace and forgiveness in Jesus Christ *and* my response of faith to this personal address.

The Bible is thus not revelation or the word of God directly, but a *record* and a *witness* to revelation. It is not the word of God directly. It is the word of God in the indirect sense that the Bible contains the normative *witness* of revelation of the past, and the *promise* of revelation in the future. The Bible is a trustworthy yet fallible witness to revelation. Although a man may unmistakably experience revelation, he never gets a *pure* communication. The revelation is always *broken* or *diffracted* through the prism of its medium. Therefore the Bible, a record of revelation, can never be directly the revelation of God nor a pure communication of it.

The neo-orthodox interpreter then looks for the Word behind the words. The religious liberal saw no Word behind the words of Scripture, but only a record of remarkable religious experiences. The orthodox identified the human words of the Bible with the Word behind the words.[72] The neo-orthodox thinker proposes to dig through the human, fallible words of the Bible to discover *the original witness to the Word of God.*

(ii). *The Christological principle.* God's Word to man is Jesus Christ. Only that part of the Bible which is witness to the Word of God is binding. This introduces the second fundamental hermeneutical principle of neo-orthodoxy, the Christological principle. Only that which witnesses to Christ is binding, and doctrines are understood only as they are related to Jesus Christ, the Word of God.

As we read the Old Testament we encounter a variety of incidents. Whatever is not in harmony with Jesus Christ the

---

[72] "Criticism has made impossible all those conceptions of the Bible which depend upon the identity of the words of the Bible with God's own 'word.'" Lewis, *op. cit.*, p. 11. "The critical movement has issued in our time in the emancipation of the Word of God from identification with the words of men and there will be no return to this bondage." *Ibid.*, p. 44.

Word of God is not valid witness. Lewis declares that there
is nothing in the Old Testament about God that is binding
upon Christian men which "cannot be reconciled with what
God has disclosed himself to be in the Incarnate Word, and
with the requirement of human life and thought and action
that is the proper issue and concomitant of this disclosure." [73]

Further, it is argued by Brunner that no doctrine is a
Christian doctrine unless it receives a Christological orientation. Such doctrines as creation and sin are not to be directly
approached in the Old Testament for only in Christ do we
truly know what it means to be a creature (and thereby
have the proper grounds for understanding creation in Genesis) and only in Christ do we know what sin is (and thereby
understand Genesis 3). The rule for understanding "all
Christian articles of faith is the Incarnate Word, Jesus
Christ." [74]

(iii). *The totality principle.* Barth, Brunner, Lewis, and
Niebuhr argue that one cannot prove a doctrine by the citation of a text of Scripture or a few texts of Scripture. The
teaching of the Bible is determined by a consideration of the
totality of its teaching. Lewis insists that crass literalism
does not yield the true meaning of Scripture. The Scriptures
are properly interpreted only when we apply the totality
principle and Brunner argues that "we are not bound by any
Biblical passages taken in isolation, and certainly not by
isolated sections of the Old Testament." [75] No doubt the
Bible interpreted *in particular* leads to orthodox doctrines.
To take the Bible seriously (as neo-orthodoxy intends to do)
without taking it with a crass literalism, is to interpret each

[73] *Ibid.*, p. 117. These sentiments can be heavily documented from
neo-orthodox literature.
[74] Emil Brunner, *Dogmatics*, II, 6. Italics are his. Cf. also pp. 8,
52, 53, 90.
[75] *Ibid.*, p. 52. This is not really a totality principle, but an ignoration principle, for under the guise of taking all the Scripture says on a
subject, they take only that which concurs with their presuppositions
and *ignore* the rest.

doctrine from the totality of the Biblical perspective guided by the Christological principle.

(iv). *The mythological principle.* The Bible contains discussions about such topics as the creation of the universe, the creation of man, the innocency of man, the fall of man, and the second coming of Christ. The liberal either rejected these teachings forthright, or altered them so as to change their Biblical character. Neo-orthodoxy seeks to interpret these doctrines *seriously* (as liberals failed to do), but not *literally* (as the orthodox do). The *via media* is to interpret them *mythologically.* [76]

The myth is a form of theological communication. It presents a truth about man's religious existence in historical dress. *Creation* is such a myth for it is a truth about religious existence in historical form. Genesis 1 is not meant to tell us actually how God created the universe. Rather it tells us on the one hand of our creaturehood, and on the other of the limits of scientific investigation. Creation really means that eventually science comes to the end of the line in its explanation of the universe and must there surrender to truth of another dimension. The *Second Coming* of Christ is a religious truth in historical form to the intent that man can never find his happiness nor his meaning in purely historical existence. The *Fall* is the myth which informs us that man inevitably corrupts his moral nature. The *Incarnation* and the *cross* are myths telling us that the solution to man's problems of guilt and sin is not to be found in a human dimension but must come from beyond as an act of God's grace.

Neo-orthodox writers make it clear that Biblical myths are radically different from pagan and classical myths. The latter are the productions of human imagination and the elaboration of tradition. The Biblical myths are a serious and meaningful (although imperfect) method of setting forth that

[76] See Anderson, *op. cit.*, Chapter X; Niebuhr, *Faith and History*, pp. 33–34; Alan Richardson, "Adam," *A Theological Word Book of the Bible*; Kierkegaard, *The Concept of Dread.*

which is transcendental about man's religious existence and can best be represented in historical form. Because myths do not actually teach literal history but the conditions of all religious existents, mythological interpretation may sometimes be called *psychological* interpretation as suggested in Kierkegaard's subtitle to *The Concept of Dread* ("A simple psychological deliberation oriented in the direction of the dogmatic problem of original sin").

(v). *The existential principle.* The existential principle of interpretation has its roots in Pascal's method of Bible study and received its initial formulation in Kierkegaard's meditation on "How to Derive True Benediction from Beholding Oneself in the Mirror of the Word." [77] According to Kierkegaard the grammatical, lexical, and historical study of the Bible was necessary but preliminary to the true reading of the Bible. To read the Bible *as God's word* one must read it with his heart in his mouth, on tip-toe, with eager expectancy, in conversation with God. To read the Bible thoughtlessly or carelessly or academically or professionally is not to read the Bible as God's word. As one reads it as a love letter is read, then one reads it as the word of God. The Bible is not God's word to the soul until one reads it as one *ought* to read the word of God. "He who is not alone with God's Word is not reading God's Word," pens Kierkegaard.[78]

Kierkegaard gives the illustration of a boy who stuffs the seat of his pants with napkins to soften the blows of the licking he is expecting. So the scholar stuffs his academic britches with his grammars, lexicons, and commentaries and thus *the Bible as God's word* never reaches his soul.

This existential approach to the reading of Scripture has

[77] *For Self-Examination and Judge for Yourselves*, p. 39 ff. Cf. Minear and Morimoto, *Kierkegaard and the Bible* for a brief sketch of Kierkegaard's hermeneutics. No doubt pietistic interpretation had existential elements in it.

[78] *Ibid.*, p. 55. Regardless of the incipient neo-orthodoxy in this essay it is one of the finest in theological literature in the field of psychological hermeneutics.

been taken up by neo-orthodoxy. The Bible contains a special history (*Heilsgeschichte*), the history of salvation. Some of it is mythological in form, and some is actual history. This history within the Bible is the record that revelation has occurred, and so constitutes a promise that as men read the Scriptures revelation may occur again. This *Heilsgeschichte* is normative for all men and the instrument of occasioning revelation. From the human standpoint revelation may be invited by reading the Bible *existentially*, i.e., as Kierkegaard suggested with eagerness, anticipation, with a spirit of obedience, with a passionate heart.

The existential situation is a profound situation of life. It is an experience involving decisions about the most fundamental issues of life. Brock defines it as follows:

Existenz is an attitude of the individual to himself, which is called forth by such concrete situations as the necessity for choice of profession or a conflict in love, a catastrophic change in social conditions, or the imminence of one's own death. It leads immediately to sublime moments in which a man gathers his whole strength to make a decision which is taken afterwards as binding upon his future life. Furthermore, Existenz never becomes completed, as does life through death. In its different manifestations it is only a beginning which is faithfully followed or faithlessly forgotten. Moreover, Existenz is not real in being known, it is real only in being effectuated, in remembrance of it, and in resolutions for the future which are taken to be absolutely binding.[79]

The Bible is not primarily history, although it contains history. It is not primarily a theological textbook although it contains theology. It is a book about existence, about life at its most comprehensive expression, about God. To understand it at this level one must read it existentially. By this existential reading the Bible may become the word of God to the reader. Speaking of this Grant says:

[79] Quoted by H. R. Mackintosh, *Types of Modern Theology*, p. 219, from Brock's *Contemporary German Philosophy*, pp. 83–84.

The deepest interpretation of Scripture is that concerned with 'existential' situations: life and death, love and hate, sin and grace, good and evil, God and the world. These are not matters of ordinary knowledge like the multiplication table or the date of the council of Nicea. There is . . . no special method for the attainment of these deeper insights; the historical method is not replaced but deepened.[80]

It is precisely at this point that the famous continental scholar, Eichrodt, levels one of his major criticisms at Fosdick. Fosdick has read *into* the Old Testament his evolutionary theory of the progress of religious ideas. Had he read the Bible with *existential* insight he would have noted more carefully the mighty redemptive and revelatory acts of God in making Himself known to the people, and the corresponding insight into the meaning of these acts which the prophets and real believers in Israel shared.[81]

Grant mentions also the German scholar Oepke,[82] who attacks the liberal's historical-critical method in that it is dead and fruitless, and suggests in its place the super-historical method—the existential method. The scholar reads his Bible with the full apparatus of his learning, yet personally he might be very nominal in his spiritual life. The scholar has an intellectual knowledge of the Bible. In contrast to this is the devout believer who has little of the scholar's critical apparatus yet who derives a rich blessing for his soul from his Bible reading. The latter reads his Bible *existentially* whereas the former reads it historically and critically.

[80] Grant, *op. cit.*, p. 162.
[81] W. Eichrodt, "Fosdick, A Guide to Understanding the Bible," *Journal of Biblical Literature*, 65:205 ff., June, 1946. Eichrodt calls Fosdick's book, "The obituary of a whole scholarly approach and investigation." P. 205. Further references on the existential approach are, Brunner, *Dogmatics*, I and II, and, Bernard Ramm, "The Existential Interpretation of Doctrine," *Bibliotheca Sacra*, 112:154–163, April, 1955, and July, 256–264.
[82] *Op. cit.*, p. 163.

(vi). *The paradoxical principle.*[83] It was Kierkegaard who
not only developed the existential principle but also the
paradoxical. This full story is too long to tell. The heart
of it is this: Hegel, a German philosopher, made much of
divine immanence and *logical rationality.* He was a pantheist
and because of his belief in the pervasiveness of his logic his
system has been called *pan-logism.* Kierkegaard challenged
these categories with the counter-categories of *divine tran-
scendence* and *logical paradox.*

If man is a limited and sinful creature, and if God is Wholly
Other (that is, very different from man), then man cannot
have unambiguous knowledge of God. The truth of God must
appear to man as dialectical or paradoxical. Any given doctrine must be defined in terms of assertion and counter-
assertion. Assertion and counter assertion appear to man as
paradoxical. Exposition of doctrine by means of assertion
and counter-assertion is what is meant by the expression
dialectical theology.

This dialectical procedure and the resultant paradoxes is
not wilful indulgence in irrationalism. It is not the contention of the neo-orthodox to assert flat contradictions. Rather,
it is the inevitable nature of theological truth, and an uncritical application of the law of contradiction leads to a premature and inaccurate formulation of Christian doctrine.

Examples of these paradoxes are: man is a creature of
nature, yet possessing spirit he transcends nature; man must
use reason to understand God, yet God is beyond human
reason; man is responsible for his sin, yet he inevitably sins;
man's historical existence is at the same time destructive and
constructive; man must lose his life to save it; God is One

---

[83] Cf. Roger Hazelton, "The Nature of Christian Paradox," *Theology
Today,* 6:324–335. R. Niebuhr, "Coherence, Incoherence and Christian
Faith," *Christian Realism and Political Problems,* pp. 175–203. H. De-
Wolf, *The Religious Revolt Against Reason.* Tillich, however, makes
a distinction between the paradoxical and dialectical (cf. "Reinhold
Niebuhr's Doctrine of Knowledge," *Reinhold Niebuhr: His Religious,
Social, and Political Thought,* p. 39).

yet Three; the cross is foolishness yet wisdom; God is absolute holiness yet unmeasured love.

The truths of man's religious existence can never be precisely or rationally defined, but are tensions between contrarities not capable of complete rational explication yet sufficiently adequate for our religious understanding. Religious reality is too rich in meaning and content to be stated in strict, non-contradictory form.

F. The Heilsgeschichtliche School

Amidst the orthodoxy and liberalism of the nineteenth century, von Hofmann of Erlangen endeavored to break through to a fresh Biblical-theological synthesis. He tried to combine the insights of Schleiermacher concerning religious experience as the point of departure for theological thought, the critical study of the Bible, and orthodox Lutheran theology. He attempted to ground religious authority on the tripod of: (i) the experience of regeneration; (ii) the history and fact of the church; and (iii) Scripture.[84]

His principal contribution to hermeneutics is his notion of holy history or salvation-history. For his basic insight he is indebted to Schelling (as Tillich is in our century), for Schelling saw history as the manifestation of the eternal and absolute and not as so many events to be chronicled. Revelation is a higher form of history reaching backward into the past and forward into the future. The supreme content of this superhistorical history, this metaphysics of history, is Jesus Christ.

With this clue from Schelling, von Hofmann said that a historical event had roots in the past, meaning in the present, and portent for the future. In the study of prophecy we must know: (i) the history of Israel, (ii) the immediate historical

---

[84] Cf. Christian Preus, "The Contemporary Relevance of von Hofmann's Hermeneutical Principles," *Interpretation*, 4:311–321, July, 1950; and, J. L. Neve and O. W. Heick, *A History of Christian Thought*, II. 132 ff.

context of the individual prophecy; and (iii) the fulfilment
intended. This is what von Hofmann considered to be the
organic view of Scripture. All Scripture was bound together
in this holy history for every event looked backwards, to the
present, and to the future. Preuss says that "it was the first
time in the history of Biblical interpretation that an organic
view of history was applied to the problems of exegesis in a
systematic way." [85]

Christ is the central point of history. God is the active
agent; Christ, the focal point. Yet this does not exhaust the
content of history, for the present age portends another age,
the millennium. Von Hofmann thus takes his place with the
Lutheran millenarians of the nineteenth century.

Further, von Hofmann taught that the Holy Spirit not only
inspired the Scriptures, but He guides the church. We are
never to formalize, dogmatize, or canonize our interpretations
of Scripture but ever be sensitive to more teaching from the
Holy Spirit. Interpretation is not to be static, but dynamic
moving along under the leadership of the Spirit.

Revelation was first historical. It is God's acts in history.
But with these events was given a divine interpretation of
them. Communication of ideas was necessary to make the
event meaningful. Scripture is thus the product of historical
event plus inspired interpretation.

Further, the older method of proving a doctrine by piecing
together a catena of Scripture from all over the Bible is
seriously challenged by Hofmann. He insists that *every*
verse or passage be given its historical setting which should
in turn give it its true meaning and its weight in proving any
doctrine.

The outstanding American representative of this school is
Otto Piper.[86] Piper admits indebtedness to von Hofmann and

[85] Preus, *op. cit.*, p. 314.
[86] Cf. Otto Piper, "Principles of New Testament Interpretation,"
Theology Today, 3:192–204, July, 1946. "The Authority of the Bible,"
Theology Today, 6:159–173. "The Theme of the Bible," *Christian*

to his Salvation history principle. He claims to be neither neo-orthodox nor liberal nor fundamentalist. One of the major theses of von Hofmann was that inspiration and criticism were not disjunctively related, and this major thesis Piper also accepted. Accordingly he is not appreciated by the liberals who deny any real inspiration nor by the fundamentalists who believe that concessions to criticism are fatal.

The authority of the Bible, according to Piper, is not its claim to verbal inspiration (for this claim is really the claim of the post-Reformation dogmatists) nor is it some higher type of knowledge which it seeks to communicate (for this is the error of gnosticism), but rather "that the Bible confronts us with facts that are more comprehensive and more important than anything else we know." [87] The Bible speaks to us of Jesus Christ and God's offer of forgiveness and salvation through faith. We find that out of our experience with life, this is precisely what our souls need, and upon faith we find ourselves blessed with the blessedness of the gospel. Hence Scriptures are not rationally vindicated, but they are vindicated out of life. The Bible is thus the Word of God (not the words of God as in verbal inspiration) because I *sense* that it is true. God speaks to me out of the Bible. He speaks of sin and forgiveness. The general address of the Bible becomes God's Word to me when I receive it by faith. Piper admits this is subjectivity (i.e., the Bible is the Word of God only to those who respond to it), but this need not alarm us. First, as long as we are willing to relate our experience to other knowledge it is not a solipsistic principle, and secondly, all *important* knowledge is subjective.

In the interpretation of the Bible Piper accepts in principle the critical treatment of the Bible for he pens, "All the attempts to exempt the Bible from the kind of criticism that

Century, 63:334 f., March 13, 1946. "The Bible as Holy History," *Christian Century*, 63:362 f., March 20, 1946. "Discovering the Bible," *Christian Century*, 63:266 f., Feb. 27, 1946. "How I Study my Bible," *Christian Century*, 63:299 f., March 6, 1946.

[87] "The Authority of the Bible," *op. cit.*, p. 163.

we apply to other historical documents are just as futile as
were the theological protests against the discoveries of pale-
ontology."[88] But to be sure he does not follow this to drastic
measures for at times he stoutly resists the efforts of the
critics to do away with the supernatural. But he does insist
that the interpreter must engage in the preliminary and
critical studies of Biblical introduction, canon, and text.

Assuming that the critical study of the Bible has been
made, the interpreter is then guided by three major hermeneutical principles (the quest for the life-movement of the
given book; the comprehension of its message; and the appropriation of its message).[89]

In the study of the life-movement of a document we perform the following: we attempt to discover the unity of the
book; we ascertain the persons to whom the book is communicated and its bearing on the interpretation of the book;
we try to follow the succession of ideas or arguments in the
book; we note the literary mold or form or structure of the
book; and we must note the basic unity of the entire New
Testament in its kerygmatic preaching and witness.

Comprehension of the document, Piper's second step, is
(i) locating each idea in the author's total view of life and
reality, and (ii) determining "the relationship which exists
between the ideas of the documents and the ideas of our own
mind."[90] This involves, among other things, the determination of the world view of the New Testament writers. The
cogency or believability of this world view lies in "the fact
that it is most comprehensive and most consistent taking all
kinds of facts and experiences into consideration and that it
reaches into depths of meaning not fathomed by any world
view."[91] If an interpreter fails to discover this world view

[88] "How I Study my Bible," *op. cit.*, p. 299.
[89] Set forth in "Principles of New Testament Interpretation,"
op. cit.
[90] *Ibid.*, 197.
[91] *Ibid.*, 198.

and insists on interpreting the New Testament from the so-called modern scientific world view he can only *misinterpret* the New Testament.

The fallacy of allegorical interpretation is that it is reading into Scripture the views already held by exegetes, rather than the discovery of the world view and system of values held by the writers of Scripture. Equally at fault is a narrow literalism, for communication is too complex to be limited to simple, literal interpretation. The *real* literal interpretation is the meaning found "in the original text when its component words are understood in the world view and according to the scale of values of the author." [92]

The final stage is appropriation which is our reply to the challenge of the Bible. Appropriation means that we critically study the Scriptures for we should not take seriously a spurious or unauthentic document. After criticism establishes the genuineness and the authenticity of a document we may proceed to its appropriation. The rationalist and liberal are so out of harmony with the supernatural character of the Scriptures that they are not able to truly appreciate them. The post-Reformation orthodox and their modern orthodox and fundamentalist counterparts equally fail to properly appreciate the Bible. The Reformers have showed us the way through the Protestant Circle. Coming to Scriptures out of faith we believe them to be the Word of God, and by properly reading them we in turn discover them to be the Word of God. Only *by* response and *in* response to Scripture do we appreciate it and truly know it as the Word of God.

G. BULTMANN AND THE NEW HERMENEUTIC

In the 1950's the theological leadership in Germany was taken over by Bultmann and the scholars trained by Bultmann in important New Testament chairs. Bultmann's main concern is with hermeneutics and therefore deserves

[92] *Ibid.*, 200.

special attention. The essentials of his hermeneutics are
as follows:[93]

(1). *The scientific principle.* All matters of fact are
settled by the scientific method, and all historical statements can be accepted only if they can be verified by the
ordinary procedures of historians. To ask a person to believe against science or against history is to ask him to
sacrifice his intellect. To ask a man to believe that Jesus
walked on water is to ask him to believe something contrary to science, and if the man does believe this he
sacrifices his intellect. The conviction that a man must
never sacrifice his intellect is a very deep conviction of
Bultmann and the Bultmannians and measurably determines their exegesis of Scripture.

(2). *The critical principle.* Bultmann studied under the
leading Old and New Testament critics of his time. He
was shaped for life in his scholarly procedures by studying
with these men. In his student days the history-of-religion-
school *(Religionsgeschichtliche Schule)* was very strong in
Germany.

The words, concepts, and expressions used in the New
Testament are to be determined by an exhaustive study of
the whole historical, literary, sociological, and religious
background of the words, concepts and expressions. Thus
the concept of "Lord" *(kurios)* is to be traced out in the
religions and philosophies that were part of the environment in which the New Testament was written. The implication of all of this is that the meaning of the New Testament concepts are not given by divine revelation and to be

[93] The Bultmannian materials are enormous because his her-
meneutics is so controversial. For initiation into Bultmann apart
from his own writings I suggest the books on the theology of
Bultmann: Walter Schmitals, *An Introduction to the Theology
of Rudolph Bultmann.* Kegley, editor, *The Theology of Rudolph
Bultmann.* Braaten and Harrisville, *Kerygma and History: A
Symposium on the Theology of Rudolph Bultmann.* Macquarrie,
An Existentialist Theology.

so understood, but not borrowed from contemporary religion or philosophy. The implications of this for Biblical hermeneutics is very great. The historical setting of a concept becomes more important in understanding the text than in a strict exegesis focussing directly on the text alone.

The second major critical tool of Bultmann is form-criticism. The German word is *Formgeschichte,* which means tracing out the history of the literary forms contained in a document. Cultures have set models, forms, literary genre by which they perpetuate their traditions. The New Testament writers were no different from writers in other cultures. So they too used forms. The larger concepts are *Gattungen* and the smaller ones *Formen.* The Gospels in particular, are to be interpreted by a research into the forms of the Gospels. This too has the general effect of making the New Testament more a culturally conditioned document than a final revelation of God.

Such typical forms are pronouncement stories, miracle stories, myths, legends and "Novellen" (short stories). Bultmann's book, *The History of the Synoptic Tradition,* shows how radical or sceptical this kind of critical interpretation can be (although it must be mentioned that some men use form-criticism without drawing from it the scepticism so characteristic of Bultmann).

This critical approach has led to the famous Content-Criticism debate *(Sachkritik).* The *Sache* of a document is what the document is attempting to communicate; it is the material substance of a document; or it is the burden of a document. Barth believes that all critical work is preliminary to the interpretation of Scripture. After these preliminary matters are settled then the interpreter follows through with a grammatical and theological exegesis of the text. So for Barth there is no Content-Criticism of the New Testament.

Bultmann rejects the idea that criticism is but the preliminary activity of the exegete before he does his exegesis, but that the criticism of the text must not be limited. It participates in all of the activities of the expositor. So with Bultmann there is *Sachkritik*. Barth maintains that when we have established the teaching of Scripture as Christians we are honor-bound to believe it. The *Sache* is part of faith. To Bultmann we may believe that the New Testament does teach the virgin birth, but Bultmann doesn't have to believe it. The *Sache* need not be accepted by modern man.

Bultmann at this point looks at *Sachkritik* from another perspective. He makes a distinction between what the New Testament says *(Gesagt)* and what the New Testament means *(Gemeint)*. So the real *Sache* of Scripture is what is meant, not what is said. This appears again in different form in the demythological debate as the distinction between what is said mythologically and what is meant existentially. Again it must be indicated that this leads to a very radical interpretation of the New Testament.

(3). *The mythological principle.* Bultmann teaches that the church of the first century expressed its faith in mythological terms. Bultmann really has three different criteria in the light of which he calls a concept mythological. (i) If the writer of the New Testament is stating his faith in a worldly way, an external way, an objective way, then he is stating it mythologically. According to this a myth is a projection from the interior of man of some concept out in the world of events and objects. (ii) If the writer of the New Testament is asserting something contrary to science such as the mysterious multiplication of bread and fish by Jesus, then it is a myth. (iii) The third criterion is nowhere stated by Bultmann but the idea comes across loud and clear. Doctrinal teachings of the New Testament that are not acceptable to modern men are myths. A distinction must always be made with Bultman between how he carefully defines myth, and what he actually does with the concept in his interpretation. Obviously he has enormously inflated the concept of myth as indicated by the way he concretely handles the texts of the New Testament.

These myths are generally derived from Jewish apocalyptic myths and Greek mystery religions myths. Furthermore these myths do not occur just here and there but the New Testament is permeated with them. This theory of myth has a very direct influence on Bultmann's hermeneutics.

(4). *The demythological-existential principle.* In 1941 Bultmann wrote a famous essay, "New Testament and Mythology." The ideas were not particularly new to Bultmann, as he had used all the concepts given in this article in his previous work. But in this essay he puts forth his method so clearly, so directly, so consistently that the article became the charter of the whole Bultmannian movement.[94]

Bultmann uses the big word, *Entmythologisierung.* The German prefix *ent-* means to take away, remove. A parallel to this in English would be the *un-* in unmask. The first duty of the interpreter is to recognize the mythological character of a passage of Scripture, for such myths are not believable by modern man. But the myth says something. The early Church used the myth to say something; so the New Testament scholar must find out what the myth says.

At this point Bultmann uses Heidegger's existential philosophy to determine what the myth is trying to say. Bultmann believes that the New Testament writings grew out of existential encounters but were unfortunately put

[94] H. W. Bartsch, editor, *Kerygma and Myth, Vol. I,* pp. 1-44. Periodically the essays on the debate over mythology are collected and published as another volume of *Kerygma and Myth.* Two volumes have already been translated and others are projected. Bultmann's own essays are collected and published from time to time as *Glauben und Verstehen.* One volume of this has been translated with the title, *Essays.* Here, too, other volumes in English are projected.

in mythological form. The modern scholar must now unmask the myth and recover the original existential meaning of the myth.

There is a lot of literature on Bultmann's use of Heidegger, but we cannot enter into the details. Basically the
issue is this. Bultmann does not believe Heidegger was
inspired of God, but that he does give us the best working
model for doing exegesis and theology in the twentieth
century. In some later date he could be replaced. But as
of now his philosophy is the most useful for Christian
theology. The critic states that Bultmann will let the New
Testament say only what passes through the screening of
Heidegger's existentialism. In addition to this, G. Noller in
Sein und Existenz claims that Bultmann does not faithfully follow Heidegger, but systematically misrepresents
Heidegger for his own theological purposes.

(5). *The dialectical principle.* Bultmann repeatedly
states that if something is objective or historical it is not
existential; if it is existential it is not objective nor historical. Faith lives only by decision and not by objective or
historical supports.

However, the cross is a unique event. It is to Bultmann
the one historical item he cannot surrender to criticism.
It is at the same time a historical event in Roman history,
and the act or event of God's salvation. But the relationship of the cross seen historically and seen by faith is
dialectical. By this Bultmann believes that a historian
cannot deduce from the historical study of the cross the
meaning of the cross in salvation known only in faith.

(6). *The revelational principle.* Whether it is true or
not, modern theologians assert that the old orthodox
doctrine of revelation believed that revelation consisted in
truths or doctrines or concepts given to the writers of
Scripture whereas modern theologians believe that revelation is an event, an encounter, the presence of God Himself.
Revelation is an existential encounter and not the impar-

tation of information known only by supernatural revelation. Bultmann belongs to the modern theologians who believe that revelation is not a quality of Scripture but, in older language, an "experience."

The "Word of God," an expression Bultmann uses, is not then Holy Scripture. Holy Scripture is a record or a witness that revelation does occur, but it is not itself revelation or directly the Word of God.

Further, revelation involves both God and man in that it is essentially encounter. In the older orthodox view revelation was in Scripture whether a man believed it or not. In Bultmann and many other modern theologians, revelation happens only when both God and man participate in the event of revelation. God speaking a supernatural Word when not heard or believed by any man is not revelation to Bultmann.

The hermeneutical importance of all of this is that the interpreter is not looking for the divine revelation in Scripture and stating it in theological form, but he is looking for the "Word within the words," for the existential stratum of Scripture, for the manner in which Scripture addresses man.

(7). *The law principle.* This will be discussed in more detail in the chapter on prophecy. Bultmann does not believe that the Old Testament in any way predicts doctrines or concepts in the New Testament. It is not a "Christian" book. It is really a book of law. It shows how man fails his existential task and only in this sense it is a negative lesson about man; but the positive message of the Scripture is in the New Testament. This position greatly influences the way Bultmann interprets the Old Testament and how he interprets all those passages in the New Testament which claim to be fulfilment of predictions in the Old Testament.

From Bultmann there sprang a radical movement in which Bultmann's scepticism about the New Testament is

carried even further, and a positive movement which attempts to push further the break-throughs of Bultmann.
This positive movement is known as the *New Hermeneutic*.[95]
Its two most articulate members in Germany are Ebeling
and Fuchs. Its philosophical writer is Gadamer.[96] It goes
beyond Bultman in the following:

(i). *The critical principle.* It is not only myths that
modern man objects to in the New Testament but to any
kind of error, historical or factual. The motto here is, "faith
elaborates," and the interpreter of the New Testament must
spot all such elaboration.

However there is another development in the New Hermeneutic that seems to go counter to this. According to
Bultmann the only historical event necsssary for the
kerygma is the cross. But his followers believe that this
historical basis is too small. So they have tried to find a
broader historical base and started what is called "The
New Quest for the Historical Jesus." Further, it was felt
that Bultmann worked with too positivistian idea of history, but history in the twentieth century is not considered
so positivistic or scientific. The influential book causing this
change of mind was that of the British philosopher, R. G.
Collingwood (*The Idea of History,* 1946). This view of
history lessens the tension between history and faith which
was so characteristic of Bultmann's theology.

(ii). *The hermeneutic principle.* The New Hermeneutic
claims that the proper translation of the Greek word for
hermeneutics should be singular and not plural. However,
the entire role of hermeneutics (we shall continue to use
the plural) is now reversed. Historically hermeneutics

95 For an introduction into the *New Hermeneutic* see Robinson and Cobb, editors, *The New Hermeneutic: New Frontiers in
Theology,* Vol. II.

96 Ray Hart's *Unfinished Man and the Imagination* is an
American attempt to give theoretical foundations of the New
Hermeneutic but unfortunately it is an incredibly difficult book
to understand.

meant the various rules given for interpreting ancient documents. Sacred Hermeneutics listed the special rules for interpreting Holy Scripture.

In the tradition of Heidegger, hermeneutics now means how the existent (the *Dasein* — Heidegger's existential word for a person) sees or understands his own world and experience and sets this out in speech. This speech is then his hermeneutics of his world and experience. Hermeneutics in the traditional sense is now a subdivision of this newer concept of hermeneutics.

The New Hermeneutic claims that its new view of hermeneutics is not just for Biblical scholarship, but is really a philosophy within itself containing its own theory of knowledge (epistemology) and the basis for a new integration of the liberal arts for the university curriculum.

(iii). *The language principle.* The New Hermeneutic moves away from Bultmann's simple division between decisions that lead to authenticity and self-understanding and decisions that lead to inauthentic existence with no self-understanding. The New Hermeneutic has really developed an existential theory of language. The whole task of preaching from the original study of the text of Scripture to the delivered sermon is to be done within the context of this new theory of existential language. Instead of using the word *encounter (Begegnung)* for man's response to God, and God's response in the act of decision or faith, it uses the word *speech-event (Sprachgeschehen* or *Sprachereignis).* Although in many ways the scholars of the New Hermeneutic will do exegesis in the traditional Protestant manner of the past one hundred years, in other ways they will make radical departures in view of their existential theory of language.

Summary: The various efforts to understand the Bible have now been surveyed. It has not been our purpose to refute each of these methods here suggested, as that in prin-

92   PROTESTANT BIBLICAL INTERPRETATION

ciple is involved in the next chapter. In this following chapter we define and defend what we believe to be the conservative Protestant method of Biblical interpretation for we deem it the only adequate one to unlock the meaning of Sacred Writ. We believe it was the essential method of our Lord, of His Apostles, and all others who have been successful in understanding the pages of God's Holy Word.

BIBLIOGRAPHY

F. W. Farrar, *History of Interpretation.*
————, *Interpretation of the Bible: A Short History.*
R. M. Grant, *The Bible in the Church: A Short History of Interpretation.*
K. Fullerton, *Prophecy and Authority: A Study in the History of the Doctrine of the Interpretation of Scripture.*
B. Smalley, *The Study of the Bible in the Middle Ages* (revised edition).
C. Briggs, *Biblical Study,* Chapter X, "The Interpretation of the Bible."
H. P. Smith, *Essays in Biblical Interpretation.*
The Interpreter's Bible, I, p. 106 ff., "History of the Interpretation of the Bible."
C. W. Dugmore (editor), *The Interpretation of the Bible.*
M. S. Terry, *Biblical Hermeneutics, Introduction,* Chapter III, "Historical Sketch."
G. H. Gilbert, *The Interpretation of the Bible: A Short History.*
Wolfgang Schweitzer, "Annotated Bibliography on Biblical Interpretation," *Interpretation,* 4:342-357, July, 1950.
Fr. Torm, *Hermeneutik des Neuen Testaments,* Section 10, "Kurze Übersicht über die Geschichte der Exegese."
(W. Schweitzer's *Schrift und Dogma,* a survey of contemporary hermeneutics, came into our hands too late to include it in this chapter.)

CHAPTER III

THE PROTESTANT SYSTEM OF HERMENEUTICS

A. INSPIRATION: THE FOUNDATION

The divine inspiration of the Bible is the foundation of historic Protestant hermeneutics and exegesis. With the Jews Protestants accept the inspiration of the Old Testament, and with the Roman Catholic and Eastern Oriental Churches they accept the inspiration of the New Testament. Protestants differ from Orthodox groups in rejecting the Apocrypha.

Historic Protestant interpretation shares much in common with the classicists in that it has documents coming from antiquity in ancient languages, and in terms of the cultures of those times. Both the Biblical interpreter and the classicist have the problem of determining the text, of translating, and of stating ancient concepts in their modern counterparts. For example, the classicist must explain that Aristotle's word for matter (*hyle*) is not the equivalent of our word *matter*. Likewise the Biblical interpreter must take a word like soul (*psyche*) and relate it by comparison and contrast with our present usage of the word in English.

The classicist has no documents he considers inspired although he may greatly value and admire them. One life-time scholar of the classics said in the hearing of the author that his idea of heaven was a group of Greek students sitting around a seminar table reading through the Greek literature again and again. The Protestant, however, is professedly dealing with inspired documents. At the point of inspiration a new dimension for interpretation is added. This new dimension has the following features:

(i). It has a *moral* or *spiritual* aspect. There is no moral or spiritual qualification necessary to understand the classics unless a man defends the brief that only a moral man can understand great art. The spiritual requisite is, however, central in Protestantism. The Bible: being a spiritual book demands of its interpreter a minimum of spiritual qualifications which are not necessary for the classicist.

(ii) It has a *supernatural* aspect so that what is suspect in classical studies is sober history in the Biblical records. The myths and marvels of Greek mythology are taken by the classicists as inventions of the human imagination. The Protestant accepts the existence of an Almighty God who in the progress of redemption performed mighty miracles. Therefore, in interpreting his text the Protestant takes soberly the miraculous whereas the classicist rejects it in his documents—and rightly so.

(iii). It has a *revelational* aspect adding new content to old words. Granted that the bulk of New Testament vocabulary is derived from classical and *Koinē* Greek, and that many of the meanings remain unchanged in the New Testament, there is yet no question that added depth is given to words in the New Testament. We are not here defending the notion—exploded by Deissmann—that there is a special or ecclesiastical Greek. But the New Testament does add new depth, new connotations, to such words as *faith, love, mercy, redemption, salvation, heaven,* and *judgment.*

The evangelical Protestant interpreter in accepting the plenary inspiration of Scripture severs company with all forms of rationalism, e.g., neo-orthodoxy, religious liberalism, or Reformed Judaism. Many of the critical judgments of the nineteenth century are today either discarded or modified. The imposition of an evolutionary theory of religion on the Scriptures has undergone some modification and even rejection by some scholars. The archeological researches have shown that much more is sober history in the Old Testament than was previously believed. Archeology has also shown the radical contrasts of Israelitish religion with surrounding religions. The conservative trend in Old Testament studies is one of the unexpected phenomenon of the mid-twentieth century.[1]

The position of the evangelical is that only a *full-fledged, intelligent Biblicism is adequate to the present day situation in science, philosophy, psychology,* and *religion.*

Because historic Protestantism accepts the plenary inspiration of Scripture certain over-all attitudes characterize it. (i) It approaches the Bible from the spiritual dimension of faith, trust, prayer, and piety. (ii) It engages in Biblical criticism to save it from being deceived or deluded or naive. It is not foundationally anti-critical. Unfortunately some representatives of the conservative viewpoint have unenlightened opinions as to the nature and purpose of criticism, but anti-criticism is not part of the necessary structure of evangelicalism. Evangelicalism, however, is patient and watchful when confronted with critical problems, trusting that further research and investigation will weigh the evidence in its favor. The rewards of such an approach have been many, particularly from archeological research. (iii) It exercises the utmost care and scruples to discover the true text of both Testaments, to discover the true rules of interpretation, and to apply them with the greatest of pains and care that the word of man may not be intruded into the Word of God. It therefore does not indulge in the wholesale reconstruction of texts, histories, and documents which characterizes liberalism.

[1] Liberals may well note that there is a considerable number of erudite scholars of the Jewish and Catholc faiths that have not capitulated to rationalism in criticism. Cf. Felix A. Levy, "Contemporary Trends in Jewish Bible Study," *The Study of the Bible Today and Tomorrow* (Willoughby, editor), pp. 98-115; and, James Harrel Cobb, "Current Trends in Catholic Biblical Research," *ibid.*, pp. 116-128. Other essays showing how liberalism has failed to really understand the Bible are: G. E. Wright, "The Christian Interpreter as Biblical Critic," *Interpretation*, 1:131-152, April, 1947; and, H. H. Rowley, "The Relevance of Biblical Interpretation," *Interpretation*, 1:3-20, January, 1947.

B. Edification: The Goal

Not only is Protestant interpretation grounded in the plenary inspiration of the Scriptures, but it takes also as the counterpart of that truth the great purpose of the Bible, namely, to produce a spiritual effect in the life of the man that reads it. Augustine was not wrong when he said the guide of interpretation was *LOVE*—love to God and love to man. All the historical, doctrinal, and practical truth of the Bible is for one purpose: *to promote the spiritual prosperity of man. The Bible is not an end; it is a means.* Its purpose is first of all to make us wise unto salvation, and secondly to benefit us in our Christian life through doctrine, reproof, correction, and instruction in righteousness (2 Tim. 3:15-17). The end result is that we might be *men of God* completely equipped in good works. The prostitution of the Bible from *means* to *end* is an ever present danger for little groups who study the Bible for no other reason than to study the Bible. Such groups frequently fall prey to such spiritual maladies as Pharisaism, spiritual pride, and popishness in interpretation.

This is to say the goal of all interpretation is *spiritual results* in the listeners. Hobart correctly says that "no man goes good interpretation who does not look for results in men as the final aim of his interpretation." [2] Nor can we gainsay Rowley when he wrote:

There is yet another principle of interpretation which remains to be mentioned without which no interpretation can be adequately relevant. . . . This means that the theological interpretation of the Bible which is often called for, and which indeed is to be desired, is not sufficient. For the Bible is more than a theological book. It is a religious book; and religion is more than theology. Its study should do more than develop right views about God, man, and duty; it should nurture right relations to God.[3]

[2] Hobart, *A Key to the New Testament*, p. 11.
[3] Rowley, *op. cit.*, p. 16.

The practical significance of this is that the crowning method of preaching is the expository method. This method puts the Holy Bible at the center of the public ministry of the preacher. It is a professed acknowledgment that the only dependable source for preaching is the Scriptures. It enables the full power and pungency of the Word of God to be released among the people of God. When resigning a church a pastor gave to his people this advice for the selection of his successor which shows directly the necessity for an expository ministry: *"Do not choose a man who always preaches on isolated texts, I care not how powerful and eloquent he may be. The effect of his eloquence will be to banish a taste for the Word of God and substitute a taste for the preacher in its place."* [4]

C. THE PROTESTANT METHOD OF HERMENEUTICS

(1) *Theological Perspectives*

The Protestant method of interpreting Holy Scripture is based on certain theological convictions. Belief in Holy Scripture as the Word of God means that interpretation must be seen in a theological context. All the specific rules of interpretation must be contained with a larger frame of reference, and that frame of reference is theological. Therefore before we come to specific rules the Holy Scripture must be set in its proper theological context. Certain very general theological assumptions govern the particular exegesis of Scripture and these guiding assumptions are as follows:

(i). *The clarity of Scripture.* Holy Scripture is an ancient book, a very large book, and a book with many perplexing passages. How sense is to be made out of individual passages and the Holy Scriptures as a whole is the problem of the

---

[4] *The Moody Monthly* (editorial), 45:261, January, 1945. Italics are ours. Cf. also Chafer's discussion of "Animation" (the power of the Bible to influence life and conscience), *Systematic Theology*, I:120-123.

clarity of Scripture. The Roman Catholic Church had its theory of the clarity of Scripture. In that both Christ and the Spirit mystically indwell the Roman Church, the Church shares in the mind of Christ and the Spirit. It is therefore its gift to know the meaning of Scripture and in the exercise of this gift the Roman Catholic Church solves the problem of the clarity of Scripture.

The Reformers rejected this view of the solution to the problem of the clarity of Scripture. It was Martin Luther in his work, *The Bondage of the Will,* who determined the Protestant theory of the clarity of Scripture.

Luther spoke of the external and internal clarity of Scripture. The solution to this problem is fundamental for both the theory of hermeneutics and the practice of interpretation. Luther said that the external clarity of Holy Scripture was its grammatical clarity. If an interpreter properly follows what has been called "the laws of language," or "the rights of language," he can know what the Scriptures specifically mean. This is the application of the humanists' philological method to Holy Scripture.

The internal clarity of Scripture is the work of the Holy Spirit in the heart or mind of the believer, illuminating his mind to see the truth of Scripture as the truth of God. By the use of scientific philology and the illumination of the Spirit we arrive at the clarity of Scripture, and there is no need to resort to the Church.

But this does not mean the Protestant interpreter knows the meaning of everything in Holy Scripture. Farrar cites the Talmudic rule: "Teach thy tongue to say, I do not know."[5] That there are passages that are puzzling and have to date yielded to the skill of no interpreter must be candidly admitted. Lindsay has put his finger on the cause when he wrote: "The obscurity of ancient documents is far more frequently occasioned by our ignorance of mul-

---

[5] *History of Interpretation,* p. 474. This anticipates the concept of "learned ignorance" of the medieval philosophers.

titudes of things, then so familiarly known, that a passing
allusion only was needed to present a vivid picture, than
any difficulties connected with the language itself."[6]

Words and sentences occur in the context of a conversation,
in the context of language, and in the context of a culture.
Their meaning depends in a large part to these contexts in
which they occur and without that context it is either
difficult or impossible to know the meaning of the words
or sentences. It is therefore no great thing nor something
out of the ordinary that we should have words, concepts,
and sentences that puzzle us in Holy Scripture.

(ii). *Revelation as accommodated.* Holy Scripture is the
truth of God accommodated to the human mind so that the
human mind can assimilate it. The Scriptures were written
in three known languages of man (Hebrew, Aramaic,
Greek). The Scriptures were written in a human or social
environment and its analogies are drawn from that environment. When we learn the content of that environment we
can know the meaning of the revealed analogy.

Through such accommodation the truth of God can get
through to man and be a meaningful revelation. Stated
another way, revelation must have an anthropomorphic
character. [7]

The accommodated character of divine revelation is
especially obvious in such instances as the Tabernacle and
in the parabolic teaching of Christ. In both instances the
human and earthly vehicle is the bearer of spiritual truth.
Our understanding of the spiritual world is *analogical* (although Brunner and Niebuhr prefer the use of the word

6 *Lectures on the Epistle to the Hebrews,* I, 169.

7 Cf. the extended discussion of this under the caption, "Does
Inspiration Exclude All Accommodation?" by Cellérier, *Biblical
Hermeneutics,* p. 266 ff., and in P. Fairbairn, *Hermeneutical
Manual,* p. 88 ff. Both agree that there is an accommodation in
the *form* of revelation but not in its *matter.* Some scholars prefer
the word *anthropic* (characteristic of the human) rather than
anthropomorphic (the divine in terms of human analogy).

mythical at this point, in that theological statements are hybrids formed of some element in this world, and indicating at the same time something about God or the spiritual order; and Tillich prefers the word *symbol* by which he means a manifestation of the truth of God in terms of our world in contrast to the more literal and the more flat word, *sign*). The fact of God's almightiness is spoken of in terms of a right arm because among men the right arm is the symbol of strength or power. Pre-eminence is spoken of as sitting at God's right hand because in human social affairs the right hand position with reference to the host was the place of greatest honor. Judgment is spoken of in terms of fire because pain from burning is the most intense pain man encounters in the ordinary experiences of life. The gnawing worm is the fitting analogy for the pain that is steady, remorseless, and inescapable. Similarly the glories of heaven are described in terms of human analogies — a costly structure of gold, silver, and jewels; no tears; no death; and the tree of life. The question as to whether descriptions of hell and heaven are literal or symbolic is not the point. The point is that they are valid, analogical descriptions of inescapable realities. The particular character of those realities will become apparent in their own time.

This anthropomorphic character of Scripture is nothing against Scripture, but it is necessary for the communication of God's truth to man. This the interpreter will always keep in mind. The point has been excellently stated by Seisenberger:

We must not be offended by anthropomorphic expressions, which seem to us out of keeping with our conception of God. It is with a well-considered design that the Holy Scripture speaks of God as of a Being resembling man, and ascribes to Him a face, eyes, ears, mouth, hands, feet and the sense of smell and hearing. This is done out of consideration for man's power of comprehension; and the same is the case when the Bible represents God as loving or hating, as jealous, angry, glad, or filled with regret, dispositions which apply to God not *per affectum* but *per effectum*. They show us that God is not coldly indifferent to loyalty or disloyalty on the part of man, but notices them well. Moreover we must not forget that man is made in the image and likeness of God, and that therefore in the divine Being there must be something analogous to the qualities of men, though in the highest perfection.[8]

The interpreter who is aware of this anthropomorphic character of the divine revelation will not be guilty of grotesque forms of literal exegesis. More than one unlettered person and cultist has taken the anthropomorphisms of the Scriptures literally and has so thought of God as possessing a body.

Before leaving this subject of accommodation of Scripture it is necessary to declare our rejection of the liberals' use of the idea of accommodation. This particular species of interpretation by accommodation comes from Semler (1725-1791). To liberalism accommodation was the evisceration or enervation of the doctrinal content of the Bible by explaining doctrinal passages as accommodations to the thought-patterns of the times of the Biblical writers. B. Bacon's work, *He Opened unto Us the Scripture,* is replete with this kind of exegesis. Thus the liberals asserted that the Scriptures were not only accommodated in form but also in matter or content. This same sort of error is true in the *nth* degree in Bultmann's theory of the mythology of the New Testament. The atonement as a vicarious sacrifice is a way in which first-century Christians thought of the cross but, it is asserted, we are not bound today to think of the cross in that manner.

(iii). *Revelation as progressive.* By progressive revelation is not meant that the Biblical revelation is a process of evolution in the cultural or religious sphere. This idea of the evolution of religion in the Scriptures was a means of

---

[8] *Practical Handbook for the Study of the Bible,* p. 466.

denying the real revelatory content of Scripture and of undermining the uniqueness of Biblical revelation. It received a clear and classic statement in Fosdick's *The Modern Use of the Bible.*

By progressive revelation we mean that the Bible sets forth a movement of God, with the *initiative* coming from *God and not man, in which God brings man up through the* theological infancy of the Old Testament to the maturity of the New Testament. This does not mean that there are no mature ideas in Old Testament nor simple elements in the New Testament. Progressive revelation is *the general pattern of revelation.* That this is the teaching of the New Testament may be argued from the following:

(a). In the Sermon on the Mount our Lord is not instructing His disciples to *break* or *loose* the law, for he came not to break the law but to fill the law full. In his *Commentary on Matthew (The American Commentary on the New Testament)* Broadus gives a magnificent exegesis of this text (Matt. 5:17-20). Christ came to bring out the wider, larger, higher significance of the law. The law was proper as far as it went, but it did not go far enough. It taught a basic morality for the children of Israel but our Lord elevates the law to a higher level of motivation and spirituality. No abstinence from killing will do, but man must now act on the higher dictates of love. Refraining from cursing is not enough, for we must now look at the full sanctity of a promise. The morality of the Ten Commandments was a necessary point of beginning in man's ethical, spiritual, and theological development, but the Sermon on the Mount summons believers in God to a much higher level of ethical conduct.

(b). In his Epistle to the Galatians Paul divides up the dealings of God into the period before Christ and after Christ. The period before Christ is designated as a period of childhood, tutelage, immaturity, "grammar school education." In the fulness of time Christ came and with him comes the full revelation with its maturity of doctrine and morality. The Old Testament was a period of learning the theological alphabet, of carnal ordinances and elementary teaching. In Christ the fulness of revelation comes, and God's sons are reckoned as mature heirs.

(c). Exceptionally clear in relation to this point under discussion is Hebrews 1:1-2. We are told that God has two great revelations, one of which was given through prophets to Israel, and the other through a Son to the Church. Three adverbs commence the book of Hebrews (in the Greek text) and they each describe part of the manner in which God spoke through the prophets to Israel. First, the Old Testament was uneven in its progress through *time*. The revelations came sporadically. The *method* of revelation greatly varied. We have such a diversity as the law written with the finger of God, and Balaam rebuked by the voice of his animal. The *period* of this revelation is the ancient times *(palai)*, that is to say, the time of man's theological infancy and youth. In contrast to the first verse is the second which asserts that God has spoken his final word through His Son. God spoke clearly, directly, and conclusively through the highest possible organ of divine revelation, His Son, and so brought into existence his full revelation, the New Testament.

It is the additional teaching of the book of Hebrews that the Old Testament revelation was a *material* revelation, the spiritual truth being encased in earthly and cultural shells, and one of *types, shadows,* and *parables* — whereas the New Testament is a *spiritual* revelation, and contains the substance, reality, and fulfilment of the Old Covenant forms.

This perspective of progressive revelation is very important to the interpreter. He will expect the full revelation of God in the New Testament. He will not force New Testament meanings into the Old, yet he will be able to more fully expound the Old knowing its counterparts in the

New. He will adjust his sights to the times, customs, manners, and morals of the people of God at any given state in the Old Testament period of revelation, and he will be aware of the partial and elementary nature of the Old Testament revelation. He will take Augustine's words *(Distingue tempora et concordabis Scriptura)* "distinguish the times and you will harmonize Scripture" as a guide so as not to create a contradiction in Scripture by forcing a New Testament standard of morality or doctrine upon an Old Testament passage. Monogamy is a distinct emphasis of the New Testament and must not be urged as a contradiction to the polygamy of the Patriarchs who apparently had no revelation at this point.

Progressive revelation in no manner qualifies the doctrine of inspiration, and it in no way implies that the Old Testament is less inspired. It states simply that the fullness of revelation is in the New Testament. This does not mean that there is no clear Old Testament teaching nor that its predictions are nullified. On the other hand, the heart of Christian theology is found in the New Testament which contains the clearer revelation of God. Christian theology and ethics must take their primary rootage in the New Testament revelation.

(iv). *Scripture interprets Scripture* (or, "obscure passages in Scripture must give way to clear passages"). There is no question that there are passages in Holy Scripture that are very obscure for modern man which may have been very clear to the authors of the passages. Or there may be some doctrinal suggestions in Holy Scripture that we do not know how to bring out into their full clarity of meaning. The Roman Catholic Church claimed that it possessed the mind of Christ and the mind of the Spirit in its teaching magisterium so that it could render obscure doctrines clear. The Reformers rejected the claim of the Roman Catholic Church that it had the gift of grace and illumination to know what the Holy Scripture taught. In place of an appeal to the teaching magisterium of the Church, the Reformers proclaimed that Scripture interprets Scripture.

In this expression the word "Scripture" is used in a double sense. As the first word of the formula, Scripture means the total Scripture; in the second occurrence it means a part of Scripture, either a verse or a passage. Restated the principle would read: "The entire Holy Scripture is the context and guide for understanding the particular passages of Scripture." If this is true then no appeal is necessary to the teaching magisterium of the Church.

In the concrete task of writing Christian theology this principle means that the theologian must basically rest his theology on those passages that are clear and not upon those that are obscure. Or to phrase it yet another way, "Everything essential to salvation and Christian living is clearly revealed in Scripture." Essential truth is not tucked away in some incidental remark in Scripture nor in some passage that remains ambiguous in its meaning even after being subjected to very thorough research.

There is no question that much mischief has been done with Scripture in the history of interpretation by interpreters who claimed to have much truth in obscure passages of Scripture. Saul's encounter with the witch at Endor is an obscure incident and from which we can draw no certain conclusions about witchcraft. Paul's reference to baptizing for the dead (I Cor. 15:29) is so enigmatic to us today that no doctrine should ever be built upon it. Or Paul might be saying something like this: "You people in the Church at Corinth who claim that the day of the Lord is past, why do you practice proxy-baptism which presumes that the day of the Lord has not come?" In either case no doctrine of proxy-baptism can be taught in the Church from this one obscure verse.

In John 3:5 our Lord says we must be born anew by the Spirit and by water. Nowhere in the text is the meaning of water specified. The closest we can come to the meaning of water is what water might have meant to a Jew when used in this context. The most obvious meaning would be "a cleansing." But to import into this text a whole theology of baptismal regeneration is not defensible. Perhaps the New Testament does teach baptismal regeneration, but it cannot be established from the occurrence of the word "water" in one text.

Cardinal Newman defends the Roman Catholic concept of the nun from the case of Anna in the Temple (Luke 2:36-38).[9] From this one passing reference to this woman mentioned here can no doctrine of nuns be justifiably defended.

Others who err at this point are those who approach I Peter 2:24 ("by whose stripes we are healed") with a detailed theology of divine healing. Here something is imported into the text that just is not there. The text does not univocally say "that just as Jesus bore our sins on the cross so that our sins may be forgiven, He also bore our diseases on the cross so that our sicknesses may be healed." That the expression is a metaphorical one speaking of the salvation of the soul is far more defensible than the notion that the clause teaches healing of our diseases. Peter gives no *extensive* discussion of healing in the atonement.

The real doctrinal element of Scripture is to be found where doctrinal topics are dealt with extensively. For example Romans 1-3 is an extensive discussion of the doctrine of sin; John 5 contains an extensive discussion of the deity of Christ; I Corinthians 15 has a long discussion on the theme of resurrection. Galatians discusses in much detail the relationship of the Law to the Gospel. It is in these great doctrinal passages that we get our stance for handling the occasional remarks on these doctrines in the other parts of Scripture.

[9] *Apologia pro vita sua* (Everyman's Library edition), pp. 253-254.

(v). *The analogy of faith.*[10] Horne defines the analogy of faith to be "the constant and perpetual harmony of Scripture in the fundamental points of faith and practice deduced from those passages in which they were discussed by the inspired penmen either directly or expressly, and in clear, plain, and intelligible language."[11]

The basic assumption here is that there is one system of truth or theology contained in Scripture, and therefore all doctrines must cohere or agree with each other. That means that the interpretations of specific passages must not contradict the total teaching of Scripture on a point. This is similar to saying that Scripture interprets Scripture *(scriptura sacra sui ipsius interpres)*. It also overlaps the problem of the unity of Holy Scripture. The diversity of Scripture is uniformly recognized. But beyond or behind this diversity is there any principle which expresses the unity of Scripture?[12]

The problem of the unity of theology, or the unity of Scripture, or the possibility of system in theology, is one of the most debated of modern issues in theology. This discussion divides itself into the following typical theories:

(a). *Theologies but no theology.* In his book, *The Religion of the New Testament,* Parsons argues that there is no one theology in the New Testament but several. This is not a new position but reflects the older conviction of New Testament scholars that we have a Johannine, Petrine, and Pauline type of theology. Parsons is by no means alone in this conviction but represents the viewpoint of a great

[10] The expression "the analogy of faith" is found in Romans 12:6. In context it means the proportion of faith given to each believer. But in the history of theology it means the system of faith or doctrine found in Holy Scripture. Cf. "Analogy of Faith," J. H. Blunt, *Dictionary of Doctrinal and Historical Theology,* pp. 18-19.

[11] *An Introduction to the Critical Study and Knowledge of the Scriptures,* I, 342. Italics omitted.

[12] Cf. Rowley, *The Unity of the Bible.*

number of Biblical and theological scholars. If this position is correct then there can be no analogy of faith.

(b). *Formal, systematic unity.* It was assumed by the authors of The Westminster Confession of Faith that there is but one system of theology contained in Holy Scriptures and they tried to summarize this system in their Confession. To put it another way, *systematic theology* — in the strict sense of the word "system" — is possible. In that the Scriptures do not tell us the whole mind of God, and in that even regenerate man is imperfect in his reasoning, there can be no completed system of theology. But the task of the theologian is to systematize the teachings of Holy Scripture the best he can. He is to aim at a final system of theology deduced from Sacred Scripture even though he knows that he could never in this life attain this final system.

(c). *Unity of perspective.* Some theologians believe that there is such diversity in Scripture that no system is possible. Rather, the unity of Scripture and therefore the unity of theology is in the persistent perspectives in Scripture. That is, God is always holy, true, and powerful; or, that man is always sinful; or that man lives by God's grace alone; etc. Theology is then unified around perspectives and attitudes like this and not by any formal system or any kind of systematic theology. Representative of this position is Torm *(Hermeneutik des Neuen Testament)*.

I presume that Bultmann would speak of the uniformity of the *existential perspective* in the New Testament. He too would agree that there are theologies in the New Testament but no unitary theology as such. The closest thing to a unity of thought is the manner in which John and Paul begin to reflect in their writings existential interpretations. If there is then any unity in the New Testament for Bultmann it must be in its common existential intention.

(d). *Theology of the cross.* The expression, "the theology of the cross," stems from Luther. He opposes it to the "theology of glory." The scholastics of the Middle Ages wrote their immense *summas* (catalogs) of theology as if they were saints in heaven doing research in the library of the New Jerusalem. But Luther sees that sin has fractured man's existence. Just as the cross puzzles us and is a scandal to us, and yet we believe in it for our salvation, so our knowledge of God is puzzling and obscure. Theologians can write only a theology of the cross and not a theology of glory.

Lutheran theologians believe that the attempt of the Reformed theologians to write a systematic theology manifests too much rationalism in Christian theology. Although Lutheran theologians do not believe theology is a series of disconnected doctrines they tend to write more topically than systematically reflecting their belief in the theology of the cross.

In neo-orthodoxy in particular there has been a new restatement of the theology of the cross and a new attempt to present a Christological unity of theology. For example, both Barth and Brunner do not believe in the older notion of serious *systematic* theology. (Although Tillich calls his theology a systematic theology he is using the word systematic more in the sense of correlation of kerygma and theology, or theology and philosophy, and not in the older sense.) Neo-orthodox theologians have not only been influenced by Luther but also by Kierkegaard. Hegel attempted to formulate a universal philosophy which Kierkegaard called "the system." Kierkegaard opposed the concept of system because finite man, existential man, cannot achieve a system.

Neo-orthodoxy has a *radial* and *Christological* theory of the unity of theology. Christ is the center of Christian theology and all doctrines are to be related to Christ. Thus all doctrines are unified in their radial relationship (like spokes

on a wheel) to Christ and not in terms of a network of dog-
mas forming a system.

Both Luther and Calvin claimed to have made Christ the
center of theology. But, according to Barth, they did not
really follow through on this belief. Barth intends to do
this (and so does Brunner). So Barth's doctrine of revelation is Christological, his doctrine of sin is Christological,
his doctrine of man is Christological. That is, the key to
these doctrines is somehow to be found in Christ. Hence
Barth has been called a *Christomonist*.

In summary of this discussion three more observations
are in order: (a) A theologian may be working with elements in each of these theories of theological unity. He
may emphasize one but include elements of the other. One
may believe (as I do) that there is a system of truth underneath the theological statements of Holy Scripture but that
this does not exclude a very concentrated use of the Christo-
ligical principle. (b) There are limits to any kind of
systematization. A theologian may achieve a high consistency in his theology which I think men like Tillich or
Bultmann have, but all theologies are eventually theologies
of the cross. (Or put in logical terms, we may try to axio-
matize Christian theology and so make it a perfect deduc-
tive system but in our sinnerhood and finitude we cannot
achieve this goal.) (c) We cannot agree with Parsons or
any other theologians who would fragmatize the Scriptures
into conflicting theological chunks. If this is the case, the
Scriptures have really lost any normative role in the writing
of Christian theology.

(vi). *The unity of the meaning of Scripture*. It has been
said that the Scriptures are like a piano or a violin. An
artist may play any composition he wishes on either of
these instruments. And so Holy Scripture is such a big
book and such a diverse book it lends itself rather easily to
the person who wants to impose on it some particular kind
of theology.

An interpreter who imposes such an interpretation on Scripture (*eisogesis,* bringing a meaning into Scripture as opposed to *exegesis* in which the meaning of Scripture is brought out) may not realize at all that he is asserting the plurality of the sense of Scripture. But this is what he really asserts.

In emphasizing the unity of the sense of Scripture we do not mean to reduce the meaning of Scripture to a narrow literalism, to an ignoration of the prophetic and typological depths of Scripture. We mean to oppose certain hermeneutically outrageous ways of interpreting the Scripture such as:

(a). *Allegory.* A study of the commentaries or use of Scripture among the early Church Fathers reveals a fantastic use of the imagination in finding New Testament truth or spiritual truth or theological truth in the Old Testament by the use of allegorical interpretation. This is really an assertion of the plural meaning of Scripture. Believing in the unity of the sense of Scripture eliminates all allegorizing of Scripture, ancient or modern.

(b). *Cults.* Metaphysical cults, theosophical cults, divine science cults, pantheistic cults all base their interpretation of Holy Scripture on the theory that the meaning of Scripture is plural. The first meaning is the ordinary historical or grammatical one; and the second meaning is the one the cultist brings to Scripture from the particular metaphysical system or religious system he is pushing. Once again the emphasis on the unity of the sense of Scripture puts an end to the cultic abuse of Scripture.

(c). *Protestant Pietism.* Many devout Christians believe that God speaks to them each day out of Scriptures and so gives them direction and guidance for the decisions of that day. Hence the Scripture is read in anticipation of *specific* directions emerging out of their reading of the Scripture that pertain *directly* to their lives and their decisions. Scripture is not only the fountain head of all theological truth and God's Word through the ages, but its phrases or sentences or verses are intended to be specific ways in which God can speak to each Christian each day he reads his Scripture in the light of the decisions and situations that Christian is confronted with that particular day.

For example, a very pious Protestant might be in a place of indecision whether he should take a certain trip or not. In his devotions he reads how the Church at Antioch sent Paul and Barnabas away on a missionary trip. So this Christian feels that God is speaking to him in that passage and it is now God's will that he should take the proposed trip.

This is a very direct assertion of plurality in the meaning of Scripture. (i) The first sense is what the record means of Paul and Barnabas setting out on a missionary trip. (ii) The second meaning is that God is telling this pious Christian of the twentieth century to take a trip.

But the pious Christian who does this has no idea that he is asserting a plural meaning of all Scripture. He does not know that much Catholic dogma is supported by allegory which is based on a plural meaning of Scripture; nor does he know that many cults base their theology in Scripture by the use of plural meanings in Scriptural texts. In short the Protestant who uses his Holy Scripture this way is unwittingly in some very bad theological company.

(vii). *Interpretation and application.* The true purpose of Holy Scripture is to be God's immediate earthly instrument for spiritually affecting mankind. The great classical verse on the inspiration of the Scripture (II Tim. 3:16), indicates what Scripture is to do to man. It is to teach, reprove, correct, and train in righteousness. Its goal is a man of God who is equipped spiritually and ready for every good work.

For this reason Barth has insisted in his hermeneutics that there is one bound from interpretation to application. Or to put it another way, interpretation intends application, or, teaching intends obedience, or, faith drives towards works. All of this is right, for Holy Scripture is not a theoretical book or a book of theological abstractions, but a book that intends to have a mighty influence on the lives of its readers.

But here we must remember the old adage: "Interpretation is one, application is many." This means that there is only one meaning to a passage of Scripture which is determined by careful study. But a given text or a given passage may speak to a number of problems or issues. Five or six different kinds of sermons could be preached from the text, "You must be born again" (John 3:7). What application the preacher makes of the text is determined by the purposes of the sermon. But the preacher must always distinguish the initial primary meaning of the text from the particular application he makes with it.

There is a real "homiletical temptation" at this point. The preacher wants the text to be relevant and contemporary. In order to achieve these purposes he may distort the text in some manner, or misrepresent it, or use it more for a motto than a point of Scriptural reference for his sermon. This can be done in such a way that it gives the congregation the false impression that his sermon expresses the original meaning of the text.

It is therefore mandatory for a preacher to realize that interpretation of the meaning of the text is one thing, and the range of application is another, and that he must always keep these two matters separate. And this warning should not be made only for preachers. In the devotional use of Scripture there is again the temptation to presume that a devotional thought or two gathered from the text is the original meaning of the text.

(2) The Philological Principle

In recent literature, philology means the technical and comparative study of words. It is roughly equivalent to linguistics. But in the larger historical context philology meant a total program in understanding a piece of literature. This included linguistics but also much more — such as history, cultural surroundings, and literary criticism. We are using the word *philological* in this second sense.[13]

Sometimes the philological method is called the historical method, or the grammatical method, or the historico-grammatical method, and sometimes the literal method where it is contrasted with the allegorical or mystical methods. It may also be called the critical method. By being critical, hermeneutical theory has become very self-conscious of what hermeneutics is all about and what criteria are necessary to insure faithful interpretation of documents. Any interpretation of a given passage or book of Holy Scripture must be given an adequate justification. Or to put it another way, the basis for accepting a certain interpretation must be made explicit. "Critical" does not mean the same as "sceptical," just as "academic" is not necessarily the opposite of the "spiritual." In essence, to be critical in the exegesis of Scripture means to bring into one's methodology the kinds of procedures that are characteristic of good scholarship. Devotional commentaries have a place in the general edification of the Church but they must never be considered as scholarly commentaries. The persistent problem of scholarship in any field is also

[13] For a general introduction to the subject of hermeneutics and for an analysis of its present status see the excellent article by James Robinson in *The New Hermeneutic* ("Hermeneutic Since Barth," pp. 1-77). For a recent American effort at hermeneutics cf. A Berkeley Mickelsen, *Interpreting the Bible.* A judicious little handbook has been written by Otto Kaiser and Werner Kümmel called *Exegetical Method: A Student's Handbook.* In German we have K. Frör, *Biblische Hermeneutik*, E. Fuch's *Hermeneutik*, and the impressive essay by G. Ebeling in *Die Religion in Geschichte und Gegenwart* (3rd edition), III, 242-262. For a compact treatment of the whole range of hermeneutics see the section on Hermeneutics in *Baker's Dictionary of Practical Theology.*

true of Biblical scholarship: all scholarly work is done by men, and men who are not pure scholars but have their presuppositions, or biases, or favoritisms, or hostilities, or in recent hippie language "hang-ups" (or being "up tight"). While commending scholarship as the critical function in the interpretation of Scripture, we do not affirm that such scholarship is free from prejudices which are common to all men, scholars or laymen.

Competent interpretation of Holy Scripture is done in a context, the context of the principles of scholarship which have not been arbitrarily chosen but have emerged from the scholarly standards and procedures of our universities since their creation in the thirteenth century. Philological interpretation of Scripture means that the Biblical interpreter does very much the same sort of thing that any competent scholar would do working in the same general area. In Chapter 1 we have listed under point 5 those elements which an interpreter of Holy Scripture must have in addition to the ordinary tools of scholarship.

The true philological spirit, or critical spirit, or scholarly spirit, in Biblical interpretation has as its goal to discover the original meaning and intention of the text. Its goal is *exegesis* — to lead the meaning out of the text and shuns *eisogesis* — bringing a meaning to the text. Or as Luther put it: *"Das ist der beste Lehrer, der seine Meinung nicht in die sondern aus der Schrift bringt"* ("The best teacher is the one who does not bring his meaning into the Scripture but gets his meaning from the Scripture").[14]

It is very difficult for any person to approach the Holy Scriptures free from prejudices and assumptions which distort the text. The danger of having a set theological system is that in the interpretation of Scripture the system tends to govern the interpretation rather than the interpretation correcting the system. The most persistent criticism of Bultmann and Tillich is that they have adopted certain theo-

[14] Cited by Farrar, *History of Interpretation*, p. 475.

logical and philosophical principles in such a set, rigid manner that it is very difficult for them to entertain an interpretation of a passage of Scripture that does not agree with their system.

Illustrative of how one's theological position can distort interpretation is the manner in which the parable of the Ten Virgins is treated. Arminian theologians use it to show that Christians may fall from grace. Advocates of the concept of a second blessing (i.e., a second major work of God in the believer following the one of his salvation) see here the proof for a second blessing. Calvinists use the text to show that there may be profession of faith without really participating in salvation. Others try to derive some doctrine of the Holy Spirit from the passage on the basis that oil is the symbol of the Spirit. Others see it as part of a prophetic program to occur in some yet future event. To the contrary it is a simple lesson on the concept of spiritual preparedness, or readiness, or as Jeremias takes it, of repentance.[15]

Calvin said that the Holy Scripture is not a tennis ball that we may bounce around at will. Rather it is the Word of God whose teachings must be learned by the most impartial and objective study of the text.

The most fundamental presupposition of the philological method in Biblical exegesis is that all exegesis must be done in the original languages if it is to be competent and trustworthy exegesis. It was the humanists who came out of the Renaissance (that movement in western culture beginning in the fourteenth century in which western culture moved from the medieval period to the modern period and whose original impetus is associated with Petrarch, 1304-1374) that called the scholars back to the Greek and Latin texts of the great classics of the Greek and Roman world. Luther, Melanchthon, Bucer and Calvin were deeply influenced by the scholarship of the new humanism. This lead them away

[15] *The Parables of Jesus*, p. 132.

from dependence upon the Latin Vulgate, the Bible of the Christian west for a thousand years, to the study of the Hebrew and Greek testaments. Calvin's *Commentaries* are considered the first real scientific, philological exegesis of Scripture in the history of the Church.

The great doctrines of our Christian faith can be established in any responsible or competent manner only by the interpretation from the original languages. This is a principle of all sound scholarship. Any philosopher posing as an authority on Plato must be able to read the Greek texts and any authority on the philosophy of Kant must be able to read German. The interpreter who interprets Scripture only in his modern langauge is always working with a linguistic veil between himself and original texts. And he never knows how thin or how thick this veil is.

At this point it is possible to give a thousand illustrations showing how a person without a knowledge of the original languages is really at a loss to do accurate interpretation. We shall be content with just one. In Ephesians 5:1 Paul exhorts Christians to be "imitators of God." The person who knows only English has no idea what is behind the concept of imitation. Unfortunately in English *imitation* usually means a cheap copy of the genuine article, or the artificial imitation of some outstanding personality. The concept of imitation is one of the fundamental concepts of the theory of art in classical times. In fact the first theory of art pronounced by Plato is that art is the imitation of nature. There is also the concept that *this* world is the imitation of a *heavenly* or *spiritual* world. The only reality or truth in this world is, therefore, that which is a copy of the other world. In Plato in particular there is the concept of the imitation of God. If God is the perfection, the model, the archetype of all things, then true religion is the imitation of God. There is also the imitation of God taught in the Old Testament: "and be ye holy for I am holy" (Lev. 11:44-45; repeated in I Peter 1:16). There is also the imitation of God taught in the Sermon on the Mount: "You, therefore, must be perfect, as your heavenly Father is perfect" (Matt. 5:48). What appears in the English text of Ephesians 5:1 as a spiritual truism is discovered to be in virtue of a knowledge of the Greek one of the great concepts of both the Greek and Hebrew traditions.

However, this is not the entire story of the use of the Scriptures in the Church. It was also a passion of the Reformers to translate the Scriptures into the language of the peoples. Luther is famous for his great translation of the Holy Scriptures into German. He did the New Testament himself while in "captivity" in the Wartburg castle or fortress. He was the chairman of a group of scholars who translated the Old Testament. Both Luther and Melanchthon insisted that the entire school system of Germany be revised so that the lay Christian could read the German Bible for himself. Luther also broke with the scholarly tradition of writing everything in Latin. He began to publish his materials in German. This was again his desire to get Biblical and theological materials in the German language for the lay Christian.[16]

Calvin wrote his theology in Latin *(The Institutes of the Christian Religion)*. However with his own hand he made a masterful translation of his book into the French language. This is again in keeping with the spirit of the Reformation to get theological materials into the language of the people.

Although the Reformers set the right standard in the Church that Christian scholarship at its best must work with the Hebrew and Greek languages, they did not want theology or Biblical interpretation to become a new Protestant priestcraft. They did not want to make Scripture the

16 The word for *people* in medieval German was *doit*. The German language can make an adjective out of a word by adding *sch* to it. Thus *Deutsch* (derived from *doit*) means "the peoples' language" in contrast to Latin, the scholars' language.

book *only* for scholars. Every Christian can profit from reading his Scriptures in his national language. In fact there is a great deal he can get from Scripture without a knowledge of the original languages. There is no intention to take Scripture away from the lay person by insisting that competent interpretation can be done only with the original languages. The lay person may read his Scriptures and learn its history, be blessed and edified by its spiritual content, and come to know much of the essential theology of Holy Scripture all in the use of the translated Scripture.

(1). *Literal.* We use the word "literal" in its dictionary sense: "... the natural or usual construction and implication of a writing or expression; following the ordinary and apparent sense of words; not allegorical or metaphorical" *(Webster's New International Dictionary)*. We also use it in its historical sense, specifically, the priority that Luther and Calvin gave to literal, grammatical, or philological exegesis of Scripture in contrast to the Four Fold Theory of the Roman Catholic scholars (historical meaning, moral meaning, allegorical meaning, eschatological meaning) developed during the Middle Ages and historically derived from Augustine's Three Fold Theory. It was particularly the allegorical use of the Old Testament that the Reformers objected to, and the manner in which Roman Catholic dogma was re-enforced by allegorical interpretation. Hence the "literal" directly opposes the "allegorical." This was programmatic with Luther and Calvin, and it does not mean that these men had no lapses back into allegorical interpretation.

The accusation so frequent in current theological literature that Fundamentalism is a *literalism* is not at all what we have in mind when we use the word "literal." The word is ambiguous. To some scholars the word "literal" means "letterism" and this is really what they mean when they say Fundamentalists are literalists. Others have thought that orthodoxy in theology is a literalism in the sense that it attaches almost magical or supernatural powers to the very words of Scripture. Some linguists believe that the literal meaning of a word is determined by counting. Ordinarily we think that the word "bear" means an animal in its literal sense; and that a speculator in the stock market who is called a "bear" is a bear by metaphor. But if the population uses the word "bear" three times more frequently for the stock speculator than for the animal then the literal meaning of "bear" is the stock speculator.

Associating certain words with such things as nouns, verbs, adjectives, etc., is called *designation*. Every language represents a certain system of designation. Language also reflects several levels of designation. Ordinary conversation reflects popular, ordinary, common-sense designation; a learned lecture on physics represents a techincal designation; a poem represents metaphorical designation. The word "literal" in the theory of hermeneutics implies an understanding of this process of designation. It takes as the primary range of designation the customary, the usual, the socially-acknowledged designations. Thus the literal meaning of a word is its designation in the common stock of the language.

The older books on hermeneutics used the expression *usus loquendi*. This means that the meaning of a word is determined how the word was used in ordinary conversation. *Designation* is a better modern semantical term to use in developing a theory of interpretation, rather than *usus loquendi*.

When we assert that the literal meaning of a word or a sentence is the basic, customary, socially designated meaning we do not underestimate the complexity of language. There is a certain parallel between the thrusts, faults, and obtrusions of rocks in geology and the structure of languages. Languages are built up through centuries of use and become laminated and encrusted. In asserting that hermeneutics must start with the literal meaning of words this assertion is made in the light of the complexity of language.

The spiritual, mystical, allegorical, or metaphorical usages of language reflect layers of meaning built on top of the literal meanings of a language. To interpret Scripture literally is not to be committed to a "wooden literalism," nor to a "letterism," nor to a neglect of the nuances that defy any "mechanical" understanding of language. Rather, it is to commit oneself to a starting point and that starting point is to understand a document the best one can in the context of the normal, usual, customary, tradition range of designation which includes "facit" understanding.

Horne has a very excellent definition of what is meant by *literal* in *literal* interpretation:

> Further, in common life, no prudent and *conscientious* person, who either commits his sentiments to writing or utters anything, intends that a diversity of meanings should be attached to what he writes or says; and, consequently, neither his readers, nor those who hear him, affix to it any other than the true and obious sense.... *The Literal Sense* of any place of Scripture is that which the words signify, or require, in their natural and proper acceptation, without any trope [figure of speech], metaphor, or figure, and abstracted from mystic meaning.[17]

Craven's excellent comments are as follows:

> *Normal* is used instead of literal ... as more expressive of the correct idea. No terms could have been chosen so unfit to designate the two great schools of prophetic exegetes than *literal* and *spiritual*. These terms are not antithetical, nor are they in any proper sense significant of the peculiarities of the respective systems they are employed to characterize. They are positively misleading and confusing. *Literal* is not opposed to *spiritual* but to *figurative; spiritual* is an antithesis on the one hand to *material* and on the other to *carnal* (in a bad sense). *The Literalist*

[17] *Op. cit.*, I, 322. Italics are his.

122   PROTESTANT BIBLICAL INTERPRETATION

... is not one who denies that *figurative* language, that *symbols* are used in prophecy, nor does he deny that great *spiritual* truths are set forth therein; his position is simply, that the prophecies are to be *normally* interpreted (i.e., according to the received laws of language) as any other utterances are interpreted — that which is manifestly literal being regarded as literal, and that which is manifestly figurative being so regarded. The position of the *Spiritualist*... is not that which is properly indicated by the term. He is one who holds that certain portions are to be *normally* interpreted, other portions are to be regarded as having a *mystical*... sense. Thus for instance, Spiritualists... do not deny that when the Messiah is spoken of as "a man of sorrow and acquainted with grief," the prophecy is to be normally *interpreted;* they affirm, however, that when He is spoken of as coming "in the clouds of heaven" the language is to be "spiritually" (mystically) interpreted.... The terms properly expressive of the schools are *normal* and *mystical.* [18]

The reader will note in these citations the emphasis on "natural," "proper," "obvious," and "normal." These are but other ways of indicating *usus loquendi* or of semantic designation within a speech culture. This is not *letterism* which fails to recognize nuances, plays on words, hidden metaphors, figures of speech, lamination of meanings in a word, etc. Nor is it the alleged "wooden literalism" which is supposed to characterize orthodox, Fundamentalist, or conservative hermeneutics. As previously indicated this is a continuation of the hermeneutics of the Reformers. What is surprising in contemporary Roman Catholic Biblical scholarship is how much of the hermeneutics of the Reformers Roman Catholic scholars now use themselves; and how embarrassed they are with the allegorical excesses of previous generations of Roman Catholic scholarship and especially the use of allegory by the papacy in its recent pronouncements. In the declaration of the bodily assump-

[18] *Commentary on Revelation* (in the Lange commentary series), p. 98. Italics are his. We are using *literal* in the meaning that Craven gives to *normal.*

tion of Mary (by Pius XII, in 1950, in *Munificentissimus Deus*) the Scriptural support was assigning certain verses in the Psalms which spoke of Israel as references to Mary which was obviously an allegorical and not a philological exegesis of these verses. On the other hand the Reformers were not pledged to a slavish literalism, for Calvin himself wrote that "to show themselves men of letters, these good doctors prohibit even the least departure from the literal signification. . . . If this canon of interpretation be admitted, all the light of faith will be overwhelmed in crudest barbarism." [19]

In defense of the literal basis of Biblical hermeneutics it may be argued that:

(a). *The literal method of interpretation is the usual practice in the interpretation of literature.* Whenever we read a book, an essay, or a poem we presume the literal sense in the document until the nature of the literature may force us to another level. This is the only conceivable method of beginning or commencing to understand literature of all kinds. The non-literal is always a secondary meaning which presumes an already existing literal understanding of literature. This previous stratum of language is the *necessary* point of departure for the interpretation of all literature. If we attempt to read some oriental, mystical book we shall first attempt to understand it literally and when we see that procedure is not doing justice to the text we then forsake the literal program for a mystical, allegorical, or metaphorical one.

Therefore, without prejudging the nature of Holy Scripture one way or another (whether there is a deeper or profounder meaning expressed typologically, allegorically, mythologically, or existentially), we must start our inter-

[19] *Institutes of the Christian Religion*, IV, 17, 23. In another place Calvin wrote these remarkable words: "I will give an interpretation, not subtle, not forced, not wrested, but genuine, natural and obvious." *Ibid.*, IV, 1, 1.

pretation of Holy Scripture from the stance of literal or philological interpretation.

(b). *All secondary meanings of documents depend upon the literal stratum of language.* Parables, types, allegories, symbols, figures of speech, myths and fables presume that there is a level of meaning in language prior to the kind of language this kind of literature is. The parable of the sower is understood only within the context of literal "farm" language. The symbolism of a lion is based upon what is asserted about lions in literal speech. Incense as a symbol of prayer is understood again within the context of the use of incense in daily life and expressed in the literal language of daily conversation. The typological or perhaps allegorical way Paul speaks of Abraham, Sarah, and Hagar in the book of Galatians is based upon the historical and factual statements about these people which in turn reflects the literal stratum of language. In that all non-literal statements are "take-offs" from the more original, more primitive literal langauge, then the literal exegesis is the point of departure in all interpretation, Biblical or extra-Biblical.

(c). *Only in the priority of literal exegesis is there control on the exegetical abuse of Scripture.* By the "exegetical abuse of Scripture" we mean all interpretation in the history of the Church and in the histories of cults which forces strange and unBiblical meanings into Scripture by some form of allegorical interpretation (meaning by the "allegorical" any kind of reading into Scripture secondary or tertiary or even quaternary meanings).

In the history of the allegorical interpretation of Scripture it is not denied that there is a literal, historical, or grammatical sense to Scripture, but it is depreciated. It is the "fleshly" or the "superficial" understanding of Scripture. However in making such a value judgment the allegorists are generally blind as to how much literal interpretation they actually employ to get their own allegorical program moving.

Furthermore there are many kinds of spiritualizing or allegorizing of the Scriptures. The Church Fathers used an uncontrolled allegorical method to find Christian theology in the Old Testament. The Roman Catholic theologians used some version of allegorical interpretation to justify their sacramentarianism and hierarchy from the Old Testament. Although some cults are deplorably literalistic in their understanding of Scripture, others of a more metaphysical or theosophical bent are given to strange allegorizing of Scriptures. For centuries the parables of the Gospels were not properly understood because they were given allegorical and not literal interpretations. How do we resolve the competition among the various allegorical schools of interpretation? There is really only one way: grant the prior right to literal interpretation of Scripture, and the right of literal interpretation to act as judge and umpire of any proposed allegorical or mystical interpretation of Scripture.

To rest one's theology on the secondary strata of meanings is to invite interpretation by imagination. That which supplies the imagination with its content is unfortunately too often non-Biblical ideas or materials. The only sure way to know the meaning of Holy Scripture is to anchor interpretation in literal exegesis. Literal interpretation is not the *Charybdis* of *letterism* nor the *Scylla* of *allegorism*. It is rather the effective, meaningful, and necessary control for the protection of the right interpretation of Scripture. This may be said even stronger. It is the theologian's or interpreter's *responsibility* to guard the use of Holy Scripture by the hedge of literal exegesis.[20]

There are three points at which the program for the

---

[20] The Ecumenical Study Conference's Report, "Guiding Principles for the Interpretation of the Bible" brands allegorical interpretation as arbitrary and in our vocabulary defends the primacy of literal interpretation. Richardson and Schweizer, editors, *Biblical Authority for Today*, pp. 240-246.

priority of literal interpretation may be misunderstood and these points must be briefly commented upon:

(a). The program of the literal interpretation of Scripture does not overlook the figures of speech, the symbols, the types, the allegories that as a matter of fact are to be found in Holy Scripture. It is not a blind letterism nor a wooden literalism as is so often the accusation.

(b). It is not true that a belief in verbal inspiration of Scripture implies letterism or wooden literalism in hermeneutics. It is hard to understand why this accusation is made but it is a frequent one in theological literature. The belief in verbal inspiration does not mean, for example, that this belief makes the interpreter interpret the book of Revelation in a completely literalistic fashion. Verbal inspiration is a theory about the origin of Holy Scripture but it settles nothing in and of itself about theory of hermeneutics.

It must be admitted that some very orthodox people think that verbal inspiration and literal interpretation belong together for to them "literal interpretation" means to take the Bible "as it is." Any other kind of interpretation is "tampering with God's Word." Their intention is genuine, but their idea of how Scripture is to be protected is both naive and wrong.

(c). Behind all discussions of hermeneutics or interpretation, about Scripture or about literature in general, are some very sophisticated theories of language. In philosophy, theory of language has become one of the major themes of modern philosophy. The defense of literal interpretation may appear to some reader informed about language theory that we presume that understanding language on the literal level is a matter of simple assertion or simple designation. Such pioneers in this field as Urban and Cassirer have shown how much metaphor or "dead metaphor" (such as the psychological word "attract" used as if it were a physical force in the statement "a magnet attracts nails") penetrates even the literal level of language. We are not unaware of this additional complex factor in language nor of the newer ideas of language dating from the Vienna Circle but a discussion of these matters is not necessary for the practical intention of this book.[21]

21 Cf. the article on "Language," *The Encyclopedia of Philosophy*, VI, 384 ff., and the extensive references to langauge theory in the Index, p. 461. Besides philosophical theories of language in the older sense (as Urban), and the newer linguistic or analytic philosophy (Wittgenstein, Ayer, Feigl, Carnap, etc.) there is a current debate about the character of theological language. There are the English theologians who wish to describe the language of theology from the perspective of contemporary analytic philosophy (e.g., Ramsey) ; and the existential theory of language stemming from Heidegger (Bultmann, and the New Hermeneutic) ; and the mythological character of theological language (Brunner and Niebuhr — a theological assertion is mythological in that part of it is a reference to this world and the other part is a reference to God or the spiritual world). and in Tillich's idea of symbols there is an explicit theory of theological language.

CHAPTER IV

THE PROTESTANT SYSTEM OF HERMENEUTICS

(Continued)

In the previous chapter the basic theory of hermeneutics was stated, explained, and defended. Our concern now is to show how it expresses itself in the concrete task of interpreting Holy Scriptures. The matters we discuss in the following are not to be concerned as the necessary chronological order in which interpretation is done. An interpreter of Scripture is thinking many things and doing many things all at the same time. But we are stating the elements which constitute the actual way in which literal interpretation is practiced.

(a). *Words*. Words are the units of thought in most of our thinking and writing; they are the bricks of our conceptual formulation. Any serious study of Holy Scripture must engage in the study of words. In the ordinary course of exegesis the meaning of words may be found in the Hebrew and Greek Lexicons. Walter Bauer spent a lifetime in writing his famous *Greek-German Lexicon* (translated into English and edited by Arndt and Gingrich with the title, *A Greek-English Lexicon of the New Testament*) in which he attempted to give an exhaustive classification of almost every word in the New Testament.

In addition to this we now have the famous Kittel, editor, *Theological Dictionary of the New Testament* (an English translation of the first six volumes and to be completed in eight) in which all the important words in the Greek New Testament are given an exhaustive philological and historical discussion. In that in most cases the Hebrew Old Testament is consulted as well as the Greek translation of the Old Testament, the Septuagint, it functions secondarily as a great treatment of words in the Hebrew Old Testament. Of course, the work is not to be taken as if it were the product of infallible scholarship but as a working tool used with discretion it is a magnificent source of information about the words of Holy Scripture and no serious exegesis can be done without reference to it. These are huge volumes running to a thousand pages or more in some volumes suggesting the amount of material packed into them.

(aa). Words may be studied *etymologically*. This means we attempt to understand the word by the way it is formed. Words may have prefixes and suffixes, and sometimes are a combination of words. The word translated "bishop" is derived from *episkopos*. It is combined from *epi* which means upon or over, and *skopeō* which means to look. Hence it means an overseer, a person with a specific office, or even a guardian, or perhaps manager or superintendent. The word translated "apostle" is from the prefix *apo* which means away from, and *stello* which means to send. Hence an apostle is a sent one, a delegated one, an official representative of an important body.

The etymological analysis of Greek and Hebrew words is of limited value. In some cases it does really help us to understand the word. More important, however, is to learn how to assess the meaning of words from studying the typical ways the Greeks put their words together. This means studying the kinds of prefixes they used and how these prefixes function, and the kind of suffixes they used and what meaning can be gathered from the manner in which they ended words. This kind of etymological study is far more important than taking compound words apart.

One of the most controversial words in the New Testament is the word "inspired" — *theopneustos* (II Tim. 3:16, "inspired of God"). When -tos is added to a Greek word, what does it intend to indicate? German scholarship has put the emphasis upon the internal state of the prophet: he is an inspired man. After a comprehensive research into words ending with -tos, Warfield came to the conclusion that it emphasizes an inspired product, the Holy Scriptures.[1] Thus *theopneustos* is not about man being inspired by God (although this is not excluded) but God producing a Book.

Even more controversial than *theopneustos* has been the word *harpagmos* in Philippians 2:6. Does it mean robbery? Something to be grasped? Here again much research has been done with Greek words put together the same way as *harpagmos*, to see if this very detailed and technical etymological research will settle the meaning of the word.

Unfortunately this kind of etymological research can be done only by linguistic experts, but it is the most significant kind of etymological research. German scholars have produced a Greek lexicon in which the words are spelled backwards. In itself it represents a very unusual kind of scholarly dedication to a problem (H. Schone, *Reportorium griechescher Worterverzeichnisse und speziallexika*). A Greek scholar can then look at dozens of examples of the manner in which the Greeks ended a word and so grasp what the Greek language intends by a particular ending.

But there are limitations to etymological research. In some instances we do not know the origin of the word, such as the Greek word for deacon *(diakonos)*. In other instances the word has had such a complicated history that very little can be learned about its meaning from its etymological construction. The Greek word for God, *theos*, is such a word. Whatever its original derivation was, it is

[1] "God-Inspired Scripture," in *The Inspiration and Authority of the Bible*, pp. 245-296. On page 282 Warfield lists 75 Greek words ending in *-tos*.

not really of any help to understand the New Testament usage of this word.[2]

(bb). Words may be studied *comparatively*. By this we mean using a Hebrew or Greek concordance to discover all the occurrences of the word in Holy Scripture. If we can see at a glance how many times the Greek New Testament uses a Greek word, and the contexts in which it is used, we can begin to get the "feel" of the word. On the other hand it may reveal how varied the use of a word is, and so save the interpreter from a premature, simplified understanding of a word. Such words as *soul* and *spirit* are complex words, and a good comparative study of these words can correct the superficial nonsense that has collected around these words. It has been asserted in some very narrow Christian circles that when God gives a meaning to a word, that is the meaning of that word for the rest of Holy Scripture. This attempt to close off with a sort of mathematical precision the meaning of a word just will not do. Any person with the ability to do it can sit down with a concordance to the Greek New Testament and see in five minutes that a word like *heart* has a plurality of meanings in Holy Scripture. Kuyper's assessment of this procedure is correct when he writes that "a sharply drawn distinction of conceptions and a constant usage of words is foreign to the Scripture."[3]

The kind of detailed and laborious work of tracing down the meaning of words by their comparative study is best reflected in recent theological work by Leon Morris, particularly the kind in exhaustive work he has done on words about the atonement in his book, *The Apostolic Preaching of the Cross.*

Another aspect of the comparative study of words is in

[2] Most pastors do not get enough Greek in their education to do even the most basic kind of etymological research. Fortunately *The Analytical Greek Lexicon* (the "Bagster's Lexicon") does give the elements that form a compound Greek word.

[3] *Principles of Sacred Theology,* p. 496 fn.

the study of synonyms. Fortunately we do have Girdle-stone's *Synonyms of the Old Testament* and Trench's *Synonyms of the New Testament*. However it must be emphasized that these are older works and Biblical scholarship desperately needs this kind of study brought up to date.

By noting what word a writer considers as a synonym for another word gives us a real clue about what the writer understood the first word to mean. (In my own reading of contemporary theological and philosophical literature one of the things I systematically do is to note what words or expressions the author uses in a synonomous way as a significant clue to his thought.)

There are two parts of the New Testament that are very important to study in which there is considerable occurrence of synonyms. There are the various passages in Paul's writings where the same ideas are discussed such as Ephesians and Colossians. There are also repeated references by Paul to church order, and to church offices or ministries, such as statements in I Corinthians, Ephesians, and the Pastoral Epistles. A study of the entire four Gospels from the standpoint of synonymous expression is also very rewarding. Out of dozens of possible examples we indicate two. Matthew 20:21 speaks of Christ being seated "in his kingdom," and Mark 10:37 of His being seated "in his glory." "In his kingdom" and "in his glory" are then identical concepts. Matthew 18:9 uses the expression "enter into life" but Mark 9:47 uses the expression "to enter into the kingdom of God." Again the phrases must mean the same thing.

The benefit of such a study is that it helps us understand an expression or word that is obscure or difficult to understand in one passage by reference to a passage where the same concept is clearly explained by the use of another expression. Or it shows us what the writers of the New Testament understood by a concept by using diverse synonyms.

There is not only exegetical clarity introduced by noting what words are synonyms and what expressions or even passages are synonymous, but there is a warning about the manner in which we understand theology. If the New Testament shows a flexibility in its vocabulary then our theology ought to reflect this flexibility. Or stated in another way, if we pack too much meaning into one specific word in Scripture we will then be embarrassed when confronted with synonyms of that word which in turn undermines the theology we have tried to pack into that one word.

For example, if we try to make a distinction between the expressions "kingdom of heaven" and "kingdom of God" by noting the passages only which use either of the two terms, we create a false alternative. By the use of a Greek *Harmony of the Gospels* (such as Hauck's) we find out that there are at least a half dozen different expressions synonymous with "kingdom." The problem is no longer that of trying to show how the kingdom of God and the kingdom of heaven are different but to show how to harmonize the half dozen or more expressions about the kingdom which are undeniably synonymous.

(cc). Words may be studied *culturally*. We may look at such a Greek word as *oikos* and say that that it is the word for *house,* or the word *oikia* and say it is the word for *household*. However, how we today understand a house, and how a house or household was understood in the first Christian century, may be different. The issue is an important one in settling the matter of infant baptism in view of "household baptism" in the New Testament. One of the usual arguments for infant baptism is that a household generally includes children or infants so that if a household were baptized then the infants were baptized. But this may prove too much. In some instances *oikos* or *oikia* included animals and we are not about to start baptizing household pets as well as infants. Therefore before we can say too much about even such simple words as *house* or *household,* we must try to include what these words mean in the culture in the first Christian century.

Often behind a word in the New Testament or Old Testament is a practice of the culture, and really to know the richness of the word we must know the cultural practice. When it is said that our Lord offered *supplications* (Heb. 5:7) a word is used that was associated with a custom of bringing an olive branch to a dignitary from whom one is requesting a favor and the branch was the assurance of a sincere appeal.

When our Lord mentioned that if we were *compelled* to go one mile, we should go two (Matt. 5:41), He was referring to a well-known Persian custom. When a Persian messenger carried a message of the empire he could compel inhabitants of a locality to carry his baggage one mile, or to perform any service the messenger commanded. Hence Christians out of love and not command should help their neighbor not for the customary or accepted one mile, but for the extra mile of love and grace.

The student of Holy Scripture today has a wealth of material available to him which will give him these historical details and cultural practices without having laboriously to go through a small library to find them out for himself. There is, as previously mentioned, Kittel's *Theological Dictionary of the New Testament* which is an enormous storehouse of these kinds of materials. Recently published is *The Interpreter's Dictionary of the Bible.* New commentaries, are being published continuously in England and America,. Some of the more important words of Holy Scripture are given a fresh interpretation in view of our newer knowledge gained in linguistics and archeology in A. Richardson, editor, *A Theological Word Book of the Bible.* Some of the older works still have some valuable information as far as the meaning of particular words are concerned, as Deissmann's *Light from the Ancient East* and Coburn's *New Archeological Discoveries* (about the New Testament).

(dd). Words may be studied in *cognate* languages and ancient translations. By cognate languages we mean languages that belong to a same language family (such as French and Spanish, or Swedish, Norwegian and Danish). A word that may puzzle us in the Hebrew in particular may be understood by investigating its equivalent in Arabic.

This kind of language study is very technical and is beyond the average student or pastor. Research in the Hebrew language includes languages from Egypt to Mesopotamia. Arabic and Aramaic are of particular importance for Old Testament studies because these languages are so close to Hebrew. The results of these kinds of technical studies are supplied for us in the recent commentaries, Hebrew and Greek lexicons, and the more philological commentaries.

In that the Old Testament and New Testament have been translated into other languages in a historical period much closer to the Biblical period than we are, we can gather something of what the ancient translators thought about Hebrew and Greek words. The two basic translations for Biblical work are the Septuagint (a translation from Hebrew to Greek beginning in the third century before Christ and obviously only of the Old Testament) and the Latin Vulgate (done by Jerome in the fifth Christian century but after twenty years of study in Palestine). There are other materials such as the paraphrasings of the Old Testament into Aramaic, the famous Targums, and other translations as the Syriac Peshitta, that are very valuable for scholars. But here again what is important for the student or pastor (who is by no means a research scholar) is contained in the kinds of materials of recent publication which we have mentioned above. We include these matters in this book to give the average reader some sense of the very technical language studies necessary for an accurate understanding of the vocabulary of the Hebrew and Greek Testaments.

(b). *Grammar.* If words are the units of a language, then the sentence is the unit of thought. Of course, dividing up a language into words and then sentences is artificial. But in all such kind of studies we must be working with parts and wholes at the same time. Although a study of a Biblical word as such is very rewarding the word occurs in a sentence, in a context, and in some instances the context tells us far more what the word means than pure philological research.

First, everything said about research for the meaning of words applies to grammar. The same sort of resources that help us understand words help us understand grammar.

Second, in the study of grammar we must understand that languages are put together in different ways. An *analytic* language is a language that basically stresses word order. That means that the very order in which the words occur is the way in which we grammatically grasp the meaning of the sentence. English is very much a word order language. The importance here for the student of Scripture is that Hebrew is an *analytic* language (but not quite so dependent on word order as English).

An *agglutinative* or *synthetic* language is a language where the meaning is understood only partially by word order and much more by word-endings or case-endings. To explain this we must explain three more words.

Inflection. All languages are inflected. This means that something is put in front of a word (prefix) or at the end of the word (suffix) or in the middle of the word, to indicate a *special* meaning of the word. We form singulars and plurals, present tense verbs and past tense verbs, masculines or feminines by making these kinds of changes. *Egg* is singular; *eggs* is plural. *Eat* is present; *ate* is past.

Decline. When we make changes with adjectives and

nouns we are said to decline them. *Declining* is the verb used to describe *inflection* of adjectives and nouns. So, *house* is singular; *houses* is plural. *He* is nominative; *him* is accusative.

Conjugate. When we *inflect* verbs this is called *conjugating* verbs. *Run* is present; *ran* is past; *will run* is future.

As previously mentioned, all languages are inflected. But when the inflection becomes very complicated then the language is called *synthetic*. This means that a lot of meaning is packed into the form of the word itself. This, in turn, means that the grammar or syntax becomes more complicated. In the English language *the* serves for singular and plural, masculine, feminine and neuter. But *the* in German has a special form for the masculine, the feminine, and the neuter; it has yet another form if it is singular or plural; and it has yet another form depending which one of the four cases it is in. So every time a German uses the word *the* he has to know the gender of the noun, the number of the noun, and the case of the noun.

Greek is a strong synthetic language and that is one of the reasons it is so difficult for Americans to learn. There is a shift from the analytic way of speaking to a synthetic way.

Knowing then the fundamental structure of the Hebrew and Greek languages, we are able to "hang the picture." We know how each of these languages expresses meaning and so we get the feel of the language, the pulse of the language, or the knack of the language. As the Germans say, we get a *Sprachgefühl* — "speech feeling" — for the language.

For example, in Greek, a participle is both an adjective and a verb as far as its grammatical construction is concerned. So in stating the conjugation of a participle one may say it is an "accusative, singular, masculine, present, active participle." The first three words apply to nouns and adjectives, the last three to verbs.

Third, the interpreter must have a general knowledge

of syntax. Grammar suggests in a general way how sentences are put together according to rules. The more technical word for the study of the structure of a sentence is syntax. Each language has its own syntax, but certain categories of syntax cover most languages. In learning Hebrew and Greek the student learns the syntax of that language. However, students of Holy Scripture who work only in English should have some understanding of such concepts as subject and predicate, number, gender, mood, tense, participle, preposition, and so forth. What is important here for the student who works in English alone is more a sensitivity than a list of rules. He will much more readily understand the text if he has a sense about grammar or a sensitivity to syntax.

At this point many books on hermeneutics go into great detail about *idioms* (ways in which a language may vary from its set grammar) or *figures of speech* (simile, metaphor) or the *specialized terms* (elipsis, paraleipsis, paronomasia) of rhetorical expression; but any good commentary will discuss such constructions in its exposition of the text. That is a far more functional way to learn these details than any attempt to memorize a list. (Young's *Analytic Concordance to the Bible* lists seventy-one Biblical idioms.)

Fourth, grammatical interpretation involves consideration of the context.

(aa). The context of any verse is the entire Scripture. This is what is meant by "Scripture interprets Scripture." Barth defends some of his odd interpretations, especially in the Old Testament, by claiming that he has a right to bring the entire contents of Scripture to bear upon any particular passage. This is a principle difficult to manage, but it does say procedurally or programmatically that the "universe of discourse," the "locale," the "habitat" of any passage of Scripture is the total Scripture. It sets the general mood, gives the general perspective, governs the fundamental assumptions, or sets the possible limits of meaning for the interpreter of Holy Scripture.

There seems to be in the hermeneutical literature two or three versions of the "hermeneutical circle" or "spiral." One of them is this: "We can understand a particular passage only if we know what the whole Scripture teaches; but we can only know what the whole Scripture teaches by knowing the meaning of its parts." And so all theological interpretation of Scripture is a rotation or "spiraling" from part to whole, and whole to part.

(bb). The second context of any passage is the Testament it is in — Old or New. Each Testament has unique features of its own. Diversity in Scripture is in many ways greater than unity in Scripture. The interpreter comes to the Old Testament or the New Testament with the proper mind set which corresponds to the essence, the composition, the peculiar historical configuration, the place in the progress of divine revelation, of the Testament.

(cc.) The third context is the particular book in which the passage occurs. The interpreter must know what the "Galatian heresy" was all about properly to interpret passages in Galatians. The interpreter of the book of Revelation must understand the history of martyrdom and the theology of martyrdom of the early Church, or else he turns the book of Revelation into a kind of Ouija board for prophetic speculation.

(dd). The fourth context of any passage is the materials immediately before it, and, immediately after it. The material before the passage is the radar which guides the approaching, and the following material is the radar of the leaving. And if we can track the material approaching and leaving the particular passage, we have the framework in which the passage is to be understood.

For example, to understand the heart of the middle and last part of Romans 3, which is in some ways the theological heart of the whole Biblical plan of salvation, we must understand the kind of a case Paul builds in the preceding materials about man's sin and guilt, and what he says in Chapters 4 and 5 about man's faith and justification.

Romans 7 is the most controversial chapter in the entire Scripture in debating the significance of the context. The bibliographical materials on the passage are enormous and the debate has not let up. According to one group of interpreters the context of Romans 7 is sanctification, and therefore Paul is describing a Christian experience. The other group of interpreters states that we cannot follow through with the context line by line, because Paul is making an excursus back to his pre-Christian days to show the helplessness of the law to sanctify. Therefore Romans 7 is about pre-Christian experiences of Paul. In this passage the manner in which we understand the context determines our total stance in how we intend to understand the chapter.

In view of the frequent neglect of context especially in preaching we may sympathize with Robertson's remark that "the first step in interpretation is to ignore modern chapters and verses."[4]

Fifth, grammatical interpretation takes into consideration *parallel passages* or *cross references*. This principle is virtually the same as the study of synonyms, only it deals with larger sections of materials. The reason for this principle is that what is said in one part of Scripture may illuminate what is said in another part of Scripture. In most literature there are no overlaps, but one of the marked characteristics of Holy Scripture is that there are many places where in one manner or other Scripture repeats itself.

(aa). *Verbal cross reference.* This is a situation in which the wording in one passage is similar to the wording in another passage of Scripture. In some instances where the wording is the same, or the expression is the same,

---

4 Cited by Miller, *General Biblical Introduction*, p. 11.

nothing is really gained by the mutual study of both passages. This is an *apparent* cross reference. This is a matter of pure verbal coincidence. The only reason for mentioning this is that some preachers think that a Scriptural word has the same meaning in all of Scripture, and so they bring verses together that simply do not belong together, and these interpretations given in a sermon can be very misleading.

A *real* cross reference is that parallelism of words or expression where the content or the idea is the same and there is profit from the mutual study of the texts.

Examples of *real* cross reference work are: (1) Looking up all the passages that contain the very important concept of *son of man;* (2) looking for all references where Paul uses the word *flesh* (Greek, *sarx*); (2) examining all the passages in Colossians that parallel similar passages in Ephesians, for in many instances the subject matter of both epistles are the same. Fortunately there exists an *Englishman's Concordance* for both the Old Testament and New Testament which can be used by a person not knowing the original languages. If a student of Scripture knows only English, he will find that if he knows how to use Young's or Strong's complete concordances to the Scriptures he can find out what the Hebrew and Greek words are in a given text.

(bb). *Conceptual cross references.* A conceptual cross reference means that there is a verse or a passage in one book of Holy Scripture that has the identical substance or content of another part of Scripture even though there is no use of common words. The concepts in the passages are identical rather than just the words being the same.

Hebrews 2 and Philippians 2 both discuss the character of the incarnation; Romans 3 and Hebrews 10 both discuss the atonement; I Corinthians 15 and Revelation 20 treat the identical subject of the resurrection from the dead;

and, Matthew 24 and 25 must be compared with II Thessalonians 2, for both deal with the end or last times.

(cc). *Parallel cross references.* When two or more books of the Holy Scriptures describe essentially the same events, to get the whole picture before the interpreter he must compare these parallel accounts. The events in the life of Christ must be compared as they are differently recorded in all four Gospels, especially the first three which are called the Synoptic Gospels, because so much of their content is the same. There are *Harmonies of the Gospels* in both English (Robertson) and Greek (Hauck and Aland).

The life of Paul is recorded in Acts, and pieces of his autobiography are spread throughout his Epistles. The material in Acts must be checked with the material in the Epistles. For this we have Goodwin, *A Harmony of the Life of St. Paul* (an older work needing some correction from newer studies but still not duplicated in any recent work).

The same historical materials are covered by Samuel, Kings and Chronicles. For this kind of study we have Crockett, *A Harmony of Samuel, Kings and Chronicles.*

(c). *Literary Mold or Genre.*

There are ways in which thought can be expressed which cannot be understood by ordinary grammatical examination. A special manner of expression is used, and these special kinds of expressions are called either the *literary mold,* where *mold* has the idea of a fixed or standard pattern, or *genre,* a French word meaning genus, way, style, or fashion. An appreciation of literary genre is indisputable for the understanding of Scripture, because so much of Scripture (in a sense *all* of Scripture) is expressed in some kind of literary genre.

For example, there is a critical debate over the genre of the Synoptic Gospels. Some critics assert that the Gospels are pre-literary compositions; they are really a sort of staccato reporting or mere cataloging of the sayings and deeds of Jesus. The opponents of this viewpoint insist that the Gospels are literary compositions, but differ so much from ordinary literature because of the uniqueness of the materials and the uniqueness in the way these materials were preserved in the Church.

There are three circles of literary genre in Holy Scripture, each circle being larger than the other.

(aa). *Figures of speech.* A figure of speech may be a phrase of a complete sentence in which the author expresses himself in a special way that goes beyond ordinary methods of assertion. The most common are metaphors, similes, and hyperboles. A *metaphor* expresses something by direct comparison, direct similarity, or direct parallelism ("Ephraim is a cake," Hosea 7:8). A *simile* functions like a metaphor, only uses the words "like" or "as" ("the glory of the Lord was like a devouring fire," Exod. 24:17). *Hyperbole* means that some idea or event is stated in an exaggerated manner to indicate its importance or its quantity ("But there are also many other things which Jesus did; were every one of them to be written, I suppose that the world itself could not contain the books that would be written," John 21:25).

The range of figures of speech is large, and again we affirm that the student of Scripture should be sensitive to their existence; and, if he uses good, grammatical commentaries the figures of speech will be explained in the exposition. Some of these other kinds of figures of speech are: ellipsis, paradox, irony, syndoche, zeugma, euphemism, brachylogy, litotes, meiosis, oxymoron, personification, paronomasia, and metonymy.

(bb). There are larger forms of special literary expression ordinarily used within the text of a larger work. Examples of these are parables, allegories, fables, myths, and riddles. Here again the interpreter needs to realize that such forms of literary genre exist, that they take more reflection and imagination to interpret than strict grammatical interpretation, and that good commentaries spell these matters out. It is better for the student to have the right sort of book that gives him this kind of information, than that he should have a rote memorizing of the details.

(cc). Every book of Holy Scripture is cast in some sort of broad literary genre. If one reads books on Biblical introduction (to the Old and to the New Testament) he will find scholars attempting to specify these literary genre. Such a Biblical scholar will classify some book as *historical* (e.g., Acts); or as *dramatic epic* (e.g., Job); or as *apocalyptic* (seeing the future in terms of familiar images of the past, e.g., Daniel); or as *poetry* (e.g., Psalms); or as *wise sayings* (e.g., Proverbs).

The issue becomes complicated when such genre are introduced as *legends, sagas,* and *myths.* The reason is that critics have both a positive and negative evaluation and many critics have used these genre against the authenticity of Scripture. We know from the study of language, literature, and communication theory that truth and fact may be conveyed in other than straight prose reporting or exposition. Holy Scripture is a book rich and varied in its literary genre and this must not be overlooked nor underestimated. Because some of these genre have been used by some critics to undermine the trustworthiness of Scripture, the temptation naturally arises to be suspicious of *all* such literary genre as related to Scripture. There is no *inherent* harm in a literary genre; there is only harm or danger in how a scholar may use such genre against a document. If such a genre plays a *positive* role in the communication of revelation and is seen as part of the organism of all of Scripture we should not shy away from it.

Expositors have, do, and will differ over what kind of literary genre any particular book or passage of Holy Scripture exhibits. Barth does not believe that any mythological material in Holy Scripture is a valid witness to revelation. A huge volume was written in the nineteenth century by an evangelical Christian who interpreted the flood of Noah as an allegory and not a historical event.

The hermeneutical principle, however, is not touched by the different ways in which expositors assess the genre of different parts of the Scripture. The genre of a passage or book of Holy Scripture sets the mood or the stance from which all the rest of the book is seen. As for sheer number of divergent interpretations, the *Song of Songs* is the most controversial book in the Scriptures. We either take it allegorically as representing some sort of relationship between God and man (Israel and the Lord, Christ and the Church, Christ and the believer, God and the believer, etc.) or we take it literally (at the same time acknowledging the great amount of poetic imagery in the book) as a theological justification and interpretation of human sexuality. Our stance about the literary genre of the book determines our entire interpretation of the book.

It has been hard to assess the literary genre of the Gospels. To some the Gospels are pure historical reporting and to radical critics of the nineteenth and twentieth centuries they are mythological (pious and well-meaning elaborations and additions of the early Church but nonetheless nonhistorical fabrications). Most modern New Testament scholarship does not think the Gospels are biographies in the usual sense of the term. By this they mean no "life of Christ" can be decoded or deciphered from them. The films, novels, and plays that so construct a life of Christ are at variance with the nature of the Gospels themselves. Also most modern scholars (and by this expression we are including evangelicals) believe that the Gospels are *witnessing* or *kerygmatic* or *preaching* or *teaching* materials. How authentic the materials are depends on the convictions about inspiration and revelation of the scholar. The evangelical accepts them as authentic materials.

If the New Testament scholar believes that the Gospels are essentially mythological or "pre-literature" that will govern his entire manner of exegeting and interpreting the Gospel incidents. If the scholar believes that the Gospels are the sum of the authentic witnessing or kerygmatic materials of the early Church faithfully delivered by the Apostles his interpretation will be otherwise.

These are just examples to show how crucial it is to employ the concept of literary genre in the interpretation of Scripture, otherwise we can make a first class mess out of a book.

Many modern books of theology indiscriminately judge all scholarship that in some broad sense is evangelical or orthodox as "wooden-headed literalism." A number of things are meant by this charge but one of them is that such scholarship has no real appreciation of literary genre and the manner in which its recognition governs the way in which Scripture is interpreted. Their favorite target is the literalistic eschatology of the Fundamentalists who take all the predictions of the events of the end-times in a strict, literal way. The most absurd thing they usually point out is that future battles of the end-times are fought with the weapons of the ancient world which means that regardless of modern development of guns, tanks, airplanes, rockets, etc., mankind will revert back to bows, arrows, and spears. It is the lack of any real appreciation of literary genre that forces Fundamentalists to make such absurd assertions about future events.

It must be made clear that the mainline Reformation scholarship — Anglican, Reformed, Lutheran — has no part with that kind of Biblical interpretation that runs roughshod over literary genre and interprets Scripture with a grinding literalism. Rather, in the best of philological tradition, it recognizes that no book can be intelligently assessed and interpreted without first noting its literary genre.[5] Disagreements about literary genre, and disagreements about degrees of literalism do exist in this tradition and it would be wrong to ignore these differences. The point is that although the tradition allows for differences it is not in principle forced to a grinding literalism in its Biblical interpretation.

One more matter must be mentioned that is more a matter of theology than of literary genre. Lutheran theologians make a distinction between Law and Gospel which the Reformed and Anglican theologians do not make (cf. P. Althaus, *The Theology of Martin Luther,* chap. 19). The differentiation of Law and Gospel is an important working tool for the Lutheran theologian or interpreter and at this point Lutheran and Reformed hermeneutics divide. The Law is God in his wrath, God in his judgment, God in his hatred of sin, God in his strange voice, God in his alien work. Gospel is God in his grace, God in his love, God in his salvation. This is not a distinction between the Old and New Testaments. Nor is it a distinction properly expressed by speaking of "law and grace." The distinction of Law and Gospel runs through the entire Scriptures and is absolutely fundamental for the understanding of Scripture according to Lutherans. It is therefore also one of the main components in the Lutheran theology of preaching.[6]

[5] It has been pointed out more than once that the pronounced literalism in exegesis of prophetic and apocalyptic passages of many of the Fundamentalists contradicts the very allegorical way in which they interpret the Tabernacle, its priesthood and its offerings. In addition to this in many of their devotional commentaries they unconsciously or unwittingly do a great deal of allegorizing or spiritualizing in order to discover the devotional possibility of a text of Scripture.

[6] We have already mentioned Law and Gospel briefly in our discussion of Luther. It is a very complicated subject with nuances that escape those who do not come out of Lutheran tradition. Cf. T. McDonough, *The Law and Gospel in Luther;* E. Schlink, *Theology of the Lutheran Confessions,* Chapters 3 and 4, P. Althaus, *The Theology of Martin Luther,* Chapter 19.

Reformed theologians look at Law as something contained within the Gospel. It expresses the moral seriousness of faith in God and the absolute necessity for repentance in salvation. The Reformed theologians are not unaware of the differences made between Law and Gospel in such books as Romans, Galatians, and Hebrews, but they do not believe that the distinction is of such a nature that it becomes a major hermeneutical principle (cf. K. Barth, *Evagelium und Gesetz*).

Strange as it may seem much pre-millennial and dispensational theology is closer to the Lutheran view of the Law and Gospel than the Reformed theology, yet pre-millennialism and dispensationalism (when they are really conscious and honest about their theological heritage) stand in the Reformed tradition of theology.

CHAPTER V

THE PROTESTANT SYSTEM OF HERMENEUTICS

(Continued)

(ii). *Cultural.*

Rhetoric became a specific skill among the Greeks who in turn transmitted it to the Romans. The great victories of the Greeks in war created a wealthy and semi-wealthy ("upper middle class") class of citizens. In the division of the many different kinds of spoils of war they were thrown into law suits against each other. This called for a specialist in briefing and argumentation, especially in a culture that had not as yet developed the necessary legal documents for their level of civilization.

It was the rhetorician that was called into service to help the Greeks with their lawsuits. The rhetorician was then a combination of scholar, debator, logician, and expert in speech. This kind of specialist also became a part of the Roman legal system. A literature began to grow up about rhetoric which included the Greek Aristotle and the Roman Quintilian, whose book, *De Institutione Oratoria,* is a great classic in the history of rhetoric.

It became more and more apparent that the rhetorician (somewhat similar to our modern lawyer) had to know of many things to help his clients in their defense. The subjects which he took to make him a more learned man were called "the liberal arts." Originally this was a list of ten to fourteen different subject matters. Martianus Capella in his work, *The Marriage of Mercury and Philology* (A.D., fifth century), schematized the liberal arts into the traditional seven liberal arts. When the universities were started in the Middle Ages the seven liberal arts were the basis of the curriculum.

When the Renaissance came into existence at the end of the Middle Ages it produced the humanists who were the scholars of the period. One of their great passions was to recover anew the great classics of the Greek and Latin authors. However they insisted that a study of the language was not enough. The student of the classics had to know the history and culture of the peoples of the ancient world as well as their languages. Philology meant to them not only the study of words and grammar but the whole or comprehensive scholarly method of investigating the culture and history about the classical period. This was as important for the interpretation of the literature as being an expert in the Greek and Latin languages.

Both Luther and Calvin were greatly influenced by the scholarship of the humanists, and when it came to the interpretation of Holy Scripture they espoused the current philological method of interpretation. Philology meant to them the same as it meant to the humanists, namely, the historical and cultural study of a period as well as its books and languages. The hermeneutics of the Reformers was then as much historical and cultural as it was grammatical. Present Protestant hermeneutics stands in the same tradition of the Reformers in the way in which they understand the expression "philological hermeneutics." (A procedure anticipated in Augustine's *On Christian Instruction*.)

Some interaction with the culture and history of a book of Holy Scripture is mandatory. This becomes very obvious in the contributions that archeology has made for the understanding of the Old Testament. Even when scholars of previous generations knew the words and the grammar, many passages were still opaque. But after a century and a half of work in archeology we can see the meaning in so many passages of Scripture because we have uncovered their historical and cultural context.

There is also striking confirmation of the need of knowing cultural and historical backgrounds in the story of New Testament interpretation. For centuries the customary procedure with scholars has been to study classical Greek in the universities and then when they came to theological studies they read and studied the Greek of the New Testament. It was inevitable for them to import the historical and cultural background of their classical studies into their New Testament exegesis. Unwittingly the history and culture of the Greek classical world became the point of departure for New Testament exegesis.

However there were occasional scholars who did not follow this pattern but rather spent much time in studying the Jewish literature of the inter-Biblical period. John Gill (1697-1791), the famous Baptist theologian and commentator, was ahead of his times in the extensive use he made of rabbinic materials. In 1900 Abrahams registered a complaint in *Cambridge Biblical Essays* that New Testament scholars were wrong in neglecting the rabbinic literature in the interpretation of the New Testament. Eventually it became clear to the New Testament scholars that the real background of the New Testament was Palestine, not Greece; it was rabbinics, not Greek classics; and it was more important in many instances to know Aramaic than classical Greek. In New Testament studies today the historical and cultural background for understanding the New Testament has been shifted from Athens to Jerusalem. Men like G. F. Moore, Joseph Bonsirven, Wilhelm Bousset, Israel Abrahams, C. G. Montefiore have greatly contributed to this shift.[1] Out of this came Strack-Billerbeck's *Kommentar zum Neuen Testament aus Talmud und Midrash*. The various authors of Kittel's *Theological Dictionary of the New Testament* borrow heavily from Strack-

[1] Cf F. C. Grant, *Ancient Judaism and the New Testament.*

Billerbeck as well as doing their own research in rabbinics. Out of this has also come a renewed study of Aramaic because Aramaic was the language of the people of Jesus' time. New Testament experts of today not only know their classical Greek and its culture; they also know ancient Palestine, ancient Judaism, and Aramaic.

By "cultural" is meant the total ways, methods, manners, tools, customs, buildings, institutions, and so forth, by means of which, and through which, a clan, a tribe, or a nation carry on their existence. It is not to be confused with "cultured," which indicates an advanced or sophisticated level of existence. Whatever men write they write from out of their cultural backdrop. Their culture modifies, determines, guides, colors, or influences the manner in which they express themselves. Even where some author reacts against his culture, attempts a deliberate break from it, or becomes a caustic critic of it, he never really escapes his culture. More realistically it is perhaps one smaller or lesser part of his culture that is the basis for the assault on the larger segment of his culture. Therefore a study of culture is indispensable in Biblical interpretation.

However there is a preventive function in understanding Scripture through its culture. From the culture we can decode the original designation of a word, its *usus loquendi*. Cultists are usually a-cultural; that is, they impose a meaning on Scripture from the perspective of their beliefs, their traditions, or their ideology. Every cult then, perhaps sects, too, violate the principle of interpretation through ignoring the culture of the original writers of Holy Scripture. For example, any doctrine of the atonement must start from understanding of Biblical writers in their particular culture; it cannot be imposed upon Christianity from some new or alien metaphysical, theosophical, or philosophical system. It can be imposed in such a movement as Christian Science by its teachers who give no real value to historical and cultural studies of the ancient Biblical world; or it can be imposed in a very sophisticated way by Tillich who, while knowing the Biblical and historical materials, nonetheless imposes a modern existential concept upon the doctrine of the atonement.

(a). The interpreter must study *Biblical geography.* If history is the temporal background of Scripture, then geography is the spatial background. The interpreter needs to know the data about mountains, rivers, plains, crops, flora, fauna, seasons, and climate. To understand the Ten Plagues of Exodus the interpreter must know the geography of Egypt, the gods of Egypt (for some scholars believe each plague is directed against a specific god of Egyptian religion), and the flora and fauna of Egypt. To understand the book of Acts the interpreter must have some idea of the geography of that part of the world in which Paul, in particular, traveled. Many of the passages in the Old Testament become much clearer when we understand their geographical location. There are many geographical references in the Psalms and those references hang in mid-air until we know their reference through a knowledge of Biblical geography.

With reference to the crucifixion of Christ we do not know what the word skull (*calvary,* from the Latin word for skull, *calvaria;* Greek, Golgatha; and that in turn from the Aramaic from the Hebrew) means. Skull may refer to an old Jewish tradition that the skull of Adam was found here, or to the idea that this was the place where criminals were executed, and therefore nicknamed "the place of the skull" (of criminals), or to a mound whose exposed vertical face looked like a skull. Historically the first interpretation may be true because there is no skull-like mound of earth at that place; but Gordon looked at the text in the second sense and founded "Gordon's Calvary" which is a spot outside of the current walls of Jerusalem.

The point need not be belabored. Every event in Scripture has its geographical locus and part of the process of interpretation of Scripture is to find out as much as possible of the geography of the event, for either in small or in large it helps with the understanding of the text.

(b). The interpreter must know *Biblical history*. If every event in Scripture has its geographical referent (or in mathematical language, its parameter), then every event has its historical referent in that all Biblical events occur in a stream of history.

Thanks to more than a hundred years and more of intense research in Biblical history we now have in many instances the embarrassment of wealth. We have the monuments of Egypt, the extensive archeology "digs" on the "tells" or "mounds" in Palestine, the monuments and inscriptions of Asia Minor, the clay tablets and the papyrus that have endured the centuries without being eroded away, and the extensive research of all kinds in the Mesopotamian valley. We also have the works of historians such as the Egyptian Manetho, the Jewish Josephus, and the Roman Tacitus.

H. H. Rowley has expressed the need for a historical knowledge of Scriptures very accurately when he wrote:

A religion which is thus rooted and grounded in history cannot ignore history. Hence a historical understanding of the Bible is not a superfluity which can be dispensed with in Biblical interpretation, leaving a body of ideas and principles divorced from the process out of which they were born.[2]

Here again, a thousand examples can be drawn from Scripture to show the absolute indispensability to know history in order to understand the text in depth, or sometimes to understand it at all.

We shall resort to just one illustration, the crucifixion of Christ. Historically we need to know how the Jews got

[2] "The Relevance of Biblical Interpretation," *Interpretation*, January 1947, p. 8.

to the place they were in space and time; we need to know the historical origin of the Jewish sects of the day (Pharisees, Sadducees, Essenes, Herodians); we need to know the Jewish legal system of the time and the function of the Sanhedrin; we need to know how the Romans happened to be in Palestine; we need to know how the Romans governed Palestine; we need to know the legal system of the Romans; we need to know what were the arrangements made between the Jews and the Romans (for this determines what powers the Jews had under the Romans); and we need to know something of the historical origin of crucifixion and how it was administered by the Romans. And I am sure that these are not all the historical elements we need to know in order better to comprehend the event of the crucifixion of Christ.

If we may add a second illustration it would be that of the interpretation of the book of Revelation. If we ignore the history of the first Christian century and read Revelation as if it were simply a list of apocalyptic symbols existing independent from history, then the interpretation of Revelation is really impossible or at best superficial and certainly misleading. But if we know the historical situation we then know why the author wrote as he did, and how the book was to function within the Church. As a result we can begin to make some real sense out of a book, even though much may still remain obscure.

(c). The interpreter must study *Biblical culture*. We are now using the word culture in the strict anthropological sense. Anthropologists divide the culture of a people into its material culture and its social culture. *Material culture* refers to all the things — tools, objects, dwellings, weapons, garments, and so forth — that the given people use in the maintenance of its life. *Social culture* refers to all the customs, practices, rites, and so forth, that a society observes in the societal on-going of the people.

Again we are faced with a deluge of materials which illustrate the necessity of understanding the various cultures we find in Holy Scripture. Many of these details can be found in books such as E. Rice, *Orientalisms in the Bible Lands;* M. Miller and J. Miller, *Encyclopedia of Bible Life;* F. Wight, *Manners and Customs of Bible Lands.* All of the standard dictionaries of Holy Scripture will contain a lot of this material especially the recent ones profiting from recent archeological research.

Some rather obvious examples in material culture are: upper rooms were large rooms and best adapted for the meeting of a large group (Acts 1:13); in the time of Christ people ate while reclining and not sitting (John 13:23-24); the Jews purified their water (they let the silt sink to the bottom) by letting it stand in large jugs (John 2:6); bread was baked in thin sheets spread on top of small clay or earth ovens heated with grass (Matt. 6:30); and ancient oil lamps at the time of Christ were very small so three or four could be held in the hand at once. The virgins who took their lamps and not their oil jugs were foolish, because a marriage vigil could last as long as three hours and so exhaust the supply of oil in the little lamp (Matt. 25:1ff.).

The scope of Scripture from Genesis to Revelation includes cultures, and so there are many social cultures represented in Holy Scripture. In the interpretation of Scripture we must do the best we can to uncover the specific social culture behind a specific passage. Genesis 1-11 presupposes a Mesopotamian background; the story of Joseph in Egypt, and the exodus from Egypt reflect Egyptian culture. Paul's travels presuppose a Graeco-Roman culture. Colossians represents a very different cultural context from the cultural context of Hebrews.

The interpreter must research out the cultural practice of any given event in Scripture, such as: puberty rites, marriage rites, burial rites, political structures, legal systems, family structures, farm practices, business practices, methods of warfare, the practice of slavery, the treatment of captives, the monetary system, the economic system, and the religious practices. To understand Paul's speech on Mars Hill (Acts 17) the interpreter must know some Greek philosophy. Behind many of Paul's references in Colossians was some kind of philosophical-religious cult.

The principal purpose for studying the cultural elements in Holy Scripture is that this aids the interpreter to know what are *the original things* referred to in Scripture. It is the original social setting of Scripture which allows us to have genuine, controlled, literal interpretation. Stated another way, cultural studies give us the *usus loquendi* of a language and so enables us to know the original, literal, socially-designated meaning of a word, a phrase, or a custom. Words, sentences, expressions are meaningful at the first level in terms of the culture in which they are embedded. "Literal interpretation" is crippled without the help of cultural studies. Again like Biblical history, cultural matters are not niceties we may search out if we have the time but which we may ignore under the pressure of time and circumstances. They are indispensable for the accurate understanding of Holy Scripture.

The most acute theological problem today is to assess to what extent or degree culture determines the character of Scripture, binding Scripture to its own particular historical period. To understand this a word of explanation is necessary.

In the eighteenth and nineteenth centuries a number of critical theories of the Old and New Testaments arose which challenged the historical validity of Scripture, the factuality of Scripture with reference to scientific knowledge, and the literary integrity of Scriptures. (That is, traditional authors of books of the Bible, traditional dates of when the books were written, traditional assumptions that each book was of one piece, were in many cases rejected.) At first it was called *neo-logism* because the critics felt free to reconstruct the Hebrew Text; it was called *Ger-*

man criticism, because so many of its advocates were German scholars; it was called *higher criticism,* because it did not stop with critical studies of the text of Scripture (lower criticism) but insisted on a literary criticism too (higher not being itself a word suggesting radical criticism but by popular usage it took on this meaning); and *radical criticism,* because it departed so radically from traditional views of Biblical criticism. The most common expression used to indicate these movements was *higher criticism.*

In terms of our present discussion this kind of criticism meant that large parts of the Holy Scripture reflected the culture of their times, and were neither binding nor believable for Christian scholars.

The whole matter of the culturally conditioned character of the New Testament was given a very radical interpretation in recent times by Bultmann. According to him much of the New Testament is in the form of a myth, and therefore cannot be accepted by modern man.

We have, then, a radical turnabout in the matter of culture and hermeneutics. In the older philological method the understanding of culture enabled the interpreter better to understand God's revelation in Holy Scripture. Now it is asserted that because so much of Holy Scripture reflects the culture of the time (which is just culture and not truth) most of Holy Scripture cannot be accepted as divine revelation.

This matter of the way things are understood in a culture and what is the truth-status of those things believed is a very complex one. The religious beliefs and beliefs about how the world is put together and how it functions of some little tribe of South American Indians are most likely in complete error. Even when retranslated into modern concepts, its entire set of beliefs can be seen to be the collected errors of their culture.

On the other hand the symbols and operations used in mathematics (or symbolic logic) are used commonly by all scholars around the world. As such mathematics and logic are completely transcultural, i.e., they assert the truth equally in all cultures. Some decades ago it was surmised that our planet might be able to communicate with life on another planet. The mode suggested was to set out in huge letters and figure the Pythagorean Formula that the hypotneuse of a right angle triangle was the square root of the sum of the squares of the two sides. It was presumed that if a culture made any intellectual headway it would at least know this much. Hence the Pythagorean formula (one of pure symbols) was considered not merely transcultural but trans-planetary! In the middle stand a number of disciplines that are part cultural and part transcultural. If I believe that the true philosophy was Plato's philosophy, I would not accept all that Plato wrote. Some of his analogies, some of his illustrations, some of his arguments are purely cultural and not valid today. So part of Plato is trans-cultural and part is cultural.

How does this matter stand with reference to Holy Scripture? Certain options to this problem have been made.

(aa.) We may say that the Holy Scripture and its contents is not too different from the case of the South American Indians. The Bible is a culturally conditioned book and its only real service is that it does contain some ancient history and some ancient literature which is of use to historians or students of literature. Perhaps there are two or three ethical maxims from which modern man can profit. But by no means is the Holy Scripture a revelation of God.

(bb). We may say that a certain slice through Scripture is theologically normative but the rest is all culturally conditioned and cannot be believed today. There are many versions of the "slice theory." Kant thought that the normative part of religion — and therefore of Holy Scripture — was its ethics. The critically assessed ethics of Scripture is trans-cultural.

Fosdick spoke of abiding categories (faith, love, trust,

grace, pity, justice) that were valid through the centuries, but the doctrinal or dogmatic part of Holy Scripture was purely cultural and not binding on modern man (such the doctrines of original sin, hell, or the Trinity).

Bultmann and the existentialists believe that there is an existential and kerygmatic slice in the New Testament. This is transcultural, but the rest is mythology which a modern man cannot believe. Tillich would say much the same thing, only from the context of his existential doctrine of New Being.

(cc). We may say that the Christological part of Scripture is transcultural and the rest is not. This expresses itself in many ways. The older liberal view was that whatever is true to "the spirit of Jesus" was transcultural in Scripture. Some of the radical theologians have taken Bonhoeffer's slogan, "Jesus as the man for other men," as that which measures anything transcultural in Scripture. Brunner in a more historical and more theological way has said that the authority of Holy Scripture was in its Christological character, and therefore whatever is Christological is transcultural.

(dd). The historic and traditional view is that the revelation of God comes in and through a cultural form, because any revelation from God must come to man in his concrete, cultural setting and speak to him in terms of his specific culture. Otherwise the revelation would be meaningless. When speaking of the real presence of Christ in the Holy Eucharist, the Lutheran theologians speak of Christ being present *in, with,* and *under* the elements. It is a way of expressing a real presence but yet without transubstantiation. We are tempted to say that revelation is present in Scripture *in, with,* and *under* the cultural so that the purely cultural is never made revelational, yet the revelation cannot be isolated from its cultural form.

We have here another version of the "scandal of particularity," namely that God's revelation came to specific people, at specific times, in specific cultures, in specific languages, and culminated in an incarnation in a specific man. And so we have the "scandal of the particularity of culture." This is the point that Karl Barth is attempting to make when he speaks of the Jewish character of divine revelation. He says that we must not be offended by it. According to Barth the Scriptures were written by Jewish people and in terms of their Jewish culture. Barth so claims that even if Scripture has this Jewish cultural backdrop God has so inspired Holy Scripture that it may become the Word of God again and again in non-Jewish cultures.

Because Holy Scripture is given by divine revelation and by divine inspiration, it is in virtue of these two characteristics transcultural from its very inception. For this reason it can be translated into the languages of the world, be read intelligently, be properly interpreted, and yield theological truth. Because Holy Scripture did come in Jewish culture it does have a specific cultural impress so that the entire Scripture is not completely transcultural. There is no easy solution to this problem and no simple formula which enables the interpreter to divide the transcultural from the cultural. We must declare that we know that this problem exists, that we must learn to live with it the best we can, and that God in his grace, his wisdom, and his mystery can speak to us today his Word in, with, and under its cultural impress.

BIBLIOGRAPHY FOR CHAPTERS IV AND V

Horne, *An Introduction to the Critical Study and Knowledge of the Holy Scriptures.*

Angus and Green, *Cyclopedic Handbook to the Bible.*

Todd, *Principles of Interpretation.*

Farrar, *History of Interpretation.*

Dana, *Searching the Scripture.*

Terry, *Biblical Hermeneutics.*

Seisenberger, *Practical Handbook for the Study of the Bible.*

162   PROTESTANT BIBLICAL INTERPRETATION

Chafer, *The Science of Biblical Hermeneutics.*
Fairbairn, *Hermeneutical Manual.*
Jowett, *The Interpretation of Scripture.*
Hartill, *Biblical Hermeneutics.*
Cellêrier, *Biblical Hermeneutics.*
Barrows, *Companion to the Bible.*
Warren, "By What Authority: Pitfalls in Pulpit Interpretation," *Interpretation*, I, 207-18, April, 1947.
The Ecumenical Study Conference, "Guiding Principles for the Interpretation of the Bible," *Interpretation*, 3:450-59, October, 1949.
Dobschutz, "Interpretation," *Hastings Encyclopedia of Religion and Ethics*, VII, 390-95.
Young, "Biblical Idioms," *Analytic Concordance.*
Torm, *Hermeneutik des Neuen Testaments.*
Berkhof, *Principles of Biblical Interpretation.*
Unger, *Principles of Expository Preaching.*
Briggs, *Biblical Study.*

Chapter VI

THE DOCTRINAL USE OF THE BIBLE

Part of the task of hermeneutics is to determine the correct use of the Bible in theology and in personal life. The doctrinal interpretation of the Bible is the work of the theologian. It is advancing beyond the grammatical and the historical sense to the fuller meaning of Scripture. Grammarians may differ over grammatical points in exegesis which may or may not influence theology, but the differences among theologians are sharper and more profound because theologians are dealing with the full implications of Biblical truth. A strictly grammatical and exegetical study may never discuss the problem of the Trinity, but the problem is inescapable to the synoptic method of the theologian.

Theological interpretation is thus characterized by: (i) an extension of the grammatical meaning to discover its fuller theological significance, and (ii) a synoptic view of all the Biblical data on a given subject.

The justification for doctrinal hermeneutics is the claim of Scripture to contain a knowledge of God which may be expressed as teaching (*didachē*). Biblical religion is not merely religious experience, nor are its teachings religious speculations. Biblical religion is grounded in the objective knowledge of God. It is in philosophical language a *revelational theism*. The constant allegations that the Bible is treated by the orthodox as a "theological Euclid" or as a storehouse of "intellectual propositions about God" are not true. Belief in an objective revelation in Scripture is not immediately re-

163

ducible to dry intellectualism in religion. Certainly the Reformers and the great Reformed theologians are not so guilty. But neo-orthodox writers have stated that orthodoxy represents intellectualism in religion (i.e., faith is assent to dogma or creed), and this has become the "standard" interpretation of orthodoxy by their followers without the followers taking the trouble to see if this really represents orthodoxy. Intellectualism is a disease which can infect *any* theological system including neo-orthodoxy.

Belief in a genuine revelation of God in Scripture, then, leads the conservative Protestant to believe that the Scriptures are capable of theological interpretation. Our Lord Himself made *teaching* one of the great items of the Great Commission. He was in His own ministry a *doctrinal* teacher. We note that people were astonished at His teaching (Matthew 7:28); He claimed His doctrine was from God (John 7:16); and He invited men to discover its divine origin (John 7:17).

Paul speaks of obeying doctrine from the heart (Romans 6:17) and warns us of false doctrines (Eph. 4:14). He warns Timothy to be careful of sound doctrine, referring to doctrine at least twelve times in the books of Timothy. In 2 Timothy 3:16–17, *the first profit of the Scripture is doctrine.*

Doctrine gives the Christian faith its substance and form. If there has been no disclosure of God in Scripture then there can be no doctrine, but if there has been a disclosure then doctrine is possible. From the divine disclosure doctrine is educed, thereby giving the Christian faith its substance and content.

That the Scriptures contain a valid revelation of God in the sense that the Fathers and the Reformers so understood was repudiated by Schleiermacher, Ritschl, and religious liberalism in general. Now that liberalism's beliefs have been pounded out quite thin on the anvil of criticism, it is apparent how mistaken they were. Orthodoxy and neo-orthodoxy concur in believing that religious liberalism is theologically bankrupt.[1] In that neo-orthodoxy so vigorously attacks propositional revelation, and accepts revelation as inward encounter, and reduces the Bible to the level of "witness" or "instrument," it is to be questioned if it has escaped what liberalism did not. How a non-propositional revelation gives rise to a *valid* propositional witness is the unsolved problem of neo-orthodoxy. It is our prediction that when neo-orthodoxy passes from the evangelistic stage to the critical stage a "propositional wing" will develop. As yet it is not clear how a contentless revelation (non-propositional) gives rise to a propositional witness (Scripture).

All forms of orthodoxy (Eastern, Roman Catholic, Protestant) have historically accepted a divine revelation which forms the grounds of a valid theology. For this reason we can give assent to Newman when he wrote:

I have changed in many things: in this I have not. From the age of fifteen, dogma has been the fundamental principle of my religion: I know no other religion; I cannot enter into the idea of any other sort of religion; religion, as a sentiment, is to me a dream and a mockery. As well can there be filial love without the fact of a father, as devotion without the fact of a Supreme Being.[2]

Doctrinal hermeneutics commences where exegetical hermeneutics leaves off. It works with the understanding that it is to be very much guided by *general hermeneutics*. Therefore a theologian builds upon general hermeneutics. The principles we suggest to govern doctrinal studies of the Bible are:

[1] See two very shrewd and important critiques of liberalism at this point in C. W. Dugmore, editor, *The Interpretation of the Bible.* T. W. Manson, "The Failure of Liberalism to Interpret the Bible as the Word of God" (pp. 92–107); and John Lowe, "The Recovery of the Theological Interpretation of the Bible," (pp. 108–122).

[2] *Apologia pro vita sua* (Everyman's Library edition), p. 65. This is in contrast to the modernists' position as defended by Sabatier in *Outlines of a Philosophy of Religion,* and, *Religions of Authority and the Religion of the Spirit.* Also, Harnack, *What is Christianity?*

(1). *The theologian is a redeemed man standing in the circle of divine revelation.* He is a changed man; he has undergone regeneration. He is a committed man; he has found the truth in Jesus Christ and in Scripture. He comes not as a religious speculator but as a man with a concern. He seeks the fullest explication he can of the meaning of the divine revelation and his personal experience of the grace of God. His motivation to engage in theology stems from his experience of the gospel, and he seeks the meaning of that Book from which the gospel is preached.

This has cardinal significance with reference to the way the entire Bible is treated. It is fundamentally a record of divine love, divine redemption, and divine salvation personally received. We are dealing with a dimension of truth in addition to that of symbolic formalism (mathematics, logic), and more than the problems of causal connections (science). In theology we deal with the personal, the moral, the ethical, the spiritual, and the invisible. Theological science must then be carried on within this circle of faith and commitment, and not as dry, abstract or impersonal investigation.

Further, this means that the main themes of theology will be the great truths about God (His love, His grace, His divine action), about man (his creation, his sin, his future), and about Jesus Christ (His birth, His life, His death, His resurrection, His ascension, His ministry as a priest, His return).

The Bible is mistreated when it becomes a handbook of prophecy and world politics (pyramidism, British-Israelism, Russellism) for such an approach misses the heart of the Bible: namely, *the Christological-soteriological nexus.*

The Bible is mistreated by hyperdispensationalism (and dispensationalism if it is not careful) when it spends its energies in delineating the unfolding of a plan of numerous and discrete periods. The chief task of the interpreter is to assign the various passages of Scripture to their correct periods. If this is not done then wrong doctrines and practices, it is claimed, are taught and enforced at the wrong times.

Such a pigeon-hole method of interpretation is far short of the great evangelical and conservative tradition in exegesis.[3]

This is not to eliminate prophetic nor dispensational interpretation, but it does assign to them their correct proportion in the divine revelation.

(2). *The main burden of doctrinal teaching must rest on the literal interpretation of the Bible.* In our treatment of general hermeneutics we maintained that the literal meaning of the Bible was the first and controlling principle for the understanding of the Bible. This principle is to be carried over into doctrinal interpretation.

This does not deny that substantial doctrinal truth is conveyed symbolically, parabolically, typically, and poetically. But as previously indicated, the symbolic *et al.* (i) depend on the literal sense for their very existence, and (ii) are controlled by the literal. For example, the effort to spiritualize the Levitical priesthood and so make it a justification for a clergy-priesthood, is to be rejected as it lacks New Testament verification.

The great doctrines of the faith should be those which can be determined by the literal approach to the meaning of Scripture. A theology which ignores this *control* could well bring us back to the confused labyrinth of so much patristic and medieval exegesis.

(3). *The main burden of our theology should rest on the teaching of the New Testament.* Although the Old is prior in time the New is prior in method. The New Testament is the capstone of revelation, and God's word through the supreme instrument of revelation, His Son (Hebrews 1:2). Because it is the *final, full,* and *clear* revelation of God, it would be foolhardy to make the New revolve around the Old.

In the New Testament is the life of Jesus Christ, God in the flesh (John 1:1, 14). In its pages are recorded His birth,

---

[3] Cf. J. C. O'Hair, *The Unsearchable Riches of Christ.* For an examination of the system cf. John B. Graber, Ultradispensationalism (unpublished doctoral dissertation, Dallas Theological Seminary, 1949).

ministry, death, resurrection, and ascension. In the epistles are the full revelation of ethical, spiritual, and theological truth. Christian theology must then plant itself squarely within the New Testament. Whatever divergences there might be among the Eastern Orthodox, Roman Catholic, and Protestant theologians, they have agreed to this point: *the worth of the Old Testament to the Christian Church is that it is in seed and preparatory form a Christian document.*

This is by no means to be construed minimizing the Old Testament, nor is it a detraction from its divine inspiration. It is the recognition of the truth taught in Scripture itself that the full light of revelation shines in the New Testament. The great doctrines of faith, sin, atonement, Christ, sanctification, resurrection, heaven, hell, and the new earth with its new Jerusalem are all most clearly developed in the New Testament.

This means that a theologian must have a historical sense in his use of cross-references and proof texts. Otherwise his Scriptural evidence is collated without any sense of proportion or relative importance. This sense of proportion of importance is indispensable in Biblical theology.

(4). *Exegesis is prior to any system of theology.* The Scriptures are themselves the divine disclosure. From them is to be derived our system of theology. We can only know the truth of God by a correct exegesis of Scripture. Therefore exegesis is prior to any system of theology.

Great mischief has been done in the church when the system of theology or its framework has been derived extra-Biblically. Pantheism was the bed-rock of Schleiermacher's theology. Logical pantheism was the pole around which Hegel interpreted Christianity. Kant's notion of Christianity was guided by his theory of ethics. Ritschl's theology is predicated on Kant's philosophy. Much of neo-orthodoxy is inspired by Kierkegaard, Heidegger, Ebner, Kant, and Buber.

If the grounds of Christian theology is the revelation of

God, then theology must be grounded in revelation and not in philosophy.

The historic Protestant position is to ground theology in Biblical exegesis. A theological system is to be built up exegetically brick by brick. Hence the theology is no better than the exegesis that underlies it. The task of the *systematic* theologian is to commence with these bricks ascertained through exegesis, and build the temple of his theological system. But only when he is sure of his individual bricks is he able to make the necessary generalizations, and to carry on the synthetic and creative activity that is necessary for the construction of a theological system.

Philosophy does have a role to play in theological construction but it is not in itself either the *data* or the *principium* of theology. Its function is ancillary. It provides the theologian with what Kuyper in his *Principles of Sacred Theology* calls "the logical action." The theologian uses the principles of formal and applied logic in hammering out his system. He familiarizes himself with the problems philosophers and theologians have had in common during the history of both philosophy and theology. He learns the validity of various types of argumentation. He discovers the criticisms by philosophers of theologians, and learns to judge wherein the philosopher has been right and wrong.

The exegetical theologian and systematic theologian seek to determine the content of the divine revelation. The philosophical theologian is the watch-dog and detective.

He keeps his eye on contemporary philosophy to see what is developing there and its possible relationship to Christian theology for good or evil. He scans the writings of the scientists to see the implications and importance of contemporary science for Christian faith. He scrutinizes theological publications to see what ancient heresy might be here disguised in modern dress, or what philosophical system or assumptions are presupposed.

The church needs both the exegetical and the philosophical

theologian, and she suffers when she is in want of either. The exegetical theologian protects the church from the misinterpretations of the heretics, and the philosophical theologian protects the church from the improper intrusion into Christian theology of non-Christian principles.

(5). *The theologian must not extend his doctrines beyond the Scriptural evidence.* A scientist is at liberty to spin as many hypotheses as he wishes. In weeding out the true from the false he is guided by logic and experimentation. He has no right to claim truth till these two judges have handed in their decision in the affirmative. All scientific speculation is controlled by logic and experimentation, and speculation is not treated as fact till it passes these two monitors.

What answers to this in theology? What is the control we use to weed out false theological speculation? Certainly the control is logic and evidence. The *evidence* is the Scriptures themselves. It is our conviction that many of our troubles in theology are due to the fact that theologians have extended themselves beyond the data of Scripture and have asked questions about which no answer can be given. There are many points about the atonement on which we can render no precise decision because the Scriptures are silent. What was the relationship *precisely* of the two natures at the moment of sin-bearing? In what *exact* sense were our Lord's sufferings penal? To what *exact* degree did He suffer? Similar such questions can be asked of the Incarnation and of the Trinity. So lacking are we of information of such pin-pointed questions that much of our theological definition is by negation, i.e., we may not know what the *exact* truth of the doctrine is, but we know what *cannot* be true.

Every sentence has implications. The sentences of the Scriptures have implications, and the sentences we say about the Scriptures themselves have implications. Science uses logic and experimentation to weed out the true implications test an implication's truthhood or falsity. The very creative and synthetic task of theology drives us beyond exegesis.

The theologian must use all the care and intelligence and learning he has to fill out *correctly* what is implied in Scripture. Therefore he must be aware of his predicament and keep as close as he can to his Biblical data.

Many are the questions asked about heaven—will we eat? Will we wear clothes? Will we know each other? Will we remember loved ones who are lost? Will family ties be reunited? Will we see the Trinity or just the Son? Will babies become adults? Will we speak Hebrew or Greek? The *best* answer will not be the most clever nor the most sentimental, but the one within the *limitations* of the Biblical data on these subjects. Where Scripture has not spoken, we are wisest to be silent.

Certainly great care must be used in formulating statements about the relationship of the divine sovereignty to human freedom. Perhaps much of our trouble in this regard is due to the posing of questions to which there is no Scriptural material for answers. The importance of the great Calvinistic-Arminian debates of the past are not to be minimized but something of the *spirit* of Faber's remarks ought to color our thinking in this regard, and could well be extended to other theological problems.

It may not be the most philosophical, but it is *probably the wisest opinion which we can adopt*, that the truth lies somewhere between the two rival systems of Calvin and Arminius; though I believe it to exceed the wit of man to point out the *exact* place where it *does* lie. We distinctly perceive the two extremities of the vast chain, which stretches across the whole expanse of the theological heavens; but its central links are enveloped in impenetrable clouds and thick darkness.[4]

Training in logic and sciences forms an excellent back-

[4] Faber, *Discourses*, I, 478–79 (cited by Horne, *op. cit.*, I, 423. Italics are in Horne's statement). The differences between Calvinism and Arminianism are not meaningless and are capable of some decision. We accept the general system of Calvinism in theology, but we do not believe that the precise relationship of sovereignty and freedom can be dogmatically stated.

ground for exegesis. It will give the interpreter the requisite background in the general rules of logic, the principles of induction and evidence, and the practical uses of the same in laboratory work. So much of exegesis depends on the logic of implication and the principles of induction and evidence, that it is unwise not to have a working knowledge of the same. Laboratory work which is properly supervised can inculcate into the student a reliable sense of what is evidence and what is not.

Ministers, Bible students, and interpreters who have not had the sharpening experiences of logic and science may have improper notions of implication and evidence. Too frequently such a person uses a basis of appeal that is a notorious violation of the laws of logic and evidence, yet may have a tremendous appeal to an uncritical Christian audience. *The pursuit of a blessing should never be at the expense of truth.*

In summary, there is no simple rule which tells us that we have gone beyond our Scriptural data. The dangers of so doing ought always be in the mind of the interpreter and the theologian so that they may be ever so careful to keep their exegetical and theological work within the limitations of the Biblical data.

(6). *The theological interpreter strives for a system.* A system is a corpus of *interrelated* assertions. A telephone book or a catalogue is not considered a system in the proper sense of the word for they are nothing more than convenient classifications of data. The theologian strives to present the *system of truth* contained in Sacred Scripture. This involves: (i) a systematic formulation of each individual doctrine of the Bible with the data gathered intelligently from the entire range of Scripture. This results in exegetical-theological studies of such topics as God, man, sin, redemption, and Christ. All the important references will be treated exegetically. Then the individual references will be used to forge the unified Biblical doctrine of the subject matter. (ii) The individual doctrines will be interrelated into a coherent systematic theology. How we understand the divine Person bears directly on how we think of the plan of redemption. Our doctrine of sin in many ways determines how we formulate our notion of salvation. This interplay and interrelation among doctrines is inevitable. The goal is a formulation of all the great doctrines of Scripture into one grand edifice of Christian Theology.

We concur with Hodge[5] that this is to be an inductive procedure. The theologian to a degree imitates the scientist. The theologian is the scientist; the "facts" to be examined are in Scripture; and the procedure is inductively directed. The theologian is to be a careful collector of facts. He tries to be as thorough and systematic as any scientist. His rules of evidence, however, are not experimentation and observation but Biblical hermeneutics. Just as the scientist strives for a systematic formulation of his knowledge, so the theologian strives for *systematic* theology.

It is true that the theologian does more than what we have here outlined. Into the formulation of any doctrine must go what may be learned from the history of both theology and philosophy. The history of philosophy is important because many of the problems of theology have been problems of philosophy; and many attacks on Christian doctrines have been made by philosophers. For example, it would be rather foolhardy to discuss the immortality of the soul without a glance at the Platonic literature on the subject, or the existence of God without taking into account the criticisms of Kant. The great schoolmen were both theologians and philosophers as were the two greatest minds of the early church —Origen and Augustine. Systematic theology demands a minimum acquaintance with the history of philosophy if systematic theology is to be written with competence.

The history of theology is indispensable for the theologian because no man is wise enough to ignore the great men of the past who have literally slaved on the great theological prob-

[5] Charles Hodge, *Systematic Theology*, I, 9 ff.

lems. The major doctrines of systematic theology have been under discussion for almost two millennia, and every theologian must also be a historical theologian, if he is to properly find his way around in systematic theology.

It has been the faith of orthodox theology in all its expressions that there is one great system of truth taught in Sacred Scripture. It is true that the Lutheran theology does not press for a system as much as the Reformed theology does, but to claim that the Lutheran theology is indifferent to system in theology is to go contrary to the nature of the theologies they have produced. However, religious liberalism and neo-orthodoxy have challenged the very existence of *systematic* theology.[6] Both agree that the Bible contains a medley of contradictory theologies. It was under this belief that there emerged such studies as Pauline theology, Petrine theology, and Johannine theology. Such theologies are even taught in some orthodox schools without a realization of their birth in religious liberalism.

Liberalism claimed the unity of the Bible to be the unity of the religious experience it proffered. What each generation has in common is not the same theology, but the same religious experience.

Neo-orthodoxy claims that the unity of the Bible is the *unity of perspective* (Aulén, Barth, Brunner). What each generation has in common with every other generation is the same theocentric attitude in faith, or the same Christological orientation to all theology.

The question is of course the nature of the unity of the Bible. Is it a unity of religious experience (liberalism), or a unity of perspective (neo-orthodoxy), or the unity of doctrine (orthodoxy)? Certainly it is not the claim of orthodoxy that we can *completely* systematize the teaching of the Bible. The

---

[6] Tillich's use of the word systematic in his work, *Systematic Theology*, does not refer to the traditional notion of systematic theology but to his method of the correlation of all methodological knowledge with theology.

very character of the Bible as a *historical* revelation prevents that. But the *ideal goal* of theology is to attain to a systematic theology which faithfully represents the teaching of Scripture. Some neo-orthodoxy reasoning is that because it is difficult of achievement it is impossible of achievement, but we do not believe that you can deduce impossibility from difficulty.

Nor are we to forget the *historical progression* of revelation. Systematic theology takes into account this process, and so claims that systematic theology is not the effort to harmonize all the teaching of the Bible as if it were all on the same flat level, but that the systematic teaching of the Scripture *is in its final intention.*[7]

We do not believe that any neo-orthodox theologian or even liberal theologian would baldly say that theology is to consist of *completely discrete doctrines.* Even Kierkegaard who affirmed that an existential system is impossible with man developed a series of interrelated propositions. The mere listing of doctrines is no more theology than chronicling is the writing of history. Although the determination of the system of theology as contained in Scripture may be difficult, we do not believe that either liberalism or neo-orthodoxy has given sufficient reason to give up the quest for unity, nor have they themselves engaged in the opposite canon—a mere listing of discrete, unrelated doctrines.

(7). *The theologian must use his proof texts with proper understanding of his procedure.*

The use of proof texts is perfectly legitimate. Both liberalism and neo-orthodoxy have strongly castigated the orthodox use of proof texts, and not with good reason. There

---

[7] For the important recent literature on the unity of the Bible see the excellent bibliographical references in H. H. Rowley, *The Unity of the Bible.* Davies (*The Problem of Authority with the Continental Reformers*) claims that one of the glaring weaknesses of Calvin's theological method was that he failed to employ the principle of progressive revelation. The result was that he treated all verses in the Bible as having the same value in theological construction.

is no doubt that the Scriptures quoted closely yield the doctrines of orthodoxy, not liberalism nor neo-orthodoxy. Neither liberalism nor neo-orthodoxy can hold their positions if
held to a strict citation of Scripture.

That both liberalism and neo-orthodoxy are inconsistent
at this point is evident to anyone who will take the care to
read their works and see how they too cite proof texts—
when the honey is to their taste. A proof text is used even
to prove that one should not use proof texts! "The letter
killeth, but the spirit giveth life," (2 Cor. 2:6). The writings
of Barth and Brunner are replete with proof texts, but with
no justification why one verse is not admitted to theological
debate, and another one is. We may cite the Bible in general
but not in particular. But how is a general truth known
apart from being forged from particulars? The method of
religious liberalism to pick and choose verses to taste is now
admitted even by the neo-orthodox as a wretched method of
treating the Scripture. Speaking of the liberals' treatment of
Scripture Lowe writes that "Those who could not bring themselves to disregard what was said by our Lord or by St. Paul
or John, unconsciously read into their texts the modern views
they liked best. It was the nineteenth century substitute for
the discarded allegorical method." [8]

The conservative insists the citation of Scripture is nothing
more than a special application of "foot-noting" which is
standard scholarly procedure. It would be a rare work of
scholarship which cited opinions of authorities without indicating the passages in which these opinions were expressed.
If a scholar claims that Anaximenes taught this, or Socrates

[8] *Op. cit.*, p. 115. Burrows (*An Outline of Biblical Theology*) cites
enough Scripture to require an index of twenty-nine pages. Evidently
proof texting is not as bad as we were told. He does say the older
method of citation without regard to historical background was mechanical and therefore wrong. But evidently proof texting correctly
done is proper. The objection against orthodoxy at this point must
then be against *how* it was done, not *that* it was done. Brunner, in his
Dogmatics, I, cites more than 400 verses in 353 pages of text. Barth
cites over 2,000 in his *Dogmatik*, I/2.

that, or Aristotle something else, he is expected to cite the evidence in terms of the writings of these men as contained in the critical editions of their works, or in writings of contemporaries or near-contemporaries who are commenting on the beliefs of these men. If a scholar claims Aquinas held a certain position about man's creation he is expected to give the reference or references. The liberal and neo-orthodox objection to the use of proof texts reflects a deep theological prejudice (both against a valid revelation of God in Scripture) rather than a rebuttal of a false method of scholarship.

There is no doubt that the proof text method is capable of serious malpractice. The mere listing of proof texts is of no value unless each verse is underwritten by sound exegetical work. It is disconcerting to discover how many verses set down in a book of theology to prove a point melt away when each is examined rather vigorously from the standpoint of exegesis. Not only does it appear that many verses are used that have no relevance but frequently a verse is used whose meaning is actually very different from the one intended by the inspired writer.

For example, Zephaniah 3:9 refers to God returning to the Jews a *pure language.* Many have taken this to mean that the Jews will speak Hebrew in the millennium. The actual meaning of the text is that God will give the Jewish people a *clean* language (morally and ethically) in contrast to an impure language.

Many of the older theologians were guilty of citing a verse in the Old Testament to prove something with reference to salvation and justification, and treating it as if it were as clear and lucid as something in Romans and Galatians. This is one of the most unhappy features of the older theologies which has been happily corrected by a much better sense of historical and progressive revelation, nor can the beneficial influence of dispensationalism be gainsayed at this point.

It is almost instinctive with conservatives to grant a point in theology if a proof text is given. Sometimes the array of texts to prove a point is rather imposing. *But there must be a sound exegetical examination of every text cited* or else we are guilty of superficial treatment of Scripture. The use of proof texts is only as good as the exegesis undergirding their citation. No theologian has a right merely to list verses in proof of a doctrine unless in his own research he has done the requisite exegetical work. It means that every theologian must be of necessity a philologian. Part of the greatness of Charles Hodge as theologian was that he was an able expositor before he was a professional theologian.[9] There is no question that the heart of the striking power of Calvin's *Institutes* is that Calvin was a great expositor and he brought the richness of his expositions into magnificent use in his theological writing.

Furthermore, the theologian must use his texts in view of their context, and in view of their place in the Scriptures. His textual evidence must have a sense of proportion, so that they will have the proper weight of evidence assigned to them. For example, the doctrines of original sin, Satan, the Holy Spirit, and the resurrection are far more dependent for their explication on New Testament passages than on Old Testament ones.

(8). *What is not a matter of revelation cannot be made a matter of creed or faith.*

It is the heritage of the Reformation that only what is taught in Scripture is *directly* binding to conscience. We can loose and bind only as we are in accord with Sacred Scripture.

We thereby object to Catholicism which adds to the revelation of Scripture the moral unanimity of the Fathers, the ecumenical creeds, the decisions of the ecumenical councils, and the *ex cathedra* utterances of the papacy. The Roman Catholic Church does not add these as additional revelation, but as authoritative interpretations of the revelation (the

[9] Note the wonderful tribute paid to Hodge's commentary on *Romans* by Wilbur Smith (*Profitable Bible Study*; p. 174).

deposit of faith in Scripture and Tradition), *and binding to the conscience.*

We thereby object to cults and sects which add to Scripture the voice of man in the form of official handbooks (Mormonism, Christian Science, Russellism, Seventh Day Adventism—with its veneration of the writings of Mary Ellen White), or the writings of their leaders which possess for all practical purposes the authority of an official handbook.

We thereby object to men who would equate their interpretations with the Word of God. To believe that one has an acceptable interpretation of Scripture is not objectionable; to forget humility and human imperfection and so to equate one's interpretation as identical with the divine revelation is objectionable.

We thereby object to speculations about matters in Scripture which lead men beyond the Scriptures themselves. Many of the older sermons on hell were far in excess of the teaching of Scripture, e.g., Jeremy Taylor's sense-by-sense description of the torments of the damned. Precise statements as to who the anti-Christ is, are not matters of faith, even though the *Westminster Confession* stated it was the pope. If the Scriptures affirm he is to be revealed (*apokaluphthē*, 2 Thess. 2:3), how are we to know who he is till he is revealed?

We thereby object to infringement on Christian liberty by men who make their own moral judgments with the certainty and authority of Scripture. What is specifically condemned in Scripture, we have the right to condemn today. What is condemned directly in principle in Scripture we may condemn today. For example, dope is not directly condemned in Scripture, but certainly the principle which condemns drunkenness condemns the use of dope. What is not directly condemned in Scripture, or what is not condemned by immediate application of a principle, must be judged by Christian conscience, but cannot be made as binding as things directly condemned or directly condemned in principle. We must apply the truth of Scripture to life today; otherwise we are not true to our trust. But in so doing we must be ever so careful not to put our interpretations of matters in our culture on the same level as Holy Scripture. The more debatable items are to Christian consciousness, the more tentative should be the spirit of our interpretation. When we brashly identify our interpretations of problems in morals, ethics, and separation with Sacred Scripture, we are making something a matter of faith which is not by its nature a matter of revelation.

There is no system of politics, economics, or culture taught in the New Testament. We may believe some system of economics, etc., is more Christian than another, but we cannot artlessly equate this system with the New Testament teaching. The surprising thing of the Church is its apparent vitality which enables it to live through a variety of political, economic and cultural systems.

The encroachment of the word of man upon the Word of God is a danger we should constantly be alert to, and with all our strength we should maintain the freedom of the Word of God from the word of man.

(9). *The theological interpreter must keep the practical nature of the Bible in mind.*

The Scriptures are not a handbook on all there is to know. They are not a handbook on *all* there is to know about God or religion. The Scriptures do not profess to be a *complete* body of knowledge. The intention of Scripture is to supply man with the knowledge of salvation (2 Timothy 3:15), and what is necessary for a godly Christian life (3:16–17). Only what is in some way related to these two themes is discussed in Scripture.

Much that our speculative appetite would desire is not there. The Scriptures do not contain typical Greek expatiations on epistemology and metaphysics. The problem of evil is not discussed in the abstract but in the concrete. The book of Job is a theodicy not about how evil exists in a good God's universe but how it is that the God of Job permits this specific man of godly character to undergo such sufferings. Habakkuk wants to know why the law is slack and judgment does not go forth (1:4). Why is it that the God of the Torah with eyes too pure to behold evil tolerates Torah-breakers in Israel? Malachi speaks of those who say there is no value in serving God (3:14) because the wicked are prospering, not the righteous.

The Scriptures' do not treat of everything because their content is controlled by their central purpose, the story of divine love and redemption. Human curiosity asks more than this. But we must stay its demand and keep our attention centered on the central message of Scripture.

The oldest saw in this regard is: "where did Cain get his wife?" Where Cain got his wife contributes nothing to the movement of the Bible, so that romantic sideline is ignored. The science of historiography informs us that no history can be exhaustive. All history writing is selective, and the principle of selection is determined by the historian. This accounts for the history of music, the history of theology, the history of art, etc. Biblical history is then that special selection which in some measure—infinitesimal or great—contributes to the story of salvation.

(10). *The theological interpreter must recognize his responsibility to the church.*

The issues proposed in the Scriptures are the greatest in man's entire range of knowledge. The Scriptures speak of an eternal penitentiary, hell, man's greatest disvalue; they speak of heaven, man's greatest bliss; and they speak of salvation, man's most wonderful experience. Further, the Scriptures profess to teach this with the authority of God, underwritten with supernatural credentials by its writers. There are no greater issues before the human race than these.

Whatever the variations in detail might be, it is nevertheless true that the Eastern Church, the Roman Catholic

Church, and the Reformers agree that: (i) the Scriptures are the truth of God; (ii) the Scriptures do teach the unspeakable woe of hell, and the indescribable bliss of heaven; and (iii) salvation from one destiny to the other was wrought by the birth, death, and resurrection of Jesus Christ, God manifest in the flesh.

All Biblical criticism and theological writing should be done in the light of these sobering considerations. This is not meant to put any check on the quest for truth, nor to impose any sort of ecclesiastical control in theological matters. But millions of people now believe the historic Christian gospel, and no man should dare shake their confidence in their belief without taking the full measure of the significance of his act.

Such a stricture applies to the critic, the theologian, and the man who would reinterpret Christianity and bring us the "true" gospel. James informs us that there should be few teachers (3:1) because the condemnation of a teacher—if he lead the flock astray—is great. All such proposed changes should be seriously pondered before being offered to the Church.

After carefully stating that the Bible is to be read and interpreted by each believer for himself, and that no priestly caste is to be the official interpreter of the Bible, Hodge says:

It is not denied that the people, learned and unlearned, should not only compare Scripture with Scripture, and avail themselves of all the means in their power to aid them in their search after the truth, *but they should also pay the greatest deference to the faith of the Church.* If the Scriptures be a plain book, and the Spirit performs the functions of a teacher to all the children of God, it follows inevitably that they must agree in all essential matters in their interpretation of the Bible. And from that fact it follows that for an individual Christian to dissent from the universal Church (*i.e.,* the body of true believers), is tantamount to *dissenting from the Scriptures themselves.*[10]

---

[10] *Op. cit.,* I, 184. Italics are mine.

(11). *No doctrine should be constructed from an uncertain textual reading.*

Doctrine should be established solely from those passages about which textual criticism has raised no doubts. The copyists made many mistakes in copying the New Testament. Sometimes they copied the same line twice or made other such mistakes of dittography. Sometimes they took a part of a later verse and for some reason or other inserted it in a former verse (cf. Romans 8:1 and 8:4). Sometimes a liturgical usage of later times is added to a verse (cf. "for thine is the kingdom, and the power, and the glory, for ever. Amen," of Matthew 6:10). The numerous types of mistakes have been collected in the various books on textual criticism, and no Bible student or minister should seek to express himself on matters of textual criticism till he has familiarized himself with the subject.

The fact is that there are textually insecure passages in the New Testament, and doctrine should not be based on that which might potentially be the voice of man and not the voice of God. The ending of Mark's gospel is a case in point. We are certain of the text through Mark 16:8. But from verse 9 on, the text is not certain. Some scholars are rather certain that the text originally ended with verse 8. Others offer reasons for the retention of the long ending. But until scholars are able to settle the text more certainly no doctrine may be built from this passage about baptismal regeneration, speaking in tongues, casting out of demons, picking up serpents, drinking poison, or divine healing.

BIBLIOGRAPHY

Cellérier, *Biblical Hermeneutics*, p. 217 ff.

Angus and Green, *Cyclopedic Handbook to the Bible*, p. 358 ff.

L. S. Chafer, *Systematic Theology*, I, pp. 114–119.

T. Horne, *Compendious Introduction to the Study of the Bible*, pp. 148–151.

E. Brunner, *Dogmatics*, I, 12, 46, 62, 72, 76 (for a repudiation of a true doctrinal unity of the Bible, and an attack upon *systematic* theology).

E. W. Parsons, *The Religion of the New Testament*, Chapter I, for a recent liberal opinion as to the lack of a doctrinal unity of the New Testament.

A. Kuyper, *Principles of Sacred Theology*.

Connolly Gamble, "The Method of Theology," *Interpretation,* 9:91–99, January, 1955.

CHAPTER VII

THE DEVOTIONAL AND PRACTICAL USE OF THE BIBLE

A. THE GENERAL USE OF THE BIBLE FOR CHRISTIAN LIVING

THE first purpose of the Holy Bible is to make men "wise unto salvation through faith which is in Christ Jesus" (2 Tim. 3:15). After a man has received this salvation, then we are told that "All Scripture is given by inspiration of God, and is profitable for doctrine, for reproof, for correction, for instruction in righteousness that the man of God may be perfect, throughly furnished unto all good works" (2 Tim. 3:16, 17). Most of the material of the Bible is for the Christian, and specifically for his growth in knowledge, holiness, and spirituality. Doctrine and theology are in primary intention aimed at making sinners into saints, and immature Christians into Christian men. The Bible and its study is one of the prime requisites for every Christian in order that he may lead an effective and genuine Christian life.

In using the Bible for moral, ethical, spiritual, and devotional purposes aimed at our spiritual growth, we suggest the following principles:

(1). *All practical lessons, all applications of Scripture, all devotional material, must be governed by general Protestant hermeneutics.*

More pointedly it could be stated this way: all such usages of the Bible must be based upon sound exegetical principles. The notorious dictum: "The ends justifies the means," is frequently baptized into the Christian fold under the guise of: "The blessing justifies the means."

If a blessing is derived from an improper interpretation of Scripture, the blessing has come not because of improper interpretation, but in spite of the misinterpretation. If a passage does not yield the help and strength the interpreter is seeking, he ought not to distort it until he does get a blessing from it, but he ought to go elsewhere in the Scripture where a blessing can be derived from the native meaning of the text.

In the intense desire to find something practical or devotional in Scripture, we are in danger of obscuring the literal or genuine meaning of the passage. It may sound harsh to so speak, but not too infrequently a very devotional message is conjured up from the Scriptures by a method of interpretation which is nothing short of trifling or tampering with Scripture.

Never should we handle a passage of Scripture in such a way as to distort its original meaning simply because we feel under pressure to find something devotional or spiritual or especially edifying in *every* passage we are called upon to teach or explain. Let the truth of God be its own blessedness.

(2). *The Bible is more a book of principles than a catalogue of specific directions.*

The Bible does contain an excellent blend of the general and the specific with reference to principles for Christian living. If the Bible were never specific we would be somewhat disconcerted in attempting a specific application of its principles. If the Bible were entirely specific in its principles, we would be adrift whenever confronted with a situation in life not covered by a specific principle. The *emphasis* in Scripture is on moral and spiritual principles, not upon specific and itemized lists of rules for moral or spiritual conduct. There are two very important reasons for this:

(i). If it were entirely specific in its practical teachings, then it would be provincial and relative. If Paul had classified sin solely in terms of specifics and therefore in terms of the culture of his day, then as new ways of sinning were devised by man, and as culture changed, Paul's teaching would no longer be relevant. As we study the terminology of Paul we are amazed how he was able to put his finger on the universal element of human sin, and so provide every generation in all cultures with a reliable guide to moral and spiritual behaviour.

(ii). If it were a legal code of rules, then the Bible would foster an artificial spirituality, and indirectly sponsor hypocrisy. If the directions were all specific, a man could live up to the letter of the rules, and yet miss the spirit of true godliness. Real spiritual progress is made only if we are put on our own. Unless we must take a principle and interpret its meaning for a given situation in life, we do not spiritually mature. It is this general nature of New Testament ethics which helps prevent hypocrisy. As long as there is a specific code to obey, men can conform without change of heart. Obedience to a moral code with no change of heart may result in the discrepancy between inner life and outward conduct which is one of the characteristics of hypocrisy. But inasmuch as we must govern ourselves by principle, we are put on our own mettle. In each important decision we shall ask ourselves: *what is the spiritual principle involved?* From this consideration we may then proceed to: *what ought I do?* If we so treat our moral and spiritual decisions we develop in spiritual insight and moral strength. Such development is central to a mature spirituality.

(3). *The Bible emphasizes the inner spirit rather than the outward religious cloak.*

The moral teaching of the Old Testament contains many rules about kinds of food permitted and banned; types of clothing which may be worn, and types prohibited. The basic purpose of these *material* regulations was to inculcate in the Jewish people a sense of *discrimination*. Right and wrong had to be learned on the obvious level of the material to help the mind to learn to discern right and wrong in the more subtle level of the spiritual. In the New Testament morality and spirituality are lifted to a higher level by being inward and spiritual.

The New Testament does not, however, condemn only improper motives, but it also condemns external acts. Gluttony, drunkenness, and revelling are specifically forbidden, and chaste, honorable behaviour before men is taught. But the *emphasis* is upon the inner spiritual life rather than upon a mere social circumspection.

Measuring spirituality entirely by outward appearances is not just to the person being judged. Judging spirituality by external matters (diet, dress, sanctimonious acts) fails to consider that our Lord taught that true spirituality was a secret activity. The external parade of piety as made by the Pharisees is specifically condemned. Prayer is to be in the secret of the closet. Giving is to be such that the right hand does not know what the left hand is doing. Fasting is to be hidden by grooming one's self before one appears in public and so to appear as if one were not fasting.

Negations ("touch not, taste not, handle not," Col. 2:21) do not measure piety; they prepare the way for true piety. True piety is faith, hope, and love. The church has had a constant battle with asceticism. If man is born a legalist in soteriology, he is a born asceticist in sanctification. Asceticism is the belief that the body and the material world are in some sense evil and that victory over them is both by abstinence from the world and by bodily suffering. That there is a measure of truth to asceticism is evident from the Biblical teaching about fasting and sexual abstinence (1 Cor. 7:5). But that asceticism as practiced at times in the history of the church is unscriptural is also evident from the words of our Lord (Luke 11:24 ff.) and of Paul (Col. 2:20 ff.).

The Bible is to be used to develop a true inner life. The Beatitudes inform us that happiness is an *inner* quality of life. Spirituality is striving toward correct attitudes, spiritual graces, the fruit of the Spirit (Gal. 5:22–23). The emphasis on outward religious show and manifest badges or banners of religious profession is not in keeping with the Biblical perspective on spirituality.

(4). *In some statements it is the spirit of the statement that is to be our guide.*

We are enjoined to cut off our hands and pluck out our eyes if they offend (Matt. 5:29, 30). People who have had the courage to conform to this literally do not impress their contemporaries with their spirituality but with their foolhardiness. Is not the *spirit* of the command that we should not pamper or nurse our sins, but deal with them with the utmost severity? If life and death are the issues, then sin certainly must be treated with the greatest dispatch and severity.

Certainly when our Lord told Peter to forgive his brother seventy times seven he was not prescribing the number of times we are to forgive a brother, but he was prescribing the *spirit* of forgiveness (Matt. 18:21 ff.). The same holds true for commands to turn the other cheek, to go the second mile, to yield the second garment. Certainly, if taken literally they become mechanical or external guides to conduct—the very thing they are intended to correct. But if the inner spirit of the command be taken, these passages teach us lessons of generosity, of kindness, of helpfulness. Rather than being covetous we ought to be generous; rather than being goaded by a spirit of vengeance we should be prompted by a spirit of love; rather than being tightfisted we should be merciful to the destitute.

(5). *Commands in terms of one culture must be translated into our culture.*

When our Lord and his apostles gave exhortations and teachings they spoke in terms of the prevailing culture. Otherwise they could not have communicated effectually with their audience. Paul's statements about women (e.g., 1 Tim. 2:9) must be reinterpreted for our culture. The same applies for Paul's statements about cutting the hair and wearing the veil. Cutting the hair was associated with paramours, and wearing a veil (not some modern perky hat) was the sign

of a decorous woman. In modern terms this means that
Christian women should avoid all appearances of immodesty,
and should be chaste and dignified in dress and behaviour.[1]

B. GUIDANCE FROM EXAMPLES

The lives of the great men of the Bible provide a great
story of spiritual guidance, and the great events of the Bible
provide a vast amount of practical wisdom for godly living.
We learn, too, by the mistakes of good men or by the sinful
careers of bad men.[2] Events in the lives of great men are
often recorded without an express comment by the Biblical
writers. Therefore guides are necessary so that we may benefit from their examples without making needless mistakes.

(1). *We must make a distinction between what the Bible
records and what it approves.*[3] Men frequently make the mistake of assuming that whatever is written in the Bible is
thereby approved. Therefore, there is a rather uncritical
justification of their activities on the basis that they parallel
the activity of men in an inspired document. The *fact* of
divine inspiration does not mean that *all* which is in the
Bible is the will of God. The Bible no more morally approves
of all that it records than an editor approves of all that he
prints in his newspaper.

Records of lying, adultery, incest, cruelty,[4] and deceit are

---

[1] Cf. Paul Woolley, "The Relevance of Scripture," *The Infallible
Word*, pp. 201–204.

[2] "When we read of the failings, as well as the sinful actions of men,
recorded in Scriptures, we may see what is in our own nature: for there
are in us the seeds of the same sin, and similar tendencies to its commission, which would bring forth similar fruits, were it not for the
preventing and renewing grace of God. And as many of the persons,
whose faults are related in the volume of inspiration, we should learn
from them, not only to 'be not high-minded, but fear' (Rom. xi:20);
but further, to avoid being rash in censuring conduct of others." Horne,
op. cit., I, 427. Italics are omitted.

[3] Miller, *General Biblical Introduction*, p. 19.

[4] Jephthah's cruel vow has been euphemized into a pledge of perpetual
virginity, because it is felt that the Bible approved his act. Although
the Bible nowhere condemns it, by the same token it nowhere approves

found in the Bible, but on each occasion the sacred writer does not necessarily add his word of condemnation. There are not only sinful acts but erroneous notions recorded. The voice of the devil is heard, the voice of Judas, the voice of demons, the voice of the opponents of Christ, and of the enemies of the apostles. Inspiration here extends only to fidelity of recording. Such words do not constitute either the will of God or the approval of God. Therefore, in every example from a man's life or from Israel's history it must be determined if in any Scripture there is approval or disapproval of this specific situation. If there is none, then we must analyze the passage to see if it is approved or disapproved by other clear teaching of the Bible.[5]

(2). *We may take direct application from all of those incidents that the Bible directly censures or approves.* The woman who poured out the valuable incense was censured by Judas but approved by Christ, and made an example for all church history (John 12:1 ff.). The equivocal behavior of Peter at Antioch was expressly condemned by Paul writing under inspiration, and is a lesson to all not to be guided by opinion but by principle (Galatians 2:11 ff.). Certainly the rebellion of Saul, the immorality of David, the pride of Absalom, the treachery of Judas, the denials of Peter, and the lying of Ananias and Sapphira stand as examples of what not to do. So the faith of Abraham, the obedience of Moses, the loyalty of Elijah, and the love of John the Apostle stand out as great examples to follow.

(3). *Express commands to individuals are not the will of God for us.* Abraham was commanded to offer up his son;

---

it. The apology to be made at this point is not to distort the very clear meaning of the vow, but simply to indicate that in an inspired record, not all the deeds of even good men are approved by the mere token of being included in the inspired book.

[5] "We should carefully distinguish between what the Scripture itself says, and what is only said in the Scripture, and, also, the times, places, and persons, when, where, and by whom anything is recorded as having been said " Horne, *op. cit.*, I, 426. Italics omitted.

that is not a standing order for each father. Joshua was commanded to slay all in his military campaign; that is not instruction for Christian soldiers. A passage of great instruction is found in the closing part of John's Gospel. Our Lord tells Peter that he will suffer a violent death (John 21:18–19). Misery loves company, so looking at John Peter said, "what shall this man do?" (v. 21) as if to say "haven't you something equally as painful for him?" Our Lord says that if He wills it, John might never die! Two disciples are offered utterly contrasting experiences, yet both within the will of Christ. It behooves us to be unusually careful that we do not try to apply uncritically the commands given to good men of the Bible. Paul's trip to Arabia is not the will of God for some, nor is Peter's call to the apostleship the will of God for others, even though both of these activities were the will of God for Paul and Peter respectively.

(4). *In the lives of men in the Scriptures determine what the outstanding spiritual principle is.* Hebrews 11 is a remarkable example of going through the Old Testament and isolating from the lives of its great men a great spiritual virtue for our benefit. There is a danger of becoming too particular in our lessons from great men, and unconsciously engaging in double-sense interpretations. But if the essential spiritual principles are the goal of our investigations, we derive positive food for the soul, and avoid the mistakes of trying to find too much meaning in trivial details.

(5). *In the application of examples to our lives we do not need a literal reproduction of the Biblical situation.* Baptism need not be done in the river Jordan nor in the land of Palestine to be Scriptural baptism. Neither do we need to go to an upper room in Jerusalem to have the Lord's Table.

C. PROMISES

"Every promise in the book is mine" is one of the overstatements of the century. Few Bible promises partake of such universality. In applying the promises of the Bible to our specific situations we need to exercise great care. If we apply promises to ourselves that are not for us, we may suffer severe disappointment. Also, promises must not be used to tempt God. A reserve and a patience should temper all our usages of promises.

(1). *Note whether the promise is universal in scope.* The classic example of a universal promise is "and whosoever will, let him take the water of life freely" (Rev. 22:18). General invitations to salvation are for all men, but invitations to prayer or to special blessings are only for the company of the saved.

(2). *Note whether the promise is personal.* When God said to Paul, "Be not afraid, but speak, and hold not thy peace: for I am with thee, and no man shall set on thee to hurt thee" (Acts 18:9-10), that was personal to Paul and may not be used generally. Missionaries in difficult situations may hope for this type of deliverance but may not command it.

(3). *Note whether the promise is conditional.* When it says "Draw nigh unto God and he will draw nigh to you" (James 4:8), there is a human condition to be fulfilled before the promise is received.

(4). *Note whether the promise is for our time.* Some promises pertain just to the Jews in their land and have ceased with the coming of the New Testament. Some promises refer to future conditions that shall prevail upon the earth at the close of the age. Evidently, in Revelation 2 and 3 certain promises were restricted to different churches.

In connection with the use of promises some have used the Bible on the same principle of animistic divination. Divination is the means whereby primitives decide whether they should undergo a proposed adventure such as hunting, fishing, or battle. Common methods among primitives to decide the portent of future events are to read the entrails of pigs or chickens; to crack a bone in the heat of the fire and decide what to do from the nature of the crack; to throw an egg on a grass roof to see if it breaks or not; to use the fire-test to determine guilt. On the sillier level divination is predicting one's future by the reading of cards or tea leaves.

Whenever we force the Bible to say something on specific items of our life, we are in danger of divination. If we do this we leave the sensible, intelligent use of the Bible for that which borders on primitive divination. Most notorious is the custom of opening the Bible and putting the finger on a verse and taking that verse as divine guidance. This method dishonors the intelligence of God, the sobriety of the Bible, puts the Christian faith in a ridiculous light, and places the method of determining the will of God on a superstitious, magical basis. It ought to be added: *no promise of the Bible is to be used that is not in keeping with sane, exegetical principles.*

The type of divination mentioned above exists on a more sophisticated level with those who every day try to find specific guidance from the Bible—not guidance in the sense of getting truth, soul-food, and principles, but in finding one particular verse that tells them exactly what to do that day, or how to resolve a given situation. To do this they have to admit that God can give a message through the Bible that is completely divorced from the native, grammatical meaning of the verse. If this is permitted, then what is to prevent the interpreter from finding anything he wishes in the Bible?

To be specific, at the outbreak of World War II, a certain individual could not decide what his course of action should be—enlist? join the merchant marine? get a theological waiver? He went to his Bible and, finding a reference to those who go down to the seas in ships, he took it as his orders from God to enlist in the United States Navy. The action could not be based upon any sensible exegetical principle, nor upon any spiritual principle; it was a haphazard coincidence between the verse that had the word *seas* in it and the United States Navy.

The will of God is determined from the Bible only in terms

of what it says in its first grammatical sense, or what can be derived from it in terms of great spiritual principles. To use the Bible as in the above example is in direct violation of the nature of inspiration and of the character of the Bible. God does not "double-talk" when He speaks in Scripture, i.e., He does not have a historical, common-sense meaning, *plus* some special message to us in a given situation. If God speaks to us in a given situation, it must be in terms of the sound exegesis of the passage.[6]

D. The Use of the Bible in Preaching or Teaching

The preaching and teaching ministry in the church is applied hermeneutics and exegesis and comes under the discussion of the practical use of the Bible. The *basic theory* of the ministry must be understood if the correct ministry of preaching will be done by the preacher or teacher. The preacher is *a minister of the Word of God.* He is not a person who has a full and free right of sermonizing before a group of people. If he is a true minister of God *he is bound to the ministry of the Word of God.* He has only one claim to the right to preach and demand decision, and that is that he is *declaring the truth of God.* It is impossible to separate the man from his calling, but as much as possible the minister must realize preaching is not *his* opportunity to express *his* religious views. His fundamental task in preaching is not to be clever or sermonic or profound but *to minister the truth of God.* The apostles were called *ministers of the word* (Luke 1:2). The apostles were ordained as *witnesses of Jesus Christ* (Acts 1:8). Their task was to preach what they heard and

[6] "The only way of ascertaining the will of God . . . is to learn it by zealous application as students of the revelation of that will contained in the Scriptures. Short cuts as pulling verses out of boxes, getting guidance by daily motto books, and letting the Bible fall open like a casting of dice are not only useless; they are deceptive." Paul Woolley, "The Relevance of Scripture," *The Infallible Word,* p. 195. His entire refutation of the magical use of the Bible is good.

saw with reference to the life, death, and resurrection of Jesus Christ. The elder (pastor) is to labor *in word and doctrine* (1 Tim. 5:17). What Timothy is to hand on to others is not apostolic succession but *the truth of Christianity* which he heard from many Christians (2 Tim. 2:2). Paul instructs Timothy not to sermonize but to "preach *the message*" (2 Tim. 4:2. Grk: *kērukson ton logon*). Peter says he is an elder by virtue of having *witnessed* the sufferings of our Lord (1 Peter 5:1).

The New Testament servant of Christ was not one free to preach as he wished, but one bound to minister the truth of Christianity, to preach the word of God, and to be a witness of the Gospel. This is very far removed from much of our contemporary preaching which is hardly more than popular, superficial, and personal discourses on religious themes.

One of the mighty issues of the Reformation was the nature of the Christian ministry. Martin Luther and John Calvin both opposed the notion of the ministry as a priesthood. The doctrine of justification by faith alone meant the end of Catholic priestcraft and sacerdotalism. What then was a minister? He was according to both Luther and Calvin *a minister of the Word of God*. In place of the liturgy and sacrament was put the singing of hymns and the preaching of the Word of God. No longer was the altar the focal point of attention, but the open Bible with the man of God preaching forth its meaning and content. The magnificent and thrilling singing of hymns was the spirited way in which the Reformed movement expressed its new joy in Jesus Christ and its freedom from the ritual and liturgy. The mass, so central to Catholic piety and ministry, was replaced by *the preaching of the Word of God*.

Again it is painful to note how these great Reformation convictions have been forgotten, and how the great emphasis on the ministry of the Word of God as God's supreme method of blessing His people has given way to popular, ephemeral sermonizing.

The rules for the practical use of the Bible in preaching are basically derived from (i) general hermeneutic theory, and (ii) the conviction about the nature of the Christian ministry.

(1). *The minister must realize he is a servant of the Lord and bound to the word of the Lord.*

His basic motivation in preaching must be to convey to people the truth of God's word. This means he should publicly read the Bible which is evidently the meaning of "give attendance to reading" (1 Tim. 4:13). He should teach God's word for one of the requirements of a pastor is "apt to teach" (1 Tim. 3:2). He should *herald* or *preach* the word of God.

(2). *The preacher must use all Scripture in accordance with the rules of hermeneutics.*

It is felt too frequently by preachers that preaching is of such a nature as to exempt the preacher from close adherence to the rules of exegesis. Proper exegesis is necessary for commentators and theologians but preachers—it is argued—have a 'poetic license' with reference to Scripture. This is most unfortunate reasoning. If the preacher's duty is to minister the Word of God, hermeneutics is the means whereby he determines the *meaning* of the Word of God. *To ask for exemptions from the strict rules of hermeneutics is then to ask for an exemption from preaching the true meaning of the Word of God.* This is precisely a repudiation of what a man is called to preach, namely, the truth of God's Word.

This does not mean that preaching is nothing but public exegesis or drab commenting on the Sacred Text. There must be energy, life, imagination, relevancy, illustration, and passion to all preaching. Bookish, dry, technical exposition is not necessarily preaching the Word of God. But whenever Scripture is used, it must be used according to sound rules of hermeneutics.

The principal mistakes in preaching in violating the meaning of Scripture are:

(i). Taking a phrase from a text because of its attractive wording. The preacher does not actually expound the meaning of the text, but uses the felicitous wording of it as the basis for his own sermonizing. Broadus says that this is not preaching Scripture, but merely the words of Scripture.[7] No matter how literary the expression nor how catchy to the ear, a phrase must not be wrenched from its content and preached upon with no real interpretation of its meaning. This is not preaching the Word of God.

(ii). A preacher may choose a text but rather than explaining it sermonize on it. The remarks in a sermon need not be as narrow as the text, but if a text or passage is employed then the preacher is under holy obligation to explain its meaning. Either the preacher ignores the text save for the topic it suggests, or else he misinterprets it altogether. This is not a wilful perversion of Scripture but a negligent or careless or ignorant method of treating the inspired Text. Broadus is not too strong when writing on this sort of an abuse of a text when he says: "It is a mournful fact that Universalists, Romanists, Mormons, can find an apparent support for their heresies in Scripture, without interpreting more loosely, without doing greater violence to the meaning and connection of the Sacred Text than is sometimes done by orthodoxy, devout, and even intelligent men."[8]

(iii). A preacher may "spiritualize" a text or a passage and so impose a meaning on the text that is not there. This is usually done under the sincere pretense that the preacher is seeking a deeper meaning of the Bible. It is actually a species of patristic allegorization, and it is astounding how many of the patristic allegories are taught in Protestantism under the guise of typology.

One of the primary causes of this Protestant allegorizing is the proper motive to be edifying. Some Scripture is plain historical narrative and it is not especially edifying for the

[7] John A. Broadus, *A Treatise on the Preparation and Delivery of Sermons* (thirtieth edition), p. 33. Broadus has a learned and unusually wise discussion of the sermon and the interpretation of the text. Part I, Chapter II, "The Text—Interpretation."

[8] *Ibid.*, p. 47

preacher to summarize so many historical incidents. But if he can read into the passage something about Christ, or the gospel, or spiritual life, then he can make the passage very interesting. But he does so at the expense of its true meaning. He then is no longer preaching the Word of God but engaging in allegorization. Again we cite with much approval the judgment of Broadus about this sort of treatment of the Sacred Text:

Among Baptists, for instance, the influence of Fuller, Hall, and others, and the wider diffusion of ministerial education, have wrought a gratifying change. But there is still much ignorance to overcome, and too many able and honored ministers continue sometimes to sanction by their potent example the old-fashioned spiritualizing [really, allegorizing]. It is so easy and pleasant for men of fertile fancy to break away from laborious study of phraseology and connection, to cease plodding along the rough and homely paths of earth, and sport, free and rejoicing, in the open heaven; the people are so charmed by ingenious novelties, so carried away with imaginative flights, so delighted to find everywhere types of Christ and likenesses to the spiritual life; it is so common to think that whatever kindles the imagination and touches the heart must be good preaching, and so easy to insist that the doctrines of the sermon are in themselves true and Scriptural, though they be not actually taught in the text,—that preachers often lose sight of their fundamental and inexcusable error, of *saying that a passage of God's Word means what it does not mean.* So independent, too, one may feel; so original he may think himself. Commentaries, he can sneer at them all; other preachers, he has little need of comparing views with them. No need of anything but the resources of his own imagination, for such preaching is too often only building castles in the air.[9]

The proper and improper limits of typological exegesis will be discussed in the chapter on typology. But the proper alternative to spiritualizing the Old Testament is to *principlize* the Old Testament. To *principlize* is to discover in any narrative the basic spiritual, moral, or theological prin-

[9] *Ibid.*, p. 52. Italics are his.

ciples. These principles are latent in the text and it is the process of deduction which brings them to the surface. It is not an imposition on the text. Allegorizing is the imputation to the text of a meaning which is not there, but *principling* is not so guilty. By principlizing we are able to obtain devotional and spiritual truth from Scripture and avoid the charge of eisegesis.

When David repeatedly refuses to slay Saul we see the principle of obedience to powers that be. When Saul is not patient with God's prophet we see the principle of disobedience. When Isaiah prays for the shadow to retreat on the sundial we see the principle of great spiritual courage. In truth, Hebrews 11 is a magnificent example of principlizing. The great faith of a multitude of men is set before us as the true principle of their lives.

BIBLIOGRAPHY

Angus and Green, *Cyclopedic Handbook to the Bible*, Chapter X. The best general account in the literature.

Terry, *Biblical Hermeneutics*, Part Second, Chapter XXIV.

Chafer, *The Science of Biblical Hermeneutics*, Chapter IV.

Pierson, *Knowing the Scriptures*, Chapter I.

Manley, editor, *The New Bible Handbook*, p. 72 ff.

Horne, *An Introduction to the Study and Critical Knowledge of The Holy Scriptures*, I, 425 ff.

Broadus, *Treatise on the Preparation and Delivery of Sermons*, (thirtieth edition), Part I, Chapter II.

Baughman, "Books on Biblical Preaching," *Interpretation*, 5:470–477. An annotated bibliography.

Chapter VIII

THE PROBLEM OF INERRANCY AND SECULAR
SCIENCE IN RELATION TO HERMENEUTICS

A. The Problem of Infallibility and Inerrancy

JUDGED by their official creeds and confessions, all the
major churches of Christendom have accepted the divine inspiration of the Bible. They are agreed that the Bible is a
book brought into existence by the special grace of God, possessing a quality which books of purely human production
do not have. Judging further from official creeds and confessions the churches have accepted the *infallibility* of the
Bible in all matters of faith and morals. Men may depend on
the doctrines and morals of the Bible with complete certitude
of their truthfulness. Going yet another step, these churches
have accepted the *inerrancy* of all the historical and factual
matters of the Scriptures which pertain to matters of faith
and morals. This is demanded by the very historical nature
of the Biblical revelation, and the plan of redemption. Some
men have tried to defend infallibility of the faith and morals
of the Bible, but not the inerrancy of the Bible.[1] What is
actually proposed is that the major historical features of the
Scriptures are reliable. The Bible is errant in historical, factual, and numerical matters which do not affect its faith and
morals.

To accept the infallibility of the faith and morals of the
Bible is *mutatis mutandis* to accept the historical trustworthiness of the historical elements in redemption. The Christian

[1] For example Gore (*Lux Mundi*) and Briggs (*The Bible, The Church,
and Reason*).

faith has taught the infallibility of the faith and morals of Scripture, and the inerrancy of all matters of history pertaining to faith and morals. No lower ground than this can be held. It is true that extremes can be found in orthodoxy in this matter. J. Paterson Smyth (*How God Inspired the Bible*) does not wish to admit more than infallibility of faith and morals. The Buxtorffs defended the inspiration of the Hebrew vowels.[2]

Careful conservative scholarship has indicated that the inerrancy of the Bible must be judged by the very nature of the divine revelation. The revelation came to men speaking human languages and living in a cultural context. To be meaningful it had to come in the language of the prophets and apostles, and employ the cultural background for figures, illustrations, analogies, and everything else associated with linguistic communication. No artificial or abstract theory of inerrancy is to be imposed on the Scriptures.

To impose a precise literalness to the number usages of the Bible is an illustration of an artificial theory of inerrancy. Some interpreters have insisted that Jesus had to be in the grave exactly seventy-two hours because he said he would be buried for three days and three nights. But the expression "three days and three nights" *must be determined by Jewish usage.* In fact to insist on exactly seventy-two hours creates confusion. If Jesus were crucified on Friday, as practically all competent scholars agree, then the resurrection would not be till late Monday afternoon. In fact, if the burial were in the afternoon—as is stated in the Scriptures that it was before sundown—the resurrection had to be just seventy-two hours later in the afternoon. If one insists that the crucifixion were on Wednesday then the seventy-two hours ends before sundown on Saturday, and not on the Lord's day.

[2] Hebrew was originally written with consonants (radicals) only. When it ceased to be a spoken language, Jewish scholars added vowels (vowel points) to indicate its pronunciation. It is now universally admitted that these vowel points are a late insertion and not part of the autographs.

In 1 Cor. 15:5 Paul says our Lord was seen after his resurrection by "the twelve." An artificial notion of inerrancy would demand twelve apostles, but Judas was dead and his successor was not appointed till after the ascension. But "the twelve" had become a regular expression for "the group of disciples."

Two other illustrations may be given to show that inerrancy must be judged by *usus loquendi* of the times and not artificially. In Mark 1:2 a citation is made from Malachi and Isaiah. Isaiah's name does not appear in the King James, but it does in the best critical editions of the Greek text. Mark attributes both citations to Isaiah. The Jewish custom in citing two or three prophets in a brief catena of Scripture was to name only the leading prophet. In Matthew 27:9 a verse from Zechariah is cited as coming from Jeremiah. The Jewish tradition was that the spirit of Jeremiah was in Zechariah and such a method of citation would not offend their historical sense.

We can sum up what we have been trying to say as follows: *in judging the inerrancy of the Scriptures we must judge them according to the customs, rules, and standards of the times the various books were written, and not in terms of some abstract or artificial notion of inerrancy.*

To those who accept the infallibility and inerrancy of Scripture, the problem of inerrancy presents a special problem to the interpreter. In dealing with this important and difficult problem we suggest the following principles:

(1). *A belief in the inerrancy of the Bible does not mean that all the Bible is clear.* The inspiration of the Bible does not guarantee its lucidity. The apostle Peter indicates that the prophets themselves were puzzled about what they wrote (1 Pet. 1:10 ff.). He further admits that Paul said many things which are hard to interpret (2 Peter 3:16, *dysnoētos*, difficult to understand). The writer of Hebrews tells his listeners that his exposition about Christ and Melchisedec is lengthy and difficult to interpret (Hebrews 5:11). Our Lord

Himself puzzled his own disciples with many of his utterances. The inerrancy of the Scriptures does not mean that it is possible to give a clear interpretation of every passage.

Above the express statements of the Scriptures to their own partial obscurity is the very nature of the Bible. We must expect obscurities from the very fact that the Bible is written in ancient languages, in a strange culture, and that the Bible refers to persons, places, and events for which no other source for corroboration exists. The Bible was composed over a vast geographical territory—from Egypt to Babylon to Rome—and written over a span of some fifteen centuries.

A considerable source of encouragement is the findings of archaeology which are clearing up some obscurities. The reference to seething a kid in its mother's milk has been a puzzler since patristic exegesis (Exodus 23:19). It is now known to be part of heathenish idolatry.[3]

The older commentators spent much time trying to unravel the meaning of the expression "daily bread" in the Lord's prayer. Deissmann has discovered the expression in the papyri and it refers to the provisions given to laborers and soldiers for the following day's work. Deissmann[4] translates it: "Give us today our amount of daily food for tomorrow."

(2). *When we assert the inerrancy of the Bible, we do not assert that the Bible speaks all its mind on a subject in one place.* It is the total Bible in historical perspective which is inerrant. The monogamous ideal of marriage is not clearly set forth till the pages of the New Testament. What is not even mentioned to a two-year-old is reprimanded in a ten-year-old. So God tolerated much in the Old Testament period while mankind (specifically Israel) was in its ethical and theological

[3] Cf. J. Finegan, *Light from the Ancient Past*, p. 148. The rite is referred to in the Ras Shamra texts.

[4] Deissmann, *The New Testament in the Light of Modern Research*, p. 86. For the better understanding of the grammar of the New Testament from research in papyri see A. T. Robertson, *A Grammar of the Greek New Testament in the Light of Historical Research* (fifth edition), pp. 1–139.

swaddling clothes. The full light of revelation burns in the New Testament. It is not proper to pit the earlier part of the Bible against the later as if they contradict. M'Intosh has argued repeatedly in his work, *Is Christ Infallible and the Bible True?* that the immature or preliminary does not exist in a state of contradiction with the mature and final, and with this we agree.

The complete mind of God on a subject matter is given (as far as revelation contains it) by a historico-synoptic view. No charge of errancy can be made against the Bible by isolating a doctrine from its complete Biblical development.

(3). *Belief in the inerrancy of the Scriptures leads us to affirm there are no contradictions in the Bible.* As much as is made over the proposed contradictions in Scripture, it is surprising how few examples of any possible merit can be supplied, and it is further surprising how difficult it is to make a successful case out of these examples. To be specific Marcus Dods lists six contradictions in the Gospels as his basis for not accepting their inerrancy, and Frederic Kenyon supplies us with another list of contradictions which prove the errancy of the Scriptures.[5] In both cases it will be discovered that in the conservative commentaries there are plausible explanations of every one of these alleged contradictions. The burden of proof is on the accuser. The believer in the Scriptures needs only to show that the evidence of errancy is not conclusive. A contradiction to be valid must be unequivocal, and as long as the proposed contradiction is alleged on ambiguous grounds no charge of errancy is valid.

Archeology has again supplied some help at this point. The difficulties about Luke's census that were once so formidable have now practically vanished, thanks to archeology. Certain other embarrassments in the Gospel accounts have been relieved.[6]

---

[5] Dods, *The Bible: Its Origin and Nature*, pp. 136–37. Kenyon, *The Bible and Archaeology*, p. 27.
[6] Cf. A. T. Robertson, *A Harmony of the Gospels*, p. 71 fn.

In considering so-called contradictions many matters must be weighed: (i) We must be sure of our original text. In the healing of the maniac of Gerasa it was assumed incredible that the pigs could run thirty-five miles to the lake and plunge in, for the town of Gerasa was so situated. Textual critics have come to the conclusion that the correct reading of the original text should be Gerasenes. To supplement this has been the work of Thompson who has found the ruins of a town named Khersa right at the edge of a steep place by the sea.[7]

(ii) Some problems, especially those dealing with numbers, may easily be corruption of the text; e.g., 1 Sam. 13:1 and Acts 13:21; 1 Kings 4:26 and 2 Chronicles 9:25. Paul declares that twenty-three thousand died in a plague (1 Cor. 10:8), whereas Numbers 25:9 records twenty-four thousand. That Paul records how many died in a day and Moses in the entire plague is a thin explanation because how would Paul know such a breakdown of the figures? A corrupt text seems to be the better accounting of this. It could also be argued that Paul contradicts Moses only if he intended to be giving the exact number. If he had *in mentis* the intent of only supplying a round number no contradiction exists. The same is true for 1 Kings 7:23 where the value for *pi* is three. It has been argued that with a flange the circumference could be reduced to 30 cubits, but if the numbers are general and not intended to be to the decimal point no contradiction can be said to exist. Further the susceptibility of numbers to corruption in ancient texts is well known.

(iii). We may misinterpret one or both of two conflicting passages. The two genealogies of Christ present a real problem. That they are contradictory has never been unequivocally established.[8] Further, the scheme of Matthew to give

---

[5] Robertson, *Loc. cit.*

[8] Cf. Robertson's discussion. *Op. cit.*, p. 259. We prefer Machen's solution to Robertson's, however. *The Virgin Birth of Christ*, p. 229 ff.

his genealogy in compressed form and in units of fourteen each is his specific intent, and not to be made thereby contradictory to a fuller account. Much care must also be used in correlating the Gospel narratives. In the healing of blind Bartimaeus, Matthew mentions two blind men, whereas Luke and Mark mention only one. In the healing of the Gerasene demoniac Matthew again mentions two, and Luke and Mark, one. Mark and Luke pick out the more notorious of the two and limit their account to him. The healing of blind Bartimaeus is stated to be while leaving the city, and while entering the city. There was a new Jericho and an old Jericho. If the healing took place between the two cities both expressions are true.

(iv). We may identify two similar events that are really different. There is the possibility of two cleansings of the Temple (John 2; Matthew 21). The Sermon on the Mount might have been given several times (Matthew 5; Luke 6). Many of the healings evidently followed similar patterns even to the conversation.

(v). The fuller account is to be used to explain the shorter account. No contradiction is to be construed if the writer condenses an account or speech for economy of space or time. What God said to Ananias in Acts 9:10–19, Paul puts in the mouth of Ananias as speaking to him (Acts 22:12–16). Acts 9 is the full account of Paul's conversion, and Acts 22 the abbreviated account.

(vi). In a given instance one writer may give direct discourse, and the second either indirect discourse or a simple statement of the content of what was said. This is a constant phenomenon in the synoptic Gospels. This is standard and accepted methodology of prose composition and not to be taken as contradictory.

(vii). Inerrancy does not mean *literalness* of detail. All of the speeches in the book of Acts are very short, and we are persuaded that Peter and Paul talked for more than one or two minutes. We have in Acts a faithful digest of these speeches and not the *ipsissima verba* of Paul and Peter.[9]

(4). *Belief in the inerrancy of the Bible does not demand the original manuscripts nor a perfect text.* That original manuscripts of the Bible existed cannot be doubted although sometimes critics of inspiration argue as if original manuscripts never existed. The Biblical writers began with copies, so it seems! Nor can it be doubted that errors of transmission took place when the autographs were copied. It is therefore entirely proper to assert that a given reading in a text might not exist in the original text. We have not by so reasoning proved the autographs to be inerrant, but on the other hand we have argued that corruptions do exist and that there may be a difference between present-day manuscripts and autographs. The fact of textual corruptions is not a denial of inspiration, but a *problem* of inspiration. It is a logical *non sequitur* to argue from a corrupted text to a denial of inspiration. There is nothing inherently contradictory in the notion of an inspired text imperfectly transmitted.

Obviously we have no autographs of either Testament. The oldest manuscript of the New Testament is the John Rylands Papyrus fragment of the Gospel of John dated by some as early as A.D. 125, although usually about A.D. 150. Until the discovery of the Dead Sea Scrolls our oldest Old Testament manuscript was the Leningrad Codex, dated A.D. 916. Now we have manuscripts of Isaiah and Daniel dated a hundred years or so before the birth of Christ, and fragments of many of the other Old Testament books.

All orthodoxy needs to claim in this regard is that errors of transmission touch nothing vital in Scripture. There is no question that the most faithfully transmitted manuscripts from antiquity are the Old and New Testaments. For proof

---

[9] *Verbal* inspiration does not mean *exact literal reproduction* of what is said or done. A study of parallel passages with a Greek harmony of the Gospels reveals how many words and expressions the Spirit considered synonymous; and it is also interesting to note variation in detail and difference of length of accounts.

of this assertion with reference to the Old Testament we cite
Green: "It may be safely said that no other work of antiquity
has been so accurately transmitted." [10] The texts of Daniel
and Isaiah in the Dead Sea Scrolls are substantially Masoretic
and so further confirm this claim of Green.

As far as the New Testament is concerned, the situation
is just as satisfactory. In the first place the number of Greek
manuscripts for critical work is now over 4000. If Latin and
other early versions be admitted, then the figure moves up
over the 13,000 mark. Further, practically the entire New
Testament can be culled from citations in the Fathers. There
is nothing in classical documents which even comes close to
this. Hort claims that less than one thousandth of the New
Testament text is corrupt. In the remarkable providence of
God the text of the Bible in the original languages forms the
most reliably transmitted texts known to classical scholarship.

B. The Problem of Science

If we accept the divine inspiration of a Book which was
written several centuries before the discoveries of modern
science we are faced with the very acute problem of relating
its statements about creation to those of modern science. To
claim that the Bible is a book filled with anticipations of
modern science does not seem to accord with the cultural
conditioning of any revelation, and to declare all its statements about nature as invalid does not seem to accord with
its inspiration. What canons of interpretation should we
follow in regard to this important and knotty question? [11]

(1). *When we assert the inerrancy of Scripture we do not*

[10] Green, *General Introduction to the Old Testament: The Text*, p. 181.
Cf. also remarks of the same commendatory nature by Kenyon, *Our
Bible and the Ancient Manuscripts*, pp. 38 and 47. For the conservative
position clearly and lucidly explained see John H. Skilton, "The Transmission of Scriptures," *The Infallible Word*, pp. 137–187.

[11] We have treated this more extensively in our volume, *The Christian
View of Science and Scripture.*

assert that the Bible uses scientific language. Classical scholars, historians, and students of the history of philosophy make a conscious effort to find modern counterparts to ancient terminology. This is not considered as depreciating the validity of these terms. Thomists insist that if present scholars would take the pains to make accurate correlations between Thomas' vocabulary and modern terms, present day scholars would find much more significance in Thomas. Others have said that much of Newton's genius goes unheralded because scholars will not bother to learn the scientific Latin jargon of Newton's day and transpose it into our contemporary language. The popular nature of the Biblical statements about nature is no argument against the validity of these statements.

The Bible is a book adapted for all ages of the human race and therefore its vocabulary about nature must be popular. It is no objection against inerrancy that the Scriptures are in popular language.

(2). *No objection can be brought against inerrancy because the language of the Bible is phenomenal.* A language which is phenomenal is restricted to terms of description and observation. Its language about astronomy, botany, zoology, and geology is restricted to the vocabulary of popular observation. What can be seen through microscope or telescope is not commented on. Phenomenal language is true because all it claims is to be descriptive. One is not deceived when he sees the sun rise and the sun set. One is deceived only if he artlessly converts his observations into theories.

The corollary to this is that the Bible does not theorize as to the actual nature of things. It does not contain a theory of astronomy or geology or chemistry. It does not seek to present knowledge which could be formed into a science text. The words of Paul Woolley are very relevant at this point:

> The Bible, then, should not be approached with a view to finding it a comprehensive treatise on, for example, natural science. A great many statements in the realm of natural science are to be found in

the Bible, and they are true statements. But the Bible offers no information as to the validity of the various modern theories concerning the nature of matter and the constitution of the physical world. There is nothing in the Bible with which to test the theories of relativity . . . One could not write a biological textbook from the Bible alone.[12]

(3). *No objection can be brought against the inerrancy of the Bible because it is a culturally conditioned revelation.* The Bible uses the terms and expressions of the times of its writers. Any revelation must be so accommodated to the human mind. The interpreter who seeks for modern relativity theory in the Bible is mistaken as he asks the Bible to speak on a subject it *ex hypothesi* will not. When the religious liberal renounces much of the Bible because it is culturally conditioned he fails to understand that inspiration uses cultural terms and expressions to convey an infallible revelation.

The mustard seed is not the smallest seed known to botanists, but among the Semites it was considered to be the smallest of seeds. Its phenomenal growth became the basis for an analogy for the growth of anything unusually small to something very large. For our Lord to have given the Latin terms of the smallest seed would have been grotesque.

John 1:13 states that the Christian is born of God, not of "bloods." It was the Jewish opinion that the seeds of inheritance were carried in the blood-stream. Does John argue that the seeds of reproduction are in the bloodstream? What John intends to teach is that a man is born of God, not on the basis of his Jewish ancestry. He had to use the culturally current terms to make his theological point. The same is true of much of the psychology of the Bible, e.g., attributing psychic properties to bowels, kidneys, heart, liver, and bones. The divine revelation came in and through these modes of expression and the infallible truth shines *through* them.

(4). *It is not proper to attempt to find numerous correlations*

[12] Paul Woolley, "The Relevance of Scripture," *The Infallible Word,* p. 190.

of Scripture and modern science. The careful interpreter will not try to find the automobile in Nahum 1, or the airplane in Isaiah 60 or atomic theory in Hebrews 11:3 or atomic energy in 2 Peter 3. All such efforts to extract modern scientific theories out of Scripture eventually do more harm than good.

(5). *It must be kept in mind that Genesis 1 is in outline form.* Contemporary works which endeavor to sketch the salient facts of the universe run up to five hundred pages. Genesis sums up creation in thirty-four verses (Gen. 1:1 to 2:3). The extreme brevity of the account must temper all our exegesis of it. Trying to read too much specific detail into this sketch can cause needless conflict with science. It is always problematic to go from the "let there be" of Genesis to the *modus operandi.*

It is the province of the sciences to fill in the details of what is in outline form in the Bible. Science should not preëmpt to itself *the first principles* of the Biblical account, nor should theologians endeavor to dictate to the scientists empirical details about which Genesis 1 is actually silent. The Church has suffered much because (i) what theologians have said about what Genesis 1 has not been clearly differentiated from (ii) what Genesis 1 actually says. A. J. Maas has stated very acceptably the relationship which science should bear to interpretation, and interpretation to science.

It would be wrong to make Scripture the criterion of science, to decide our modern scientific questions from our Biblical data. . . . It is well, therefore, to temper our conservatism with prudence; prescinding from 'matters of faith and morals' in which there can be no change, we should be ready to accommodate our exegesis to the progress of historians and scientists in their respective fields, showing at the same time that such harmonizing expositions of Scripture represent only a progressive state in Bible study which will be perfected with the progress of profane learning.[13]

[13] "Hermeneutics," *Catholic Encyclopedia,* VII, 275.

Maas suggests in this citation that our interpretations about science and Scripture should be kept fluid. Exegesis and science are both developing and progressing. It would be improper to make hard and fast interpretations if this is the situation. Just as history gives us clues to the meaning of prophecy, so our knowledge of science gives us greater insight into the Biblical statements about natural things. No interpretation of Genesis 1 is more mature than the science which guides it. To attempt to interpret the scientific elements of Genesis 1 *without* science is to attempt the impossible for the concepts and objects of the chapter have meaning only as they are referred to nature, and the subject matter of science may be called simply "nature."

One more observation must be made, however, before we conclude this chapter. The older polemic against the inspiration of the Bible was directed at specific contradictions. One unequivocal contradiction could, it was urged, bring down the doctrine of inerrancy. The critics thought they could produce examples but the orthodox felt the examples to be equivocal. The attack has taken a new, drastic and serious turn. It is not so much directed at finding contradictions or discrepancies in Scripture as it is in finding deep-seated contradictions in the very nature of the record.

One example of such an alleged deep-seated contradiction is the assertion that the historical record of the Old Testament does not contain the true order. The prophets were actually before the law. The Jewish canon which governs the order of the books in the Bible is the reverse order of history.

Further, the discussion over this or that fact in Scripture and science gave way to a new problem. The allegation was that the Scriptures represented the cosmological schemes of antiquity and were in very violent contrast to the world as understood by modern science. To attempt to reconcile Genesis to geology was repudiated because in the eyes of the critics it amounted to trying to harmonize some ancient Babylonian cosmology with the cosmology of modern science.

214 PROTESTANT BIBLICAL INTERPRETATION

A third deep-seated contradiction alleged by the critics is that there was a moral contradiction between the Old and the New Testaments. Some of the practices of the Old Testament are primitive or barbaric or cruel and in stark contradiction to the ethics of the New Testament.

Finally, the critics have proved to their satisfaction at least that the Bible represents no theological unity, but is a veritable congeries of theologies. The Old Testament books reflect a variety of religious beliefs, and several main strands of divergent theological thought can be found in the New Testament. Priest is set against prophet, the New against the Old, Paul against Peter, and John against James.

This is where the older problem of "discrepancies and contradictions" have moved and evangelicalism must reply in kind to maintain the unity of the divine revelation.

BIBLIOGRAPHY

Angus and Green, *Cyclopedic Handbook to the Bible*, p. 259 ff.

R. A. Torrey, *Alleged Discrepancies in the Bible.*

H. E. Guillebaud, *Some Moral Difficulties in the Bible.*

J. R. Van Pelt, "Discrepancies," *International Standard Bible Encyclopedia*, II, 852–54.

Terry, *Biblical Hermeneutics*, p. 404.

W. Arndt, *Does the Bible Contradict Itself?*

Barrows, *Companion to the Bible*, p. 543.

T. Horne, *An Introduction to the Critical Knowledge and Study of the Holy Scriptures*, I, Bk. II, Chapter VIII.

J. Urquhart, *The New Biblical Guide*, Vol. VIII, Part II, "The Question about the Inerrancy of Scripture."

C. A. Briggs, *The Bible, The Church, and Reason*, Chapter IV, "Is Holy Scripture Inerrant?"

J. W. Haley, *Alleged Discrepancies of the Bible.*

C. Daniel, *The Bible's Seeming Contradictions.*

G. Dehoff, *Alleged Bible Contradictions Explained.*

Bernard Ramm, *The Christian View of Science and Scripture*, "A Classified Bibliography," pp. 355–60.

CHAPTER IX

THE INTERPRETATION OF TYPES

THE content of special hermeneutics is rather large. Terry (*Biblical Hermeneutics*, revised edition) has a large list of subjects comprising special hermeneutics, e.g., Hebrew poetry; figurative language such as tropes, metonym, personification, synedoche, apostrophe, interrogation, hyperbole, irony, simile, metaphor, fables, riddles, and enigmas; parables; allegories, proverbs, and gnomic poetry; types; symbols (actions, numbers, names, colors); dreams; prophecy (general, Messianic, apocalyptic); Old Testament quotations in the New; accommodation; progress of doctrine and analogy of faith; and the doctrinal and practical use of the Bible. Out of this list there are three items in particular which need special attention due to their importance, namely, typology, prophecy, and parables.

A. JUSTIFICATION OF TYPOLOGY AS A BIBLICAL DISCIPLINE

It has been the contention of critics that typology is forced exegesis rather than an interpretation rising naturally out of the Scriptures. Some exegesis of the Old Testament in the name of typology is forced, to be sure. However such excesses—past and present—do not destroy the Christian contention that the typological method of interpretation is valid. The justification for typological interpretation is as follows:

(1). The general relationship which the Old Testament sustains to the New is the very basis for such a study. The strong *prophetic element* in the Old Testament establishes a real and vital nexus between the two Testaments. The fact of prophecy establishes the principle that the New is latent in the Old, and that the Old is patent in the New. The form of prophecy may be either verbally predictive or typically predictive. The former are those prophecies which in poetry or prose speak of the age to come (e.g., Psalm 22, Isaiah 53); the latter are those typical persons, things, or events which forecast the age to come. Thus a type is a species of prophecy and should be included under prophetic studies. Typological interpretation is thereby justified because it is part of prophecy, the very nature of which establishes the nexus between the two Testaments.

Torm makes it even stronger than this. Torm prefers to speak of the typological method of thinking (*Betrachtungweise*) rather than the typological method of interpretation (*Auslegung*). The reason for this is two-fold: typological interpretation is based on the unity of the Testaments. It shows that the divine revelation is of one piece.[1] We are thus able to relate part to part and understand their places in the divine revelation. Torm claims, secondly, typological interpretation is really a philosophy of history! He writes: "Typological interpretation is not so much an interpretation as a historical consideration, a method and manner of judging historical events and relations—a sort of philosophy of history, if you please."[2] It is the special Christian perspective on a very special segment of human history.

(2). Our Lord's own use of the Old Testament is His invitation to us to find Him in the Old Testament. In Luke

---

[1] "Die Bedeutung der typologischen Betrachtungweise ist die, dass sie uns den Blick für die Einheit in der Offenbarung Gottes öffnet und gerade dadurch uns die bleibende Bedeutung, die jeder kleine Teil der Offenbarung für die Gesamheit hat, erkennen lässt." F. Torm, *Das Hermeneutik des Neuen Testaments*, p. 224.

[2] "Die 'typologische Auslegung' ist also nicht so sehr eine Auslegung als eine historische Betrachtung, eine Art and Weise, die geschichtlichen Ereignisse und Verhältnisse zu beurteilen,—eine Art Philosophie der Geschichte, wenn man will." *Ibid.*, p. 223.

24:25–44 Christ teaches the disciples about Himself, beginning at Moses and following through *all* the Scriptures. Luke 24:44 mentions the divisions of the Jewish canon (Moses, Prophets, Psalms) thus making the reference as wide as the Old Testament canon. In John 5:39–44 Christ invites men to search the Scriptures for *they testify to him* inasmuch as Moses wrote of Him. Paul uses the sacrificial language of the Old Testament in speaking of the death of Christ (Eph. 5:2) thus showing that Christ is in the offerings. Hebrews clearly teaches that the Tabernacle which was, is now realized in a present heavenly tabernacle of which Christ is the minister of the sanctuary (Hebrews 9:9–11, 23–24). Thus Christ is to be found in the Tabernacle. And certainly from Paul's reference in 1 Cor. 10:4 Christ was in the wilderness wanderings. It is the conviction of many scholars that the Christian interpretation of the Old Testament stems directly from the teachings and example of our Lord.

(3). Even more specific is the vocabulary of the New Testament with reference to the nature of the Old.[3] The following words are used in the New of the Old. *Hypodeigma* means a sign suggestive of anything, a representation, a figure, a copy, an example. *Typos* and *typikos* (from the verb, *typtō*, "to strike") mean the mark of a blow, the figure formed by a blow, an impression, a form, a letter, a doctrine, an example, a pattern, a type. *Skia* (from *skēnē*, a tent) means a shade, a sketch, an outline, an adumbration. *Parabolē* means a placing by the side, hence a comparison, a likeness, a similitude. *Eikon* means an image, a figure, a likeness. *Antitypon* means a repelling blow, an echoing, a reflecting, a thing formed after a pattern, a counterpart, an antitype. *Allegoreō* means to tell a truth in terms of a narrative.

These New Testament words referring to the nature of the Old Testament establish the typical character of the Old Testament. In addition to this is the weight of the entire

[3] Cf. H. S. Miller, *The Tabernacle*, p. 19 ff.

book of Hebrews, for it is almost completely devoted to a study of the typical character of the Old Testament.[4]

The fact that the Old Testament prophecy includes the typical, the invitation of our Lord to find Him in all the Old Testament which includes the typical, and the vocabulary of the New Testament indicating the typical element of the Old, is adequate justification of the theological study of typology.

B. Schools of Typological Interpretation

In the history of typological exegesis certain schools of interpretation are discovered.[5] As a preparation for a discussion of the rules of typological interpretation we shall briefly note these schools.

(1). One group of interpreters *saw too much as typical*. The motivations of the various subgroups of this family are diverse. The apostolic Fathers and early apologists were apologetically motivated. Part of their proof for the divinity of Christianity was its antiquity, and its antiquity could be demonstrated by a typological interpretation of the Old Testament. Other fathers were motivated to see Greek philosophy taught in the Old Testament (Origen and Clement) and at this point the typological loses itself to the allegorical as Darbyshire observes.[6] Others, following the rules of Philo, sought to obviate supposed difficulties in the literal interpretation of the text. The medievalists and other Catholic theologians realized that typical interpretation of the Old Testament could strengthen the Biblical evidence for many of the Church's doctrines. The Protestant schools of Cocceius and Hutchinson regarded the Old Testament as a larder

---

[4] Note also 1 Cor. 10:6, and 10:11 for the typical character of some Old Testament history. Davidson (*Old Testament Prophecy*) has two excellent chapters on typology (XIII, XIV).

[5] The subject is treated historically in Fairbairn, *The Typology of Scripture*, I, pp. 1–40; and in Darbyshire, "Typology," *Hastings Encyclopedia of Religion and Ethics*, XII, 501 (Part 3, "History of Typology").

[6] *Op. cit.*, 502.

richly stored with New Testament teachings. In the effort to find devotional and edifying truth in all Scripture, and to find Christ veritably in *all* Scripture, some dispensationalists have pressed typological interpretation beyond its proper measure.

Although the motivation of these different subgroups is varied, and their emphases different, and even their procedures divergent, they yet agree to this one point: *the Old Testament is a rich mine of New Testament truth and the spiritual interpreter can dig it out.*

(2). Directly opposite to this group are those *rationalists and critics* who see the entire typological method of interpretation as a case of forced exegesis. These men have broken with the doctrine of special revelation, denied the doctrine of plenary inspiration, and accordingly renounced the supernatural world view of Biblical religion. In that prophecy as prediction is obviously a case of supernatural inspiration, it must be denied in either the form of didactic prediction or typical prediction. Thus to the rationalistic critics there are two types, and hence there can be no typological interpretation. Darbyshire's judgment is that "modern writers of the critical school have unduly ignored the importance of typology." [7] It is really more than this. They have not only ignored it; they have denied it.

(3). Bishop Marsh proposed in his *Lectures on the Criticism and Interpretation of the Bible* his famous principle that a type is a type only if the New Testament specifically so designates it to be such. This is a very strict principle and was advocated to curtail much of the fanciful and imaginary in typological interpretation. Because it is a stern and precise formula it has exerted a great influence on theological thought. Many Protestant exegetes if not adhering to the very letter of Marsh's principle certainly follow it very closely.

(4). Salomon Glassius propounded in his *Philogia Sacra*

[7] *Ibid.*, p. 503.

(5 vols., 1623–36) that types were of two sorts, *innate* and *inferred*. He has been followed in basic theory by such typologists as Cocceius, Keach, Horne, Fairbairn, and Terry. This school we may designate as the *moderate school*. The moderate school agrees with Marsh that the New Testament is the point of departure in typological studies, but insists that Marsh did not dig out the full teaching of the New Testament on the subject. An *innate* type is a type specifically declared to be such in the New Testament. An *inferred* type is one that, not specifically designated in the New Testament is justified for its existence by the nature of the New Testament materials on typology.

The most able defender of the moderate school has been Fairbairn and he is supported by Terry.[8] Fairbairn's criticisms of Marsh are as follows: (i) The relationship in Marsh's system between type and antitype is too artificial. The Old Testament and New Testament contain the same basic system of theology. They run side by side like two parallel rivers. Their parallelism is indicated by occasional channels (types) which connect them. These channels (types) are possible only because the two rivers run parallel. The Marshian principle fails to realize that other channels may be cut through which are not specifically named in Scripture, otherwise the relationship of the two Testaments is rather mechanical. Terry criticizes this principle when he writes: "But we should guard against the extreme position of some writers who declare that nothing in the Old Testament is to be so regarded as typical but what the New Testament affirms to be so." [9] (ii) In order to escape from the lawless aberrations of other schools the system of Marsh limits itself to too meagre a field. (iii) As we do not wait for the fulfilment of prophecy to declare a passage to be a prophecy, so we do not need the New Testament to declare everything a type that is a type. (iv) The very implication of Hebrews itself is that only a

[8] Terry, *Biblical Hermeneutics* (revised edition), pp. 255–56.
[9] *Ibid.*, p. 248.

fraction of the great parallels between the two Covenants is considered, and that it is left to our Christian maturity to draw the other parallels. (v) If the whole (e.g., the Tabernacle, the wilderness journey) is typical, then the parts are typical. (iv) The avoidance of extravagances in typology is not to be accomplished by narrowing typology mercilessly to a small field, but by establishing typology from an empirical investigation of Scriptures themselves.

At the present time typological interpretation is undergoing a revival. To be sure we still have the rationalists who deny the very existence of types, and to be sure we have extremists.[10] Some scholars would adhere rather closely to Marsh, and more to Fairbairn. But due to the new interest in theology, Biblical theology, and exegesis we have a new interest in typical interpretation. The revival in Old Testament theology has produced a new interest in typological interpretation. It is through the typological interpretation of the Old Testament that these recent scholars preserve the Christian character and value of the Old Testament. It must also be noted that Catholic scholars have been thinking seriously of typological interpretation and they have tried to rescue the study from the excesses to which the Fathers seem to have committed it. This new sober spirit of typological exegesis among Catholics may be noted in such works as *A Catholic Commentary on the Holy Scriptures;* the articles on "Exegesis" and "Hermeneutics" in *The Catholic Encyclopedia* (by A. J. Maas); and in the writings of Dean Daniélou (e.g., *Origen*, Part II, Chapter II, "The Typological Interpretation of the Bible").

C. Typological and Allegorical Interpretation

In the history of interpretation the question has been occasionally asked whether allegorical and typological interpreta-

[10] A very remarkable and blessed work is C. H. M., *Notes on the Pentateuch* (6 vols.). Although filled with much insight and spiritual truth, yet, from the strict hermeneutical standpoint, it abounds in allegorisms and excessive typological interpretations. Its redeeming worth is its emphasis on Christ, grace, salvation, and Christian living.

tion are one method of interpretation mistakenly called by two different names, or actually two different methods of interpretation.[11] One group insists there is but one method of spiritual interpretation but that it passes under other names such as typological, allegorical, or mystical. Jewett's contention is that there is but one such method but that among evangelicals it is called typological if proper, and allegorical if improper. Those who insist that the typological and the allegorical are two different methods of interpretation maintain that the genius of each method is peculiar enough to separate it from the other.[12]

Although to some theologians the problem might be academic, to others it is vital. A dispensationalist is anxious to preserve the distinction, for one of his strongest charges against amillennialism is that it uses the improper method of allegorizing, yet the dispensationalist must retain the typological method as valid. The amillennialist finds it to his advantage to efface the difference. He would assert that there is a mystical or spiritual sense to Scripture, and such mystical interpretations are valid if they conform to New Testament truth and invalid if they do not.[13]

The issue should be settled apart from these vested theological interests, on purely hermeneutical considerations. Is there a genius peculiar to each of these methods calling for a valid distinction, or do we have two words describing essen-

[11] Cf. the discussion by Darbyshire, *op. cit.*, p. 500; by Jewett, "Concerning the Allegorical Interpretation of Scripture," *The Westminster Theological Journal*, 17:1–20; by Torm, *Hermeneutik des Neuen Testaments*, p. 223 f.; by Horne, *Introduction*, I, 364; by Angus and Green, *Cyclopedic Handbook to the Bible*, p. 221; by Dana, *Searching the Scriptures*, p. 38; by Meyer, *Critical and Exegetical Handbook to the Epistle to the Galatians*, p. 201, fn. 7.

[12] Thus the etymology of the two words would indicate their respective genius: "allegory"—one story in terms of another, and "type" an impression made on a material by the master-copy.

[13] Berkhof actually uses the word *hyponoia* for the mystical sense of Scripture which is the word used in the classics for allegorical interpretation. (*Principles of Interpretation*, p. 59.) Note this classical use of *hyponoia* in Geffcken, "Allegory, Allegorical Interpretation," *Hastings Encyclopedia of Religion and Ethics*, I, 328.

tially one method of interpretation? We believe it is possible to find a specific genius for each of these methods calling for their separation.

Allegorical interpretation is the interpretation of a document whereby something *foreign, peculiar,* or *hidden* is introduced into the meaning of the text giving it a proposed deeper or real meaning. Geffcken notes that in allegorical interpretation "an entirely foreign subjective meaning is read into the passage to be explained," [14] and Hoskyns and Davey note that the "allegory expresses the relationship between certain persons and things *by substituting a whole range of persons or things from an entirely different sphere of experience.*" [15]

Typological interpretation is specifically the interpretation of the Old Testament based on the fundamental theological unity of the two Testaments whereby something in the Old shadows, prefigures, adumbrates something in the New. Hence what is interpreted in the Old is not foreign or peculiar or hidden, but rises naturally out of the text due to the relationship of the two Testaments.

To find Christ or the atonement in the sacrificial system, or to find Christian salvation or experience in the Tabernacle follows from the character of the divine revelation. If the problem could be rested at this point, all would be well, but such is not the case. When Philo or Origen or Clement find Platonic philosophy in the Old Testament we might cite this as clearly allegorical interpretation; and when the writer to the Hebrews finds Christ in Old Testament institutions we may cite this as a clear example of typological interpretation. But what sort of interpretation is it when the Fathers find all sorts of adumbrations in the Old Testament with reference to the New? Each piece of wood is discovered to be a reference to the cross, and every pool of water speaks of baptismal regeneration! Here scholars admit that the typical and the

[14] *Op. cit.,* I, 328.
[15] *The Riddle of the New Testament,* p. 127. Italics are ours.

allegorical methods are difficult to differentiate.[16] Should this be called improper typological interpretation, or straight allegorical interpretation?

Jewett's case for the identity of the two methods is based on Wolfson's definition of the allegorical method: "The allegorical method essentially means the interpretation of a text in terms of something else, irrespective of what that something else is." The critical words in this definition are: "in terms of something else." Our impression of Wolfson's treatment of Philo and the allegorical method is that the *something else* means something foreign, secret, hidden, imported—which was the burden of our previous citation of Geffcken. But if typological interpretation rises *naturally out of the text* then it is not an interpretation of *something else* and is therefore a method of interpretation within its own rights. Or as Fairbairn puts it, the typical meaning "is not properly a different or higher sense [as allegorical interpretation demands], but a different or higher application *of the same sense.*" [17]

The history of allegorical interpretation has brought to the surface the emphasis on the hidden, secret, and imported meaning. Further, the list of rules for the detection of an allegory (e.g., Philo and Origen) reveals that an entirely different spirit is at work in allegorical interpretation than in typological interpretation.

Attention to the literature on the subject reveals that many scholars do believe that a genuine distinction obtains between the two methods of interpretation. Dana states that the difference is that the typological method is based on the theological connectedness of the two Testaments, whereas allegorical interpretation is "assigning to Scripture an as-

[16] Cf. Darbyshire, *op. cit.*, pp. 500–501. Darbyshire notes that in such instances it is arbitrary whether the interpretation is allegorical or typological. Jewett (*op. cit.*) is able to make one of his strongest points with this problem.

[17] *Op. cit.*, I, 3. Italics are ours.

sumed meaning different from its plain literal meaning, derived deductively from some abstract or philosophical conception. It takes the events and ideas of Scripture as symbols beneath which are concealed profound or hidden meanings." [18]

Darbyshire reviews the attempts to define the two methods apart.[19] Marsh finds the difference that in typology the facts and circumstances of one instance are *representative* of other facts and circumstances; whereas in allegorical interpretation they are emblematic. Mildert indicates that that which makes a type a type is *divine intention* (and presumably there is no divine intention in allegorical interpretation). Wescott notes that typology presupposes a purpose of God being accomplished from age to age so that matters in one age may represent a subsequent age, whereas in allegorical interpretation the imagination of the interpreter supplies the connection between the two levels of meaning.

Torm also discusses this problem and finds a difference between the two. In allegorical interpretation the interpreter finds alongside the literal sense of the text a different and deeper meaning which may even completely exclude the literal meaning. ("Man versteht unter dieser Auslegung, die—auch wenn nach dem Textzusammenhang kein bildische Rede vorliegt—neben dem buchstäblichen Sinne des Textes ober bisweilen auch unter vollständigem Ausschluss deselben eine andere hiervon verschiedene und vermeintlich tiefere Bedeutung findet.")[20] And in speaking directly to the problem of their difference he states that the allegorical meaning goes alongside the literal meaning of the text, and that it is independent of the literal meaning, and may even exclude it; whereas the typological interpretation proceeds directly out of the literal explanation. ("Der Unterschied zwischen der typologischen Auslegung [oder Betrachtungweise] und der

18 Dana, *Searching the Scriptures*, p. 38.
19 *Op. cit.*, I, 500–501.
20 Torm, *op. cit.*, p. 213.

226 PROTESTANT BIBLICAL INTERPRETATION

allegorischen ist m. a. W. der: Die allegorische Auslegung geht neben der buchstäblichen Erklärung ihren Weg [ist von ihr unabhängig, ja kann sie sogar auschliessen], während die typologische Auslegung [Betrachtungweise] gerade von der buchstäblichen Erklärung ausgeht.")[21]
It would seem that an investigation of Gal. 4:24 would settle the issue but it does not. The following interpretations have been put on this text: (i) that it is an *illustration* and therefore says nothing in justification of allegorical interpretation; (ii) that it is a page out of rabbinical exegesis and therefore improper and indefensible; (iii) that it is a page out of rabbinical exegesis, to be sure, but it is a proper form of interpretation which the rabbis abused; (iv) that it is an *argumentum ad hominem* and therefore does not constitute a justification for allegorical interpretation; (v) that it is one instance of an inspired allegorical interpretation; Paul definitely makes note that he is departing from usual methods of interpretation, and it therefore constitutes no grounds for allegorical interpretation in general; (vi) that it is an allegorical interpretation and thereby constitutes a justification of the allegorical method; and (vii) that it is in reality a typological interpretation, or similar to one, regardless of the use of the word allegory in the text.

Lightfoot[22] says Paul uses the word *allēgoria* in much the same sense as he uses the word *typos* in 1 Cor. 10:11. Meyer[23] believes that by *allēgoroumena* Paul really means *typikōs legomena*. Findlay claims that "in principle the Pauline allegory does not differ from the type." [24] Lambert[25] thinks that Gal. 4:24 is part of the general typology of the New Testament and thinks that this particular example is a blend-

[21] *Ibid.*, p. 223, fn. 2.
[22] J. B. Lightfoot, *The Epistle of Paul to the Galatians* (first edition), p. 180.
[23] *Op. cit.*, p. 201, fn. 7.
[24] Findlay, *The Epistle to the Galatians*, p. 289. He also speaks of "legitimate" and "illegitimate" allegories.
[25] Lambert, "Type," *Dictionary of the Apostolic Church*, II, 623, 624.

ing of the allegorical and typical. Vincent presses for a distinction of type and allegory while commenting on Gal. 4:24:[26] whereas Robertson does not.[27] Lenski thinks that any connection between Paul's use of the word *allegory* in Gal. 4:24 and what is understood by the expression "allegorical interpretation" is purely verbal and not real. "What Paul presents is akin to type and antitype, but only akin," he writes. "Hence also he does not speak of a type. All types are prophetic; Paul is not presenting prophecy and fulfilment. Paul does not go a step beyond the Scriptural facts; what he does is to point out *the same nature* in both." [28]

An appeal to Gal. 4:24 to settle the issue is inconclusive for it is evident that the expression Paul used is not capable of unequivocal interpretation. Interpreters evidently have settled their minds on the proposed difference or lack of different between the allegorical and typological methods of interpretation on other grounds than Gal. 4:24.

D. NATURE AND INTERPRETATION OF TYPES

The interpretation of a type depends upon the nature of a type. Terry quoting Muenscher defines a type as: "In the science of theology it properly signifies the *preordained representative relation which certain persons, events and institutions*

[26] Vincent, *Word Studies in the New Testament*, IV, 149.

[27] Robertson, *Word Pictures in the New Testament*, IV, 306.

[28] Lenski, *The Interpretation of St. Paul's Epistles to the Galatians* (etc.), p. 237. Italics are his. It is also interesting to note that the outstanding French Biblical scholar, Daniélou thinks there is a difference between typological and allegorical interpretation (*Origen*, pp. 139 and 174). Burton (*A Critical and Exegetical Commentary on the Epistle to the Galatians*) believes that "which things are allegorical utterances" refers to Paul's interpretation of the passage, not to the original meaning intended by the writer of Genesis. He is not sure if the argument is *ad hominem* or if Paul is really giving us an example of spiritual exegesis. Pp. 253–56. Johnson (*The Quotations of the New Testament from the Old*) finds no objection in taking this as an allegory. Paul does not impugn the historicity of the passage. Allegorical interpretation is part and parcel of all great literature and the Biblical allegories are closer to the literary allegories of the classics than the allegories of the Jewish rabbis. P. 118 ff.

of the Old Testament bear to corresponding persons, events, and institutions in the New." [29] Miller's definition is: "Typology is the doctrine of symbols and types; the doctrine that persons and things in the New Testament, especially the person and work of Christ, are symbolized, or prefigured, by persons and things in the Old Testament." [30] Moorehead says that types are "pictures, object lessons, by which God taught His people concerning His Grace and saving power." [31]

By analyzing these definitions the following *elements* of a type are manifest: (i) In a type there must be a *genuine resemblance* in form or idea between the Old Testament reference and the New Testament counterpart. The connection between type and antitype must not be accidental nor superficial but real and substantial. (ii) This resemblance must be *designated*. The problem of designation is the crux of the Marshian principle. In fanciful systems of typology designation springs from the imagination of the interpreter either on arbitrary or superficial grounds. Previously in this work we have defended the principle of Fairbairn that types are *innate* and *inferred*. A type is properly designated when either it is so stated to be one in the New Testament, or wherein the New Testament states a whole as typical (e.g., the Tabernacle, and the Wilderness Wanderings) and it is up to the exegetical ability of the interpreter to determine additional types in the parts of these wholes. (iii) *Dissimilarity* is to be expected. There is no one-to-one correspondence between type and antitype. Great care must be taken to lift out of the Old Testament item precisely that which is typical and

[29] Terry, *op. cit.*, p. 246. Italics are his.
[30] Miller, *The Tabernacle*, p. 15.
[31] Moorehead, "Typology," *The International Standard Bible Encyclopedia*, V, 3029. Ludwig Koehler's definition of a type is: "Typus ist eine Gestalt, eine Begebenheit, ein Zusammenhang, der nicht um seiner selber willen Gewicht und Bedeutung hat, sondern dessen Zweck und Wert darin besteht, dass er eine andere Grösse auch sie eine Gestalt, eine Begebenheit, ein Zusammenhang, andeutet, vorbildet, weissagt." "Christus im Alter und im Neuen Testament," *Theologische Zeitschrift*, 4:252, July–August, 1953.

no more. There are points of pronounced similarity and equally so, points of pronounced dissimilarity between Christ and Aaron or Christ and Moses. The typical truth is at the point of similarity. One of the cardinal errors in typology is to make typical the elements of dissimilarity in a type.

The heart of typology is the similarity between the two Testaments. If the two covenants are made too dissimilar then the justification of typology is either weakened or broken. The Old Testament system is complex and care must be taken in treating it. The New Testament stresses the contrast of law in its legislative elements with the gospel, but sees marked similarities between the gospel and the ceremonial part of the law.

It is also apparent that there is a fundamental harmony between the Old Testament theology and the New ("Novum Testamentum in Vetere latet; Vetus in Novo patet"). It is shown by Paul that the act of faith is the same in both Testaments (Romans 4); that the process of justification is the same (Romans 4:22–24); that the same basic system of sacrifice underlies both Testaments (Hebrews 9, 10); that the life of faith in the Old Testament is the model for the New Testament saints (Hebrews 11); that the doctrine of sin is the same as Paul proves by his catena of Old Testament quotations in Romans 3; that the Messiah of the Old Testament is the Savior in the New (Hebrews 1). It is this profound similarity of the two Testaments which makes predictive prophecy and typology a possibility.

Returning to our central subject we note that *types are prophetic symbols* or as Davidson puts it, "Typology is a species of prophecy." [32] We suggest the following rules of interpretation:

(1). *Note the typology of the New Testament and see how it treats the subject.* This much immediately is apparent: *the New Testament* deals with the great facts of Christ and redemption; with the great moral and spiritual truths of Chris-

[32] A. B. Davidson, *Old Testament Prophecy*, p. 210.

tian experience, when it touches on typology. It does not deal with minutiae, and with incidentals. We should then learn that in typology we should restrict our efforts to major doctrines, central truths, key spiritual lessons and major moral principles. A typology which becomes too fascinated with minutiae is already out of step with the spirit of New Testament typology.

(2). Note that the New Testament specifies the *Tabernacle* with its priesthood and offerings, and the *Wilderness Wanderings* as the two major areas of typical materials. This indicates the wholes which have typical parts. By no means is typology restricted to these areas, but these are the areas where most of the typical material is to be drawn.

It is of course a matter of convention to affirm whether some passages are types or predictions. Is the flood a type of coming judgment or a prediction? Is Jonah a type of Christ or a prediction? Are the children of Isaiah types of believers (Hebrews 2:13)? Or were they analogies of believers? Is the call of Israel out of Egypt a type of Christ, or an analogy of Christ, or a prediction of Christ? (Matt. 2:15).

It should go without saying that if an interpreter proposes a typical interpretation, he should search the New Testament to see if it has any reference at all to the Old Testament passage under consideration. Obviously anything so treated as a type in the New Testament is proper for us to treat likewise.

(3). *Locate in any given type the typical and the accidental.* What is typical must be judged from New Testament considerations and the general hermeneutical skill of the interpreter. Hence a good exegete will restrain his imagination when he discusses the Tabernacle. Much about the Tabernacle has no typical significance and this ought to be clearly apprehended. Not all the actions of the priests, nor all the elements of the sacrifices have precise New Testament counterparts. The interpreter who presses beyond the typical into the accessories of the text, then brings forth what is not there *by designation*.

Temptations to be novel, clever, original or shocking should be resisted. Typology is not always appreciated as it should be because some students of it have gone to extremes and thereby soured the subject to other students. Certainly a teacher of the Bible should not boast of finding more types than other teachers because he is more spiritual than they. To be spiritual minded is not a license to abuse the rules of hermeneutics.

(4). *Do not prove doctrine from types unless there is clear New Testament authority.* Hebrews plainly proves some theological points from typological considerations, but we may not do the same because we are not inspired. Types may be used to *illustrate* New Testament truth. The central rod of the construction of the Tabernacle wall cannot properly be used to prove the unity or security of believers, but it may be used to illustrate the same.

In general a humble spirit should characterize our interpretations of typology. What is clearly taught in the New Testament may be asserted with confidence, but beyond that restraint should be the rule. Typology involves two layers of meaning and this allows for the intrusion of imagination. Therefore we must proceed with care and check the play of our imagination. To do otherwise is to obscure the word of God.

E. Kinds of Types

We may note six kinds of types in Scripture:

(1). *Persons* may be typical. Adam is a type of Christ as the head of a race (Romans 5:14, "who is the figure of him that was to come"). Abraham is the father and type of all who believe by faith. Elijah is the prefiguration of John the Baptist. Joseph is the rejected kinsman, yet future Savior. David is the type of the Great King. Solomon is the type of the Chosen Son. Zerubbabel is the type of the Head of a new society.

(2). *Institutions:* The sacrifices are types of the cross. Creation and the Promised Land are types of salvation rest. The passover prefigures our redemption in Christ. The Old Testament theocracy looks forward to the coming kingdom.

(3). *Offices:* Moses, the prophet, was a type of Christ, as was Aaron the high priest and Melchisedec the priest of the most high God.

(4). *Events:* Paul writes that the things which happened in the Wilderness Wanderings were types for our benefit (1 Cor. 10:6, 11).

(5). *Actions:* The lifting up of the brazen serpent is a type of the crucifixion (John 3:14–16). The ministries of the high priest were typical of the ministries of our Lord.

(6). *Things:* The Tabernacle was a type of the Incarnation —the presence of God with his people. Incense is a type of prayer. The curtains of the Tabernacle express principles of access to God.

F. SYMBOLISM

Properly speaking symbolism is a special study of its own. However, any discussion of typology suggests the study of symbolism. Types differ from symbols in that "while a symbol may represent a thing either past, present, or future, a type is essentially a prefiguring of something future from itself . . . A symbol has in itself no essential reference to time." [33] A type (as previously indicated) is a species of

---

[33] Terry, *op. cit.*, p. 246. For further studies of symbolism cf. Farbridge, *Studies in Biblical and Semitic Symbolism;* Wilson, *This Means That;* Pierson, *Knowing the Scriptures* (p. 341 ff.); Harwood, *Handbook of Bible Types and Symbols;* Angus and Green, *Cyclopedic Handbook to the Bible,* p. 221 ff.; Barrows, *Companion to the Bible,* p. 555 ff. All standard Bible dictionaries and encyclopedias contain articles on symbolism. Cf. also the elaborate discussion in Lange, *Revelation* by the American editor, Craven. Pp. 10–41.

prophecy, but a symbol is a timeless figurative representation. A lion as a symbol of strength or of voracious hunger does not predict anything in the future.

Symbolization occurs early in written history and literature, and is deeply rooted in human nature which seeks to represent the abstract by the concrete and pictorial.[34] The presentation of the ideational in pictures and images is also more forceful than mere verbal explication. The Hebrew Scriptures are full of symbols because in addition to these general considerations it is known that the Semitic and Oriental mind of the Hebrews was much more given to symbolism than the Western analytic, philosophical, and scientific mind.

In any symbol there are two elements: (i) the idea which is mental and conceptual, and (ii) the image which represents it. In a given culture these ideas and images are kept close together through the familiarity of constant usage. But when a culture is gone leaving but a segment of its literature it is not always easy to discover the ideas associated with symbols. To interpret the symbolism of a culture when that culture has not left us a convenient handbook to symbols is a difficult task, and for this reason there are some significant gaps in our knowledge of Biblical symbols.

For the interpretation of symbols we suggest the following:

(1). *Those symbols interpreted by the Scriptures are the foundation for all further studies in symbolism.* When the Scripture interprets a symbol then we are on sure ground. These interpretations may be used as *general guides* for all further studies in symbols. Ferocious beasts in the book of Daniel stand for wicked political leaders or nations, and we are not surprised to find them again in the book of Revelation bearing the same general idea. The lamb is a frequent symbol of either sacrifice, or the waywardness of the human heart. The context readily decides which is meant in the passage. Incense stands as a symbol of prayer.

[34] Cf. Farbridge, *op. cit.*, pp. 3–4.

(2). If the symbol is not interpreted we suggest the following:

(i) Investigate the *context* thoroughly. It might be that in what is said before or after, the idea corresponding to the symbol is revealed. (ii) By means of a concordance check other passages which use the same symbol and see if such cross references will give the clue. (iii) Sometimes the nature of the symbol is a clue to its meaning (although the temptation to read the meanings of our culture into these symbols must be resisted). The preservative character of salt is common knowledge, as is the ferocity of lions, the docility of doves, the meekness of lambs, and the filthiness of pigs. (iv) Sometimes comparative studies of Semitic culture[35] reveal the meaning of the symbol. Perchance too in archeological materials the clue will be discovered. If we are not able to turn up any clues to symbols uninterpreted in the text it is wiser to be silent than to speculate.

(3). *Be aware of double imagery in symbols.* There is nothing in the symbolism of the Bible which demands that each symbol have one and only one meaning. This appears to be the presupposition of some works on symbolism, and it is a false presupposition. The lion is at the same time the symbol of Christ ("the Lion of the tribe of Judah") and of Satan (the lion seeking to devour Christians (1 Peter 5:8). The lamb is a symbol of sacrifice and of lost sinners (1 Peter 2:25). Water means "the word" in Ephesians 5:26; the Spirit in 1 Cor. 12:13, and regeneration in Titus 3:5. Oil may mean the Holy Spirit, repentance, or readiness. Further, one entity may be represented by several symbols, e.g., Christ by the lamb, the lion, the branch, and the Holy Spirit by water, oil, wind and the dove.

In general, care and good taste should govern one's interpretation of uninterpreted symbols. An uncritical association of cross references in determining the meaning of symbols may be more harmful than helpful.

[35] Cf. Farbridge, *op. cit.*

There is no question that there is a basic symbolism of numbers in the Bible.[36] A study of the Tabernacle reveals a very even or regular proportion among the various dimensions, and in the articles of furniture themselves. Daniel and Revelation are especially rich in the symbolic use of numbers. Apart from a few basic agreements on some of the numbers, fancy characterizes most studies on the subject.

The parent of all excessive manipulation of Bible numbers is to be found in the Jewish Rabbinical method known as *Gematria*. Examples of such are as follows:[37] The numerical value of the word Branch in Zechariah 3:8 is 138. This has the same value as Consoler in Lam. 1:16 so that it is one of the names of the Messiah. In Genesis 49:10 the Hebrew numerical value of "Shiloh come" is 358, which is in turn equivalent to Meshiach, and so Shiloh is identified with the Messiah. There are never less than 36 righteous in the world because the numerical value of "upon him" of Isaiah 30:18 is 36. Genesis 11:1 says that all the inhabitants of the world were of one language. Both "one" and "holy" equal 409 so Hebrew was the primeval tongue of humanity.

A certain minimum number of judgments may be made on the symbolism of number. For example in the ancient Semitic world *three* stood for "some," a "few," i.e., a small total although in some instances it stood for "many" or "enough." *Four* stood for completeness and was used repeatedly with the diffusion abroad of blessings and cursings. Some have thought *seven* represented the covenant of grace. *Ten* sometimes signifies an indefinite magnitude, and sometimes "perfection." *Forty* represented a generation.

[36] Cf. Farbridge, *op. cit.* (Chapter IV, "Symbolism of Numbers"); Terry, *op. cit.,* pp. 288–98: Chafer, *The Science of Biblical Hermeneutics,* p. 23; Wilson, *op. cit., im passim;* Rogers, *Things That Differ,* p. 23; Harwood, *op. cit., im passim;* Craven, *loc. cit.;* Smith, "Number," *The International Standard Bible Encyclopedia,* IV, 2157–63; Philpott, "Number," *Smith's Bible Dictionary,* III, 2192–94; Zenos, "Numbers, Significance and Symbolic," *A New Standard Bible Dictionary.*

[37] From Farrar, *History of Interpretation,* pp. 98 ff., and 445.

Closely associated with symbolism is the symbolism of metals and colors. In the Tabernacle gold, silver, and brass were used. In Daniel 2 we have another symbolic usage of metals. The gold and silver of the Bible are apparently the same metals we know today, but modern brass is composed of copper and zinc whereas Biblical brass was a combination of copper and tin. It resulted in an alloy almost as hard as steel.

The symbolism of metals has been a matter of considerable debate. P. Fairbairn insists that their only symbolism is in their *value* indicating that God is to be worshipped by our very best. However most writers on symbolism and typology would press for more specific meanings. For example, silver was the universal medium of exchange in Old Testament days and the money for redemption was silver and was called atonement money.[38] Thus silver would stand for redemption.

It is urged that the use of brass in connection with the brazen altar, the blazing feet of Christ (Rev. 1:15), and the brazen serpent lifted up in the wilderness points toward judgment as the symbolic meaning of brass.[39] Gold stands for the highest and holiest ("Pure gold [is] is the light and splendour of God . . . as he dwells in his holy temple").[40]

The acacia wood of the Tabernacle was added to give frame and rigidity to the Tabernacle and its furniture. The wood is hard, close-grained, orange in color with a darker heart, and well-adapted to cabinet making. It is light, fragrant, sheds water, and is not attacked by insects. The Septuagint calls it "wood that does not rot." It was used in the Tabernacle for its lightness, durability, and resistance to insects. Symbolists uniformly identify it with human nature.

The symbolism of colors is far more difficult, for it was not until art was well-established that there was a strict and uniform association of one word with one color. Ancient

[38] Cf. Miller, *The Tabernacle*, p. 52. "The kopher."
[39] *Ibid.*, p. 53 for an excellent discussion.
[40] Terry, *op. cit.*, p. 303.

literature simply does not make the fine color distinctions that are necessary in modern times. For example, the Latin word *purpureous* was used to describe snow, the swan, the foam of the sea, a rose, a beautiful human eye, and purple objects.[41] "Both the Old Testament and the New Testament," writes Pratt, "illustrate the general fact that ancient literature knows little of the modern sensitiveness to color-effects and their subtle gradations." [42]

Blue (Hebrew, *tekeleth*) is a difficult hue to determine. It sometimes means violet or purple. Gesenius derives it from the verb, "to peel, to shell," with reference to a shell-fish from which came a purple blue dye. Bevan advocates violet;[43] Barrows calls it bluish purple.[44] It is apparent that there is some red in the blue of the ancients giving it a violet tinge, but the bluish cast predominated. For practical purposes blue is an adequate translation.

Scarlet (Hebrew, *tola'ath shani*) is derived from the scarlet worm. The Greek and Latin versions mistook the "shani" for the similar word meaning *two,* and so translated it *twice-dipped.*

White (Hebrew, *shesh*) is identical with the word for white linen, and usually stands for holiness or purity or righteousness.

Like metals the symbolism of colors has been a matter of debate. Some interpreters believe that colors represent only such a general notion that a king's presence is indicated by rich tapestry or drapery. Likewise the rich colors of the Tabernacle indicate that it is the dwelling place of God. Others attempt to give the colors specific symbolic meaning. With reference to blue Terry writes that "blue, as the color of heaven, reflected in the sea, would naturally suggest what is heavenly, holy, divine." [45] Delitzsch calls blue "the mai-

[41] *Exodus (The Holy Bible Commentary)*, p. 366.
[42] Pratt, "Colors," *The New Standard Bible Dictionary*, p. 142.
[43] Bevan, "Colors," *Smith Bible Dictionary* ,I, 480.
[44] *Sacred Geography and Antiquitiees*, p. 546.
[45] *Op. cit.*, p. 301.

esty of God in condescension." [46] Purple is usually acknowledged as the color of royalty having been worn by kings, great officials, the wealthy, and the highest in priestcraft. The meaning of scarlet is more difficult to determine though most commentators favor sacrifice as its idea. Interpretations vary from associating the word with red-earth and thus suggesting sacrificial humility to those who take it to mean a full, free, joyous life. In such a case our interpretations must be tentative.

There is at least one general principle to guide in such matters of symbolism. Careful investigation must be made of the meaning of the terms in the original, of their derivations etymologically or culturally, and a close examination of their associations to see what the natural symbolism might be.

G. RECENT DEVELOPMENTS

In that the Old Testament is still a body of literature under continuous investigation in the Christian Church, and even more so in the context of the recent revival of Biblical studies and Biblical theology, the problem of typology is always current. The following indicates general moods or attitudes among the recent Old Testament scholars:

(i). There is almost universal agreement that the older views of typology are inadequate. The older view simply looks at the Old Testament as having specific types more or less inserted in the record which in turn find their fulfilment stated or implied in the New Testament. The basis of this objection is that the previous Old Testament scholarship was not working with the right kind of doctrine of revelation, and, not working with the right of historical understanding of the very nature of the Old Testament revelation.

---

[46] Delitzsch, "Colors," *Schaff-Herzog Encyclopedia of Religious Knowledge*, I, 514 (third edition).

(ii). Some scholars, such as Bultmann, believe that there can be neither prophecy nor typology in the Old Testament. This is argued on two bases: First, a true typology would involve supernatural knowledge in the Old Testament writers about what would eventually happen in the New Testament period. But the days of supernaturalism are over with in the interpretation of Scripture. Second the kind of typological interpretation the New Testament writers do use is either artificial or a kind of perspective on religion current in their time but not valid in ours. For example the idea of the continuous repetition of events, or the so-called "continuous re-occurrence" of all things — the basis for typology — are concepts of history no longer valid.

(iii). If an Old Testament scholar does believe in typology today it is because he has come to a newer understanding of the historical and revelatory character of the Old Testament. Two concepts are of importance at this point. The first is that the Old Testament is eschatological. The Old Testament is not the pure narration of event, nor the pure theological description of events, but history and the revelation bound with it are "on the move." History which is on the move anticipating future history is eschatological history. And so typology is part of the eschatology character of the Old Testament revelation.

The second is that the Old Testament is not so much a record of specific anticipations to be fulfilled in the New Testament period but it contains God's promises. In the Old Testament God tells Israel not only what kind of a God He is now, and what He is doing now, but He is a God who tells the prophets how He shall act in the future. Hence the promises of God in the Old Testament are indications of the future character of history. Typology is then to be seen, and to be justified, within the structure of the Old Testament view of God's promises of how He will act in the future.

The concept of "the repetition of events," which is the theological basis of typology, is now seen in a new light. It is not an artificial, static, or contrived, or deterministic (i.e., the cyclical view of history in which the same thing happens over and over again such as the cycle of 33,000 years according to some Greek philosophers) view of history. The "repetition" is now based on the fidelity of God, that God is a God of the future as well as the present, and of the basic unity of the actions of God, i.e., the God who acts now in such-and-such a way will in the future also act in such-and-such a way. If God is a God of love, grace and mercy *now,* He will also be that kind of a God *then.* How He will act in the future in a specific way can only be known when the future becomes the present.

BIBLIOGRAPHY

Terry, *Biblical Hermeneutics* (revised edition).

Miller, *The Tabernacle.*

Davidson, *Old Testament Prophecy.*

Fairbairn, *The Typology of Scripture* (2 vols.).

Moorehead, "Typology," *The International Standard Bible Encyclopedia,* V, 3029.

Wilson, *This Means That.*

Pierson, *Knowing the Scriptures.*

Harwood, *Handbook of Bible Types and Symbols.*

Angus and Green, *Cyclopedic Handbook to the Bible.*

Torm, *Das Hermeneutik dese Neuen Testaments.*

Darbyshire, "Typology," *Hastings Encyclopedia of Religion and Ethics,* XII, 501 ff.

Chapter X

THE INTERPRETATION OF PROPHECY

A. Confusion of Terminology

In the interpretation of the prophetic part of the Old Testament there is much divergence and confusion about what terms are to be used in the description of prophetic interpretation. For example the word *literal* may mean to somebody like Luther or Calvin the general philological approach to the Old Testament in contrast to the allegorical interpretation of the Church Fathers. But to a dispensationalist *literal* not only means a philological approach but that the things predicted will be literally fulfilled. A reference to God reigning in Zion means that in the millennium Jerusalem will be the capitol of the world. The expression cannot be diluted into a general affirmation that God's rule in history will eventually be victorious. In our use of the word *literal* we have in mind *literal* in the philological sense.

The word spiritual is also somewhat ambiguous. Ordinarily it refers to a man's piety and devotion. But with reference to prophecy it means that a given prediction is not to be fulfilled in a literal way but in a different way, in a different key. The descriptions of the great prosperity of Israel is "spiritualized" into meaning the great successes of the Christian Church. However most dispensationalists and premillennialists would object to this kind of spiritualizing in that God says very much what He means in the Old Testament passages and no interpreter has the right to "spiritualize" away the intention of these passages.

Sometimes the verb "allegorizing" is used synonymously with "spiritualizing." Allegorizing was a very prominent method of interpretation in the early Christian Church. It was an inflated typology. In a simple way allegory means one story on top of another. This usually meant that the literal or historical sense of a passage was "fleshly" but the allegorical content was "spiritual."

The Roman Catholic theologians of the Middle Ages developed their doctrine of hermeneutics into the so-called Four Fold Method. A given passage of Scripture may have four meanings: (i) a literal or historical; (ii) a moral or ethical; (iii) a prophetic, or allegorical, or typological and (iv) an anagogical. "Anagogical" means "to lead up" and refers to the possible future or eschatological element in the text. It was step number three, the allegorical, which has caused so much trouble in the history of hermeneutics.

Contemporary Roman Catholic scholars know of the miserable abuse of this method in the Church Fathers. They therefore have tried to correct the Fathers by saying that they meant well (i.e., there is a depth to the meaning of Scripture beyond its literal or surface meaning) but they worked their theory a bad way. Recent Roman Catholic scholarship attempts to maintain some version of the allegorical method without giving it that name or else so interpreting the Old Testament so as to avoid the abuses of the Fathers or to develop the concept of the fuller meaning of a prophetic passage beyond its immediate reference (*sensus plenior*).

Sometimes the word *mystical* is used. In this sense the word *mystical* has the idea of a hidden meaning. The lamb of Exodus 12 whose blood was put on the lintels of the door has as its mystical or hidden meaning the Lamb of God of John's Gospel. The German word *pneumatische* (*pneumatic*, "mystical," "spiritual") is used at times to indicate the kind of interpretation that goes beyond the literal and historical meaning of a passage. In this sense *pneumatische* and *mystical* are synonyms.

Some scholars attempt to short-cut this confusion of terminology by using *typological* in an expanded way. There is the narrow meaning of typology discussed in the previous chapter. But in the enlarged sense it means the fundamental unity of the revelation of God and therefore the kind of revelational concepts, categories, and notions of God that are found in the Old Testament are found in changed, altered, or improved form in the New Testament.

The issue among evangelical interpreters is not over the validity of grammatical or literal exegesis. For most of the didactic parts of the Old Testament, and practically the complete New Testament there is agreement that we follow the grammatical method. In fundamental theory there is no difference between Berkhof's *Principles of Biblical Hermeneutics* (amillennial) and Chafer's *The Science of Biblical Hermeneutics* (dispensational). Both agree that the grammatical, historical method is basic to understanding the Bible.

Nor is the issue one of the figurative or non-figurative language of the prophets. The literalist in prophetic interpretation admits the presence of poetic and figurative elements, and the amillennialists who think they deny this are wrong. Some amillennialists think that the figurative and poetic elements weaken the case of the literalists, but their difference from the literalist is not as great as they imagine.

If we may provisionally define the spiritual as the non-literal method of the exegesis of the Old Testament we may further state that the issue is not between a completely literal or a completely spiritual system of interpretation. Amillennial writers admit that many prophecies have been literally fulfilled, and literalists admit a spiritual element to Old Testament interpretation when they find a moral application in a passage, when they find a typical meaning, or when they find a deeper meaning (such as in Ezekiel 28 with reference to the kings of Babylon and Tyre). Nobody is a strict literalist or a complete spiritualist.

Further, some Old Testament passages present *idealized* pictures. For example, in Zechariah 14 Jesusalem is exalted to the top of a mountain, the surrounding mountainous country is made a plain, and two great rivers pour out of Jerusalem one going east and other west. A strict literal interpretation of this passage fails to catch the spirit and vision of it. Prophecies involving horses or chariots or camels are dealing with *transportation;* prophecies speaking of spears and shields are about *armaments;* and prophecies about surrounding nations are about *God's enemies.* A strict literalism would hardly be appropriate in such matters and Davidson says that to call for the complete restoration of all these ancient peoples on the basis of strict literal interpretation *"may not unjustly be called the insanity of literalism."* [3]

The real issue in prophetic interpretation among evangelicals is this: *can prophetic literature be interpreted by the general method of grammatical exegesis, or is some special principle necessary?*

B. Principles for the Interpretation of Prophecy

There can be no question that Girdlestone's judgment that "there is no royal road to the scientific study of prophecy" is correct.[4] Many royal roads have been advocated but none has been so obvious as to compel the total assent of interested scholars. We have not lacked for advocates of various royal roads and this has led to the hopeless division of evangelical Christianity in prophetic and eschatological matters.

There are two reasons why there is no royal road to prophetic interpretation (and thereby accounting for such wide divergences of prophetic interpretation). First, the prophetic language itself partakes of a measure of ambiguity. It is

[3] Davidson, *Old Testament Prophecy,* p. 476. Italics are ours.
[4] *The Grammar of Prophecy,* p. 104.

visionary in that it is speaking of the future and painting it in word pictures. We are not in the position in most instances to compare the picture painted by the prophet and the fulfilment of it. If we could the ambiguity of the passage would drop away, but in that we cannot it remains. The richness of the Christological elements in Psalm 22 and Isaiah 53 are noticed by Christians because they read these passages in the light of the historical existence of Jesus Christ. We should not be surprised if these passages are puzzling to Jewish scholars who do not share this insight. If the language of prophecy were unambiguous the differences among interpreters could be assigned to the superior intelligence of one group and the inferior intelligence of another. But the source of this ambiguity is not in the interpreters but in the visionary character of a record which is speaking of future historical events.

The second reason why interpreters differ so widely is the extent of the prophetic Scriptures. The prophetic material of Scripture is to be found from Genesis to Revelation. To assemble each passage, to thoroughly digest its meaning, to arrange the passages in a prophetic harmony, would involve a prodigious memory, years of exacting work, a masterful knowledge of Biblical languages, an exhaustive reading of prophetic literature, a keen exegetical sense, a thorough knowledge of the histories of many peoples and a knowledge of all relevant archaeological materials. And yet some claim that prophetic Scripture is as easy to interpret as the prose passages of the New Testament! With such a great body of Scripture to keep in focus all at once, with its inherent complexity, and with the requisite learning to interpret it, it is not surprising that there is such a variety of schools of prophetic interpretation.

(1). *Fundamentals in the interpretation of any passage of prophetic Scripture.* Regardless of our millennial views (the *crux interpretum* of prophetic interpretation) certain principles must be followed by all exegetes of the prophetic Word.

(i) We must, to begin with, *give careful attention to the language of the prophetic passage.* We must determine the meaning and significance of all proper names, events, references to geography, references to customs, references to material culture, references to flora and fauna, and references to climate. A proper noun whose meaning or significance is not known stands enigmatical in the text. For example in Hosea 11 these nouns occur: Israel, Egypt, Ephraim, Assyrian, Admah, Zeboim, and in Isaiah 21 we find: Elam, Media, Babylon, Dumah, Seir, Arabia, Dedanim, and Kedar. We must not presume we know the meaning of a term because it is familiar. The word Arabia, by way of illustration, is used in Scripture to indicate different territories than the word signifies to us. The meaning of proper nouns may be ascertained by referring to Bible dictionaries, Bible encyclopedias, or commentaries.

In Daniel 11 numerous historical events are referred to and no interpretation of this chapter is adequate which is not familiar with the necessary historical information. Joel mentions the locust, canker-worm and the caterpillar and the careful interpreter will acquaint himself with requisite information about these matters of natural life. A knowledge of the history of Jerusalem and Edom is necessary to properly interpret Obadiah 10–14, and we need to understand some of the geography of Jerusalem's environs to understand the reference to the *crossway* (v. 14).

With further regard to the language of a prophetic passage the interpreter should note the *figurative, poetic,* and *symbolic* elements. We do not debate here the issue between the amillennialists (who claim dispensationalists underplay the significance of the figurative elements in prophecy) and the dispensationalists. We refer to matters which *all* interpreters must recognize. Figures of speech recur repeatedly in the prophets and the Psalms. Certainly much of the prophetic literature is poetic, and none can deny the numerous symbolic passages in Daniel, Ezekiel, and Zechariah. It was a convinced premillennialist who wrote:

That which makes the language of prophecy so vivid and yet so difficult is that it is always more or less figurative. It is poetry rather than prose. It abounds in peculiar words and expressions which are not usually to be found in prose writings of the same date. It is rich with allusions to contemporary life and to past history, some of which are decidedly obscure. The actions recorded in it are sometimes symbolical, sometimes typical. The present, the past, and the future, the declaratory and the predictive, are all combined and fused into one. The course of individuals, the rise and fall of nations, the prospects of the world at large, are all rapidly portrayed in realistic language.[5]

Girdlestone buttresses this by making a Scriptural study showing the different meanings of such terms as: earth, earthquake, sea and river, sand, stars of heaven, the darkening of the sun and moon, and the falling of stars. Sometimes the prophets use these terms literally and sometimes figuratively. Whether the usage in a given passage is literal or figurative must be a matter of careful attention.

Further, as Girdlestone[6] explains, *much of the prophetic description of the future is in the language of past, historical events*. The new creation is the analogue of original creation; the blessedness to come is in terms of paradise past; future judgment is likened to the flood of the past; destructive judgment finds its type in the destruction of Sodom and Gomorrah; great deliverance is paralleled after the deliverance of the exodus. Girdlestone notes that besides past events being used as forms for future events, past persons and past natural events are used as forms for future persons and future events.

The strict literalist would *ex hypothesi* have to call for not only the restitution of Israel, but all the nations which surrounded Israel. The going is rough, no doubt, and one of the ways out suggested by Girdlestone is to make these ancient enemies representative of Israel's future enemies.

(ii). *We must determine the historical background of the*

[5] Girdlestone, *op. cit.*, p. 48.
[6] *Ibid.*, Chapter IX.

prophet and the prophecy. This establishes the universe of discourse in which the prophet writes. Much of Isaiah is illuminated by a knowledge of the political maneuvers in Israel and among the surrounding nations. A knowledge of the captivities is indispensable for the interpretation of Jeremiah and Ezekiel. To understand Obadiah the history of Edom must be studied and to know Jonah properly a history of Syria must be examined. The so-called automobile prophecy of Nahum 2:4 is not defensible because a study of the prophecy and its historical background reveals that the prophecy alluded to has been fulfilled in ancient times.

Habakkuk 1:5 ff. has been interpreted as a dispersion of the Jews ("behold ye among the nations"), yet if the historical situation is carefully recovered it will be discovered that no such interpretation is possible. The prophet is complaining of the sin and evil unpunished in Israel. God tells the prophet that the wicked will be punished. He invites the prophet to look among the nations. What the prophet beholds among the nations is not Israel in dispersion, but the *avenger* of the ungodly in Israel—the Chaldeans ("For, lo, I raise up the Chaldeans"). The one thing which Israel could not bring himself to believe was that God would ever use a Gentile nation for his punishment. Yet God did precisely this very thing, and so it parallels that day when God shall save the Gentile to the bewilderment of Israel (Acts 13:37 ff.).

If all the examples were given to prove the importance of a thorough study of the prophet's background almost the entire body of prophetic literature would have to be cited. The importance of this principle cannot be underestimated especially when it is a frequent charge that premillennialism too easily passes by historical considerations.[7]

A further observation is that although history is necessary to understand the prophet, and that some historical event occasioned the giving of the prophecy, prophecy is not to be

[7] Cf. the strong words against premillennialism with reference to this spoken by Berry (*Premillennialism and Old Testament Prediction*, p. 8).

limited by purely historical considerations. Radical criticism has tried to eviscerate the supernatural character of prophesy by means of historical interpretation.[8]

(iii). Although it is a principle of general hermeneutics it needs to be reëmphasized here that *diligent attention must be paid to the context and flow of the discussion in the interpretation of prophecy.* Chapter and verse divisions are man-made and frequently arbitrary and misleading. The interpreter will look beyond these divisions and discover the natural divisions and connections of the Scripture. For example, to understand Malachi 3:1 properly the interpreter must go back at least to 2:17 to pick up the proper context, and the context necessary to understand Malachi 4 is deep in chapter 3.

(iv). *The interpreter must be mindful of the nonsystematic character of prophetic writings.* The prophets were preachers and visionaries and not academic lecturers. Prophetic writings are not organized like lecture notes but bear a peculiar impress. The prophets are not systematic in their presentation of sequences. The future may appear present, or nearby, or indefinitely remote. Widely separated events on the actual calendar of history may appear together in the prophetic sequence. The Jewish scholars unable to decipher pictures of Messianic suffering and Messianic glory were not properly prepared for the advent of humiliation of our Lord. Only in the pages of the New Testament are these two pictures properly related in terms of *two* advents of the Messiah (cf. 1 Peter 1:10–12 and Hebrews 9:28).

(v). *Every interpreter of prophetic Scripture should search the entire body of prophetic Scripture to find what passages parallel each other.* Such concepts as the day of the Lord, the remnant, the shaking of the nations, the outpouring of the Spirit, the regathering of Israel, and the millennial blessings occur repeatedly in the prophetic writings. Similar images

---

[8] A good statement in this regard is made by Wace (*Prophecy: Jewish and Christian*, p. 144 ff.). Fairbairn said that "History is the *occasion* of prophecy, but not its *measure*." (*Prophecy*, p. 40, italics are his.)

and symbols also occur. All of this must be reckoned with carefully and intelligently in the interpretation of prophecy.

(2). *The interpreter must determine the distinct essence of the passage of prophetic Scripture.* The essence or genius of a passage means its very nature, its innermost characteristic.

(i). The interpreter must determine whether the passage is *predictive* or *didactic*. Not all prophecy is foretelling the future. It is necessary to determine whether the passage is predictive or if it deals with moral, ethical, or theological truth. The opening verses of Zechariah (1:1–6) are didactic but the following vision is prophetic (1:7–21). Most of Zechariah 7 is didactic but the preceding and following materials are prophetic.

(ii). The interpreter must determine whether the passage is *conditional* or *unconditional*.[9] The Scriptures may or may not state if the passage is conditional.[10] The great promises of a Saviour and his salvation are certainly unconditional. On the other hand it is not difficult to suggest some conditional prophecies (Jer. 18:8, 10 and 26:12–13 and 3:12. Jonah 3:4. Ezekiel 33:13–15 and 18:30–32). Another class of passages is that which sets forth two possible destinies of which only one can be realized, such as the curses and blessings of Deut. 28.

The statement of Girdlestone is a remarkably strong one: "It is probable that hundreds of prophecies, which look absolute as we read them were not fulfilled in their completeness because the words of warning from the prophet produced some result, even though slight and temporary, on the hearts of the hearers. God does not quench the smoking flax."[11]

(iii). If the passage is prophetic determine further if it is

---

[9] An excellent treatment of the subject is Girdlestone's (*op. cit.,* chapter IV).

[10] "A prophet may set down a prophecy in his book without indicating whether it was fulfilled or set aside." Sutcliffe, "Prophetical Literature," *A Catholic Commentary on the Holy Scripture,* p. 536. Cf. also Girdlestone, *op. cit.,* p. 25, and Fairbairn, *op. cit.,* Chapter IV.

[11] *Op. cit.,* p. 28.

fulfilled or *unfulfilled*. A prophecy that is conditional and unfulfilled is at the end of the line, so to speak. The interpreter must search the New Testament to see whether the passage is cited there as fulfilled. If the passage is cited in the New Testament then a careful study must be made of both the Old and New Testament passages. It may turn out that the prophecy was made in the Old Testament and fulfilled in Old Testament times such as the prophecy of Genesis 15 fulfilled in the latter chapters of Genesis and the book of Exodus or the captivity-restoration prophecies of Isaiah and Jeremiah as fulfilled in the books of Daniel, Ezra and Nehemiah.

This problem pushes us to the next major consideration, namely, (3) *the problem of fulfilment in prophecy*. If the prophecy is fulfilled (i) then a study of the text with the historical materials which contains the fulfilment must be made. Most students will not have such materials available and must rely on good commentaries to supply it. From a study of fulfilled prophecy we gain some valuable insights. We have already noted that in the prophetic language things which are widely separated in time appear close together, and that orders of events are somewhat obscure. Fulfilment of prophecy brings these matters to the surface. But most important is that the fulfilled prophecies indicate how careful we must proceed from the prophecy to its *manner* of fulfilment. Sometimes the prophecy is very obviously fulfilled as was the case with Elijah's prediction of a drought (1 Kings 17:1) or his prediction of Ahab's death (1 Kings 21:17 ff.). Other times the prophecy is very cryptic (e.g., Gen. 3:15) or symbolic (Zech. 5:5-11). Interpreters should be cautious in the interpretations proposed for unfulfilled prophecy, for these examples demonstrate that in some instances little can be gained about the manner of fulfilment from the prophecy itself.

(ii). If the prophecy is *unfulfilled* we must take the lesson gleaned from the previous point—proceed with caution. The essence of the prophecy must be ascertained. Is it about

Israel? or Judah? or the Messiah? or the inter-Biblical events? Determine whether the prophecy is expected to be fulfilled before or after the advent of Christ. Some of the restoration prophecies certainly refer to the return of the Jewish people from Babylon and not to some future period. If the prophecy is pre-Christian, then pre-Christian history must be searched for materials of its fulfilment. If it is apparently to be fulfilled after the first Advent of Christ then we must proceed on considerations we shall subsequently discuss.

Determine what is local, temporal, cultural in the prophecy and what is its fundamental idea awaiting fulfilment. Not every detail of Psalm 22 is about the Messiah, and some scholars have asserted that not all the particulars of Isaiah 53 are about Christ. In the famous prophecy of 2 Samuel 7 where Christ is prefigured in terms of Solomon, the expression "if he commit iniquity" cannot refer to Christ. In Isaiah 7:14–15 Christ is immediately in the foreground, but verse 16 ("for before the child shall know how to refuse evil, and choose the good, the land that thou abhorest will be forsaken of both her kings") is a local reference. In Psalm 16 David's sweet meditation does not become Messianic until verse 8.

(iii). There is the possibility of *multiple fulfilment*. There is a difference between "multiple sense" and "multiple fulfilment." [12] Misunderstanding has arisen due to the failure to distinguish double sense from double fulfilment. Beecher speaks of *generic prophecy* which he defines as "one which regards an event as occurring in a series of parts separated by intervals, and expresses itself in language that may apply indifferently to the nearest part, or to the remoter parts, or to the whole—in other words a prediction which, in applying to the whole of a complex of event, also applies to some of the parts." [13] To be sure, Beecher affirms, if the Scriptures had many meanings interpretation would be equivocal, but

---

[12] Cf. Beecher, *The Prophets and the Promises*, p. 129 ff., and Johnson, *The Quotations of the New Testament from the Old*, p. 197 and 231 ff.
[13] Beecher, *op. cit.*, p. 130.

manifold fulfilment of a generic prophecy preserves the one sense of Scripture. Both promises and threats work themselves out over a period of time and therefore may pass through several fulfilments. Or one may view the same event from more than one perspective. The destruction of Jerusalem is prophesied by our Lord and through it we have a perspective through which to envision the end of the world.

Johnson has an extended discussion of *double reference.* Double reference is characteristic of all great literature, and the Bible being great literature contains it. Hence deeply buried in the events, persons, and words of the Old Testament are references to events, persons, and words of the New Testament. An Old Testament prophecy may find a fulfilment in a pre-Christian event and later in the Christian period, such as the astonishment of the Jews (Habakkuk 1:5-6), which was fulfilled in the Old Testament with the destructive armies of the Chaldeans and in the New Testament with the salvation of the Gentiles.

The presupposition, and a valid one certainly, that the Old is profoundly typical of the New intrudes itself all the way through Johnson's excellent discussion. This is somewhat similar to what Catholics call *compenetration.*[14] In an Old Testament passage the near meaning and the remote meaning for the New Testament so *compenetrate* that the passage at the same time and in the same words refers to the near and the remote New Testament meaning.

(3). The interpreter should take *the literal meaning of a prophetic passage as his limiting or controlling guide.* How else can he proceed? This is the footing for the interpretation of any passage of Scripture. Davidson makes this point with great force and although he later adds a qualification he insists that prophetic interpretation commence with literal interpretation. To the Jew Zion meant Zion and Canaan Canaan. "This I consider the first principle in prophetic interpretation," writes Davidson, "to assume that the literal

[14] Sutcliffe, *op. cit.,* p. 537.

meaning is *his* meaning—that he is moving among realities, not symbols, among concrete things like people, not among abstractions like *our* Church, world, etc." [15] Davidson treats with a measure of scorn those interpreters who blithely make Zion or Jerusalem the Church, and the Canaanite the enemy of the Church, and the land the promises to the Church, etc., as if the prophet moved in a world of symbols and abstractions.[16]

But Davidson is just as much opposed to a forced literalism. He objects to the millennial restitution of the Old Testament worship system, and to press for the restoration of Israel's ancient enemies is the insanity of literalism.[17]

The balance in prophetic interpretation is not easy to attain. The strict literalist attempts to embarrass the "spiritualizer" by asking him how he stops spiritualizing once he starts. Bales puts the shoe on the other foot and asks how the literalist stops "literalizing" once he gets started (i.e., the literalist does not plow through all figures of speech and symbols with a mechanical, literal exegesis). Further, Bales argues, in that the literalist also accepts Biblical symbolism and typology he must state how he limits his symbolic and typological interpretation. If the literalist states that it is the nature of the passage with the attendant considerations

[15] *Old Testament Prophecy*, p. 168. Italics are his.

[16] Cf., "Certainly the extreme anti-literal interpretation which considers the names Zion, Jerusalem, Israel, and the like to be mere names for the Christian Church, without reference to the people of Israel, does no justice either to the spirit of the Old Testament and its principle, or to the principles on which the apostle reasons." *Ibid.*, p. 490. The essay of Neale and Littledale (*A Commentary on the Psalms*, Vol. I, Dissertation III, "On the Mystical and Literal Interpretation of Scripture," pp. 426–470) is a perfect illustration of this sort of exegesis Davidson refers to, and also constitutes a very stout defense of the traditional mystical system of interpretation. For a more recent defense of mystical interpretation see Darwell Stone, "The Mystical Interpretation of the Old Testament," *A New Commentary on Holy Scripture*, pp. 688–697.

[17] Insufficient attention has been payed to the *idealized pictures* in the Old Testament which are not properly interpreted either by a strict literalism or a vapid spiritualizing.

which tells him when to stop "literalizing" or to limit symbolic and typological interpretation, then Bales replies these are the considerations which guide the spiritualizer.[18]

If one maintained a strict literalism he would require that David sit on the millennial throne and not Christ, yet most literalists would say at this point that David is a type of Christ. However, in so doing, his literalism is modulated and all we are arguing at this point is that literalism requires a measure of modulation.

The measure to which literal interpretation is to be followed in Old Testament interpretation is directly related to the problem of the restoration of Israel. Davidson lists four opinions in this regard: (i) those who assert that God's dealings in Christianity are completely personal so a restored national Israel is unthinkable; (ii) those who believe in Israel's conversion but not restoration; (iii) those who believe in a conversion and restoration but with no special prominence for Israel; and (iv) those who believe in a conversion of Israel, a restoration of Israel, and the millennial preëminence of Israel.[19] Mention should be made too of the almost dramatic record that we have of Fairbairn. As a young man he defended the conversion and restoration of national Israel with great ability and persuasiveness; and then as a mature scholar he takes a non-chiliast view of the problem and denies the restoration of Israel.[20]

In general, the premillennialists concur with Girdlestone when he says that: "Israel has a great future is clear from Scripture as a whole. There is a large unfulfilled element in the Old Testament which demands it, unless we spiritualize it away or relinquish it as Oriental hyperbole." [21] A literal

---

[18] Bales, *New Testament Interpretations of Old Testament Prophecies of the Kingdom*, p. 21.

[19] *Op. cit.*, Chapter XXIV, "The Restoration of the Jews."

[20] These two essays are contained in one volume with their story entitled *Fairbairn versus Fairbairn*.

[21] *Op. cit.*, p. 138.

interpretation calls for the fulfillment of many Old Testament passages in a future millennial age.

The premillenarians are not all in one camp, being divided into the dispensational premillenarians and the non-dispensational premillenarians. The former are insistent that the promises made to Israel be fulfilled in Israel; and the latter build their doctrine of the millennium on the progression of the kingdom of God through several stages including an earthly, glorious manifestation as the prelude to eternity. They would approve a measure of sentiment in the words of Frost:

> We are a generation of Christians who have learned the dangers of 'liberal protestantism' [whose entire eschatology was that we die and go to heaven]. What he [the liberal protestant] is to make of this world—both literally and figuratively—he does not know. In this situation, I venture to suggest that perhaps millenarianism which also finds a place in Revelation, was too readily scorned by the Alexandrians and evaded by Augustine. There are values attaching—in so sacramental and incarnational religion as Christianity—to the material and the temporal which must be conserved for the Age to come; it may be that a return to the entire eschatology of the Bible, that is, the eschatological 'form' which we have called the 'double-eschaton,' would provide a means whereby the preservation of those values could be presented to our minds.[22]

Hermeneutically the premillenarians are then divided between the strict and the moderate literalists.

The postmillenarians are convinced of the spread of the Christian Church by the power of the Spirit until it brings the millennial conditions upon the earth. Some postmillenarians accept the conversion of Israel and some do not. Among those who accept the conversion of Israel some accept the

[22] *Old Testament Apocalyptic*, p. 246. Note also Quistorp's sharp criticism against Calvin because Calvin failed to understand the eschatological character of the millennium of Rev. 20, and did not therefore fit it into the necessary events by which time is ended and eternity commenced. *Calvin's Doctrine of the Last Things*, pp. 161–162.

national restoration and some do not. But a measure of literalism pervades postmillennial hermeneutics. To be sure some of the promises made to Israel are transferred to the Church and thereby postmillennialists cross with the dispensationalists, but yet the promises are interpreted as fulfilled here on the earth.[23]

The amillenarians believe that the prophecies made to Israel are fulfilled in the church. If these prophecies are so fulfilled no millennium on earth is necessary. The hermeneutical method of the amillennialists (by which they accomplish this claim) is variously called allegorical, mystical, or spiritual.

It must be strongly reiterated here that amillenarians are just as strong in rejecting baseless allegorical speculations as are the ardent literalists. Wyngaarden rejects it as the work of man. Acceptable "spiritualization" is the interpretation of a passage in which the interpreter finds a broadened or figurative or typical meaning *given to it by the Holy Spirit*.[24] To accuse the amillenarians of being allegorists and implying that their allegorizations are of the same species as that of Philo or Origen is simply not being accurate with or fair to the amillenarians. In speaking of the hermeneutics of amillennialism Chafer wrote: "In sheer fantastical imagination this method surpasses Russellism, Eddyism, and Seventh Day Adventism since the plain, grammatical meaning of the language is abandoned, and simple terms are diverted in their course and end in anything the interpreter wishes." [25]

[23] To equate the postmillennialism of godly, devout, Bible-believing men with the kingdom speculations of religious liberalism is (to say the very least) tragic and lamentable.

[24] Wyngaarden, *The Future of the Kingdom in Prophecy and Fulfilment*, pp. 85–86. This could be extensively documented in hermeneutical literature.

[25] *Systematic Theology*, IV, 281–282. A similar comment with reference to postmillennialism is made by Blackstone: "Why! the same process of *spiritualizing* away the literal sense of these plain texts of Scripture will sap the foundation of every Christian doctrine and leave us to drift into absolute infidelity, or the vagaries of Swedenborgianism." *Jesus is Coming*, p. 22.

Equally contestable is the frequent allegation that the amillenarians are Romish. This allegation must be made with a weather eye to the counter-charge. Are there not millennial cults? Millerism? Seventh Day Adventism? Millennial Dawnism? British Israelism? If similarity of the millennial doctrine of premillennialism with some millennial cults does not constitute a refutation of premillennialism, neither does similarity with Catholic doctrine refute amillennialism. It is true that Augustine marks a definite shift in eschatological thought. Augustine (and Calvin after him)[26] made the kingdom of God the spiritual rule of Christ in the church. It was, however, a subsequent development which identified the visible Roman Catholic Church with the kingdom of God. The Romish doctrine is that the visible Catholic Church is the kingdom of God. This to our knowledge was not the claim of Augustine.[27]

However, it is also to be most certainly noted that it is not unusual for the amillenarians to misrepresent both dispensationalism and premillennialism. Feinberg has caught them with their foot considerably off base at more than one point.[28]

If it be granted that the literal interpretation is the point of departure for prophetic interpretation the question to be asked is: *does the Old Testament prophetic Scripture admit of any additional principle besides the strict, literal principle?* Such a principle would of necessity exclude the sort of exegesis characteristic of Philo, Patristic allegorizing and Christian Science spiritualizing. It must also exclude that sort of fanciful typological exegesis which can find New Testament truth in the Old Testament anywhere it wishes. Is there, then, an *expanded typological principle* employed in Old

[26] Calvin calls Ezekiel's temple "the spiritual kingdom of Christ" (*Institutes*, IV, 20, 13). The same term is used in IV, 20, 12. He also speaks of the "spiritual and internal reign of Christ" (IV, 20, 21).

[27] Robertson, *Regnum Dei*, Lectures V and VI.

[28] Feinberg, *Premillennialism or Amillennialism?* This material will be found in the appendix to the second edition which is really a treatise in itself containing a rebuttal of the amillennial and anti-dispensational literature which appeared since his first edition.

Testament prophetic exegesis? The answer to this must be that there is.

(i). The conviction of the early Church was that the Old Testament was a Christian book. It recognized its inspiration no doubt. But a sheer appeal to the inspiration of the Old Testament without the profound conviction that it was a Christian book would not have made its case. The heresy of Marcion—that the Old Testament was not a Christian book—has been vigorously contested in the Christian Church wherever and whenever it has appeared and in whatever form it has appeared. The entire Patristic period is uniform in its testimony that the Old Testament belongs to the Church because it is a Christian book.

There is absolutely no doubt that this conviction stemmed from the manner in which our Lord and his apostles used the Old Testament. Our Lord said that the Old Testament was his witness (John 5:39), and that he fulfilled it (Matt. 5:17, Luke 4:21). Paul found Christ in many places in the Old Testament; he found justification by faith; he found moral instruction for Christians. The Christian Church has concurred with Vischer's verdict that "The Christian Church stands and falls with the recognition of the unity of the two Testaments." [29] Without too much sense of guidance, and without too much understanding of principles of hermeneutics, the Fathers found Christianity and its doctrines in the Old Testament by improper methods. But regardless of their hermeneutical ineptitude we must recognize their inspiration, namely, *that they were seeking the Christian faith in what they deemed to be a Christian book.* In short, an expanded typological interpretation (to distinguish it from typology proper) was characteristic of the interpretations of the Old Testament by our Lord, by his apostles, and by the early Church although in the latter it suffered from malpractice.

Such typological exegesis (as previously defined) is no return to Philonian or Alexandrian exegesis, nor can it by one

[29] *The Witness of the Old Testament to Christ,* I, 27 (E.T.).

hair's breadth go beyond the implicit and explicit teaching of the New Testament. For example, it would be very improper on the basis of this principle to state that Aaron is a type of the pope because he was the chief of the priests (as the Catholic interpreters insist) because not a line from the New Testament can be found to support it, and the entire tenor of New Testament typology is against such an identification. Further, we must agree with Davidson that a thin spiritualizing of the Old Testament with no proper recognition of the literal meaning of the passages is not to be permitted. And we must further agree with Davidson when he argues that "any hermeneutic which goes so far as to eliminate from the prophecies of the Old Testament which refer to the New Testament times, *the natural race of Abraham, seems to go against the methods of interpretation applied by the apostles.*" [30]

(ii). Again we must agree with Davidson that the coming of Jesus Christ gives us a new perspective for interpreting the Old Testament. The Old Testament was given in a specific *dispensational* form and if Old Testament truth carries over into the New Testament some of the dispensational form must be dropped as it most certainly is in typology proper. That is to say, the fulfilment of the prophecy is not to be expected to be in the exact form of the prophecy. The amillennialist makes the greatest divorce between the form and the fulfilment of prophecy and that is why the more literal-minded postmillenarians and premillenarians are restive with it. The dispensationalists judge that the distinction between the form and the idea of prophecy is spurious, and therefore they look for the fulfilment of prophecy to be very similar to the precise form in which it was given in the Old Testament.

Davidson's point is that with the advent of Christ *some change in the form of fulfilment* must be expected. With Davidson's strong insistence on the primacy of the literal meaning of the Scripture this does not at all prejudice the case for amillennialism, although it does prejudice the case against an extreme and indefensible literalism.

(iii). Contemporary scholars like Hebert and Vischer are advocating a return to a typological (Vischer) or mystical interpretation (Hebert) as the only means of counter-attacking the prophetic negativism use of the grammatico-historical method of exegesis in the hands of the religious liberals. In a very real sense radical criticism was a return of Marcionism, and an unusually narrow use of the grammatical principle in Old Testament exegesis spelled the death of any predictive element in it. This exegetical negativism is to be escaped by a return to an expanded typological exegesis (although Vischer has been accused of being too free in his use of it).[31] Again the inspiration for a return to the typological exegesis of the Old Testament is the firm belief that in some significant sense the *Old Testament is a Christian book.*

We have now come to the issue which can be delayed no longer: *what hermeneutical method does the New Testament use in employing the Old?* Certainly this should be decisive if it could be unequivocally settled. This does not mean that we cannot garner some hermeneutical insights by a study of the Old Testament. The literal fulfilment of some of the prophecies within the Old Testament period indicates the validity

---

[31] Cf. Vischer, *op. cit.*, I, Chapter I; and Hebert, *The Throne of David* ("Clearly, in this general sense the mystical interpretation of the Old Testament is for Christians a matter of obligation." P. 256). Hebert's mystical interpretation is similar to Vischer's typological, and Hebert makes it clear he is advocating no return to previous excesses of this method. Ludwig Koehler has brought four major criticisms against the revived typological exegesis of Vischer ("Christus im Alten und im Neuen Testament," *Theologische Zeitschrift*, 4:253, July–August, 1953). (i) Vischer robs the Old Testament of its own individuality by making its function exclusively that of a pointer to the New; (ii) all the promises within the Old Testament for its own time period have no meaning to Vischer until related to the New; (iii) his typological exegesis is too much an appeal to the understanding and not enough to the heart and conscience; (iv) and he judges interpretations by their effectiveness not their truthfulness.

of that principle, and Wyngaarden has pointed out a measure of typological interpretation within the Old Testament itself of such terms as Zion, Israel, and Jerusalem (to mention a few). But if the New Testament contains an inspired interpretation of the Old Testament then we ought to be able to settle the basic issue at least. Wace properly writes that "no interpretation of prophecy can be compatible with the claims of the Christian faith which is not in harmony with that of our Lord, and of the Evangelists and Apostles." [32] How does the New Testament use the Old?

(i) Sometimes it is cited to *prove* a point (John 6:45) or a doctrine (Mat. 22:32, 43–44). (ii) Sometimes it is cited to *explain* a point such as bringing out the fearsomeness of Mt. Sinai (Hebrews 12:20). (iii) Sometimes it is cited to *illustrate* some New Testament truth (Rom. 10:18) or to illustrate forcibly by using the language of the Old Testament when some other thought is intended. (iv) Sometimes it is cited as being *literally fulfilled* in the New Testament as with our Lord's birth in Bethlehem (Mat. 2:5–6). Sometimes the New Testament cites the Old Testament *in an expanded typological sense*.

First, the New Testament contains typological interpretations of the Old Testament with reference to its moral teachings and spiritual teachings. The evidence of 1 Cor. 10:6, 11 and Rom. 15:4 is simply incontrovertible at this point. Whenever we draw out an ethical principle, a spiritual rule, or a devotional from the Old Testament which is not a matter of its literal expression we have made a typological interpretation. No doubt all caution and hermeneutical care is to be followed in such instances, but much of the use of the Old Testament in the preaching and teaching ministry would be lost if we denied this use of the Old Testament.

Second, the New Testament contains typological interpretations of theological elements in the Old Testament. This is the province primarily of typology proper but its extended

[32] *Prophecy: Jewish and Christian*, p. 131.

usage cannot be denied. Creation is a type of new creation in Christ (2 Cor. 4:6), as it is of the complete salvation in Christ (Hebrews 4:4). Further, all that has been said previously of *multiple fulfilment* (and compenetration) applies here. Multiple fulfilment is possible only if a much deeper and pervasive typical element is recognized in the Old Testament than typology proper.

Third, the Greek word *epouranios* ("heavenly") is approximately equivalent to typological. The earthly calling of the Hebrew people is typical of the heavenly calling of the Christian (Hebrews 3:1), and the earthly blessing of Israel is typical of the heavenly gift in Christianity (Hebrews 6:4), and the earthly land of Palestine is typical of the heavenly country of Christian promise (Hebrews 11:6), and the earthly Jerusalem of the coming heavenly Jerusalem (Hebrews 12:22). The typical character of much of the Old Testament economy therefore cannot be denied.

Fourth, the deep-seated typical character of the Old Testament economy (and thereby requiring typological exegesis) is noted in those instances where Israel and the Church are spoken of interchangeably. Paul's use of the Israel of God in Galatians 6:16 bears this out. What avails in Christ, Paul argues, is the cross and the new creation, not circumcision. Upon those who walk according to *this rule* (that which counts is the cross and the new creation in Christ) Paul invokes a blessing. Then he adds: "and upon the Israel of God." If this expression meant the Jewish people, or even Jewish Christians he would be directly contradicting himself. The true people of God are not the Judaizers who wish to circumcize their converts, but those who glory in the cross and are new creations in Christ. Further, the peace and mercy invoked in this passage *on the basis of this rule* is invoked upon those who walk according to it (and as the parallel Greek construction demands) upon the Israel of God. It is inescapable that the *Israel of God* means the true people of God (in contrast to the Judaizers) who glory in the cross and count the new birth as that saving act of God and not circumcision.

In Hebrews 8:8 the new covenant is made with the house of Israel and Judah. The strict literalists insist that this means Israel and Judah and not the Church for if it meant the Church we would have an unequivocal instance in which Israel is spoken to when the Church is meant and the essential distinction between Israel and the Church would be obliterated. The following is to be noted: (i) The New Covenant is one of the several items discussed in Hebrews all of which are now realized in the Church and the present age. That Christ is our Moses, our Aaron, our Sacrifice the strict literalists readily admit. To isolate the New Covenant and forward it to the millennium is to disrupt the entire structure of Hebrews. (ii) The writer of Hebrews applies the New Covenant to Christian experience in Hebrews 10:15–17. Bales makes a sharp but accurate observation here. If the New Covenant belongs to Israel alone and that during the millennium, then the writer of Hebrews has erred in applying it to present Christian experience.[33] To say that we are under the benefits of the Covenant without actually being under the covenant is to clandestinely admit what is boldly denied. (iii) The multiplication of covenants becomes confusing. When our Lord initiated the Lord's Table he mentioned the new covenant. Dispensationalists observe the Lord's Table and must so admit that some new covenant is now in effect, but deny that the New Covenant of the Lord's Table is the same as the New Covenant of Hebrews 8. We thus have two new covenants. (iv) The terms of the New Covenant are distinctly Christian and that is why they are applied to Christians in Hebrews 10. Yet to strict literalists the millennial age is an age of the restitution of the law.[34] But the very

[33] *Op. cit.*, pp. 110–111.
[34] The Sermon on the Mount is called the constitution of the millennial kingdom (*Scofield Reference Bible*, p. 999) and is labeled as *pure law* (p. 1000). So much so that even the petition for forgiveness of sins in the Lord's Prayer is called *legal ground* (p. 1002).

wording of the New Covenant is so clear at this point. It is declared that it will not be like the Covenant made at Mount Sinai (Hebrews 8:9).

Fifth, the context of the passage associates the mediatorial office of Christ with the New Covenant. Christ is the *mediator* of a new covenant and this is speaking of his *present work as mediator*. If his mediatorship is *present*, the covenant which he founded and upon which his mediatorship is based is *present*. To remove the covenant from its present operation is thereby to remove the grounds of the mediatorship of Christ. Strict literalists who would push the New Covenant on to the millennium have not calculated properly with the implications of such an interpretation upon Hebrews 8:6.

In short, the only consistency in Hebrews is to admit either that *all* items refer to the Jews during the millennium or that *all* pertain to the Christian dispensation. But no interpreter would dare remove the precious truths of Hebrews *en toto* from the Christian Church and make them valid only for the millennium. We are compelled to believe that the New Covenant spoken of in Jeremiah spoke of Israel and Judah as typical of the New Testament people.

Finally, we have some examples of typological exegesis in Paul's use of the Old Testament. Physical circumcision is typical of spiritual purification (Col. 2:11, Romans 2:29, Phil. 3:3, and Eph. 2:11). The care given the treading oxen of the Old Testament is typical of the care to be given the servants of Christ (1 Cor. 9:9). The veil covering the face of Moses is typical of the spiritual darkness of present unbelieving Israel (2 Cor. 3:13–16). The law written on tablets of stone is typical of the gospel written on the human heart (2 Cor. 3:1). The darkness and light of creation are typical of the darkness of human sin and the truth of the gospel in illumination (2 Cor. 4:6). The passover lamb is typical of the saving death of Christ (1 Cor. 5:7).

Supplementary to this is similar treatment of the Old Testament in the closing chapter of Hebrews. The altar of the

Old Testament is typical of the cross of Christ (13:10–12). The burning of the sacrifice without the camp is typical of the rejection of Christ, and so we too ought to go without the boundaries of "official religion" and fellowship with the sufferings of Jesus (13:13). The city of Jerusalem is typical of the city to come (13:14). The Old Testament sacrifices are typical of the spiritual sacrifices of Christians (13:15).

As Girdlestone put it, "Israel is thus a representative or typical nation, in its origin, its history, its bondage, and its deliverance. Its story is prophetic, inasmuch as it is the key to the philosophy of all history. It is also provisional and there is an anticipation running through it which is fulfilled in Christ." [35]

An extreme literalism or an extreme typological approach is equally contrary to the method by which the New Testament interprets the Old. But just as the ellipses of the planets have two foci while the sun is only at one of them, so there must be a controlling principle between the typological and the literal interpretation of prophecy. One must be the point of departure, and in keeping with the system of hermeneutics proposed earlier in this volume we make the literal the control over the typological. Therefore, *interpret prophecy literally unless the implicit or explicit teaching of the New Testament suggests typological interpretation.*

Obviously this does not immediately settle the millennial question, the *crux interpretum* of Old Testament prophetic interpretation, and it is not the function of hermeneutics as a science that it should. A particular belief is the product of an applied hermeneutical theory. However the position here stated favors a millennial interpretation of the kingdom of God.

In some passages of Old Testament prophecy it is difficult to determine whether the deliverance spoken of refers to the return from the Babylonian captivity or to millennial deliverance. Further, passages of great salvation and joy usually

[35] *Op. cit.*, p. 85.

referred to the millennium could refer to the future state in glory. Further, the *raison d'être* of the millennium must most assuredly be (as John Gill so forcibly points out in his great *Body of Divinity*) the manifestation of the glory of Christ.

(4). *The centrality of Jesus Christ must be kept in mind in all prophetic interpretation.* Millennialism degenerates into cultism whenever prophetic interpretation ceases to be dominantly Christological. Some premillennialism has been branded as excessively Jewish and perhaps those premillennialists are misunderstood because they have failed to be sufficiently Christological in their interpretation. Girdlestone's advice can be well taken in this connection: "To study the prophets without reference to Christ seems as unscientific as to study the body without reference to the head. The Spirit of Christ was in the Prophets all the way through (1 Pet. 1:11), and each book is to be read as part of a great whole." [36] The Roman Catholic exegetes have erred at this point, finding far too much Catholicism in the Old Testament rather than Jesus Christ.

The finest statement of the Christological principle in Old Testament interpretation is that of Francis Roberts who lived in the seventeenth century:

Now that we may more successfully and clearly understand Scripture by Scripture, these ensuing particulars are to be observed: (I) *That Jesus Christ is our mediator and the salvation of sinners by Him is the very substance, marrow, soul and scope of the whole Scriptures.* What are the whole Scriptures, but as it were the spiritual swadling clothes of the Holy child Jesus. (1) Christ is the truth and substance of all types and shadows. (2) Christ is the matter and substance of the Covenant of Grace under all administrations thereof; under the Old Testament Christ is *veyled*, under the New Covenant *revealed*. (3) Christ is the centre and meetingplace of all the promises, for in him all the promises of God are yea, and they are Amen. (4) Christ is the thing signified, sealed, and exhibited in all the sacraments of the Old and New Testaments, whether

[36] *Ibid.*, p. 107.

ordinary or extraordinary. (5) Scripture genealogies are to lead us on to the true line of Christ. (6) Scripture chronologies are to discover to us the times and seasons of Christ. (7) Scripture laws are our schoolmaster to bring us to Christ; the moral by correcting, the ceremonial by directing. And (8) Scripture gospel is Christ's *light*, whereby we know him; Christ's voice whereby we hear and follow him; Christ's cords of love, whereby we are drawn into sweet union and communion with him; yea, it is the power of God unto salvation unto all them that believe in Christ Jesus. Keep therefore still Jesus Christ in your eye, in the perusal of the Scripture, as the end, scope, and substance thereof. For as the sun gives light to all the heavenly bodies, so Jesus Christ the sun of righteousness gives light to all the Holy Scriptures.[37]

The *apocalypse* is one of the modes of prophetic communication. Religious liberalism and radical critics have had some very harsh things to say about the Biblical apocalypses but recent scholarship has more properly assessed them and taken a far more wholesome attitude toward them.[38] Apocalyptic language is *prophetic, historical,* and *symbolic.* The rules are easy; the interpretation difficult. (1) In interpreting apocalyptic literature all that has been said of the rules and praxis for general interpretation applies at this point. (2) In the interpretation of apocalyptic imagery a complete literalistic method is impossible. Those who claim to be complete literalists with reference to Revelation cannot consistently follow their program out. The issue is not between spiritualization and literalism but between lesser and greater degrees of spiritualization. To be thoroughly literal we would have to insist that a literal (actual) woman sat literally upon seven literal hills! that Jesus Christ has a literal sword coming out of his

[37] *Clavis Bibliorum* (1675), p. 10, cited by Briggs, *Biblical Study,* p. 363. Italics are his.
[38] Cf. H. H. Rowley, "The Voice of God in Apocalyptic," *Interpretation,* 2:403–429, October, 1948; E. F. Scott, "The Natural Language of Religion," *Interpretation,* 2:420–429, October, 1948; Raymond Calkins, "Militant Message," *Interpretation,* 2:430–443, October, 1948; and Charles T. Fritsch, "The Message of Apocalyptic for Today," *Theology Today,* 10:357–366, October, 1953.

mouth! and that beasts can act and talk like men! To be literalistic in interpreting Revelation really means that the symbols of Revelation pertain to real, visible occurrences here on earth in contrast to some sort of gradual or historical fulfilment of the symbols in a thinner form. (3) Every effort must be made to discover whether the symbol had any meaning in the culture of the writer. This demands a very careful and exacting historical research by the exegete. (4) The passage in which the apocalyptic symbol appears must be carefully examined to see whether the meaning of the symbol is there revealed. (5) An examination must be made of history if the apocalypse is fulfilled in history. Fortunately, with reference to much of Daniel and Zechariah this is possible. (6) With reference to New Testament books, inter-Biblical apocryphal literature must be examined to see whether it contributed any of the symbols. (7) With special reference to the book of Revelation the Old Testament must be searched thoroughly for every possible clue to the symbols there used.[39]

C. The Meaning of 2 Peter 1:20

This verse of Scripture has been given three major interpretations. The first is that the Catholics use it to prove that

[39] Once again it must be said that if the student works with the genuinely scholarly works, commentaries and other reference works, he will find much of these details already settled. A comprehensive survey of all the types of apocalyptic symbols used in the book of Revelation will be found in J. P. Lange, *Revelation* (E. R. Craven, American editor), pp. 1–41. Another substantial list of apocalyptic symbols is in *The Holy Bible Commentary*, IV (New Testament), pp. 468–86. A sensible set of rules for interpreting Revelation, which could be applied to all apocalyptic literature is in Henry Cowles, *The Revelation of John*, p. 39 ff. Terry, *Biblical Hermeneutics*, gives two chapters to the interpretation of apocalypsis, but merely for illustration. He says that "the hermeneutical principles to be observed in the interpretation of apocalyptics are, in the main, the same as those which we apply to all predictive prophecy," p. 340. There is no rule of thumb method to unlock the mysteries and perplexities of apocalyptic imagery. Hermeneutics is an art and a science, and the specific interpretations of the interpreter reveal to what degree he is an artist and scientist.

the church, not the individual, is to interpret the Bible. Some Protestants use it to prove that no prophetic passage is to be interpreted in isolation from other passages. And the third, and that which appears to be the correct one, is that it has nothing to do with prophetic interpretation at all, but with the divine origin of prophecy.

The theme that Peter is discussing is the divine origin and nature of prophecy. He is talking about the sure word of prophecy, that it is well for all of us to reckon with, for it is a shining light in a dark place. Having said this, he then tells us that the reason for these remarks is that the prophetic utterances come not from man but from the Holy Spirit. Thus the *context* has nothing to do with the interpretation of prophecy, but its inspiration, and verse 20 should be so interpreted.

In justification of this is the most evident parallelism of thought between verses 20 and 21. (a). *Private inspiration* of verse 20 is apposite to the *will of man* in verse 21. (b). The *origination* of prophecy is denied to man in verse 20, but affirmed of the Holy Ghost in verse 21. (c). Personal, private, self-inspiration of verse 20 stands opposite to the holy men of God in verse 21.

Moreover, a careful study of the Greek text of verse 20 seems to bear the interpretation we give it. The King James Version translates the Greek *ginetai* very weakly with an "is." If it were translated more accurately, it would have been rendered *came*, or *came into existence*, anticipating the *were moved* of verse 21. The word translated by *interpretation* is not the customary word for such but is from the verb meaning "to loose." There is a sense in which *to loose* means to interpret, in that the meaning of a passage is explained releasing its sense, and it is so used in Mark 4:34. Rendering the expression painfully literally, it would read "private unloosing." That is, no Scriptural prophecy originated through personal, individual, inspiration (loosing or releasing) but by the unloosing, releasing, or inspiration of the Holy Spirit.

Robertson[40] translates *epiluseos* as *disclosure.* As such it makes the verse speak of inspiration, not of interpretation. In his *Word Pictures in loco,* he says: "It is the prophet's grasp of the prophecy, not that of the readers that is here presented, as the next verse shows." [41] Fronmüller, in Lange's *Commentary,* says: "The reference is to the origin, not to the interpretation of the prophecy, as is evident from v. 21." [42] The American editor of the same cites Alford and Bengel as agreeing with this view. Williams, in the *American Commentary* on the New Testament, shows how the Catholics take the usual interpretation of this verse much to their own advantage and then says: ". . . but the best view seems to be this: 'That no prophecy of the Scripture is a matter of one's own explanation'—that is, the prophets do not originate their own prophecies; they receive them entire from above as is clear from the fact given in the next verse. Peter, therefore, must be understood as saying nothing whatever relative to interpreting the Scriptures." [43]

Alford gives quite an extended note in his *Greek Testament* substantiating the interpretation we are defending. Others interpreting the verse this way are Huther in Meyer's *Commentary,* and Lumby in *The Holy Bible Commentary.* Fairbairn also takes this to be the meaning of the passage and brings out the same point we have about *ginetai.*[44] However, Bigg[45] makes *ginetai* simply equivalent to "is," and says that the text does not state who the authoritative interpreters are. Bigg says the important question is: what is the opposite of private interpretation? It

[40] *A Grammar of the Greek New Testament in the Light of Historical Research* (fifth edition), p. 514.
[41] Vol. VI, p. 159.
[42] Vol. IX (second German edition), p. 21.
[43] *Peter,* vol. VII, p. 91.
[44] P. Fairbairn, *Prophecy,* p. 497.
[45] C. Bigg, *The Epistles of St. Peter and St. Jude* (The International Critical Commentary), p. 269 ff. Bigg does not even mention this alternative interpretation suggested here and defended by a number of scholars.

can only be that (a) no prophetic passage can be interpreted by itself since all prophecy is by the same author and must be therefore correlated, or (b) that there must be a "public" authority to interpret Scripture. But Peter is not talking of possibilities of misinterpreting Scripture, but of the divine origin of prophecy and its usefulness to the Christian.

D. RECENT DEVELOPMENTS

The end of World War I saw a new burst of enthusiasm and scholarship for both theology and the interpretation of Holy Scripture. The new names appearing were Barth, Brunner, Bultmann, and Gogarten. It was out of this movement that the inspiration of Kittel's great *Theological Dictionary of the New Testament* came. Also emerging were a number of Old Testament scholars pushing forth the understanding of the Old Testament in many different directions. From this came a number of Old Testament theologies written by such men as Jacob, Eichrodt, Knight, Vriezen, and von Rad.

The issue contained in the question of the interpretation of prophecy became focused at a particular point: how does the Church use the Old Testament? Or, in what sense is the Old Testament a Christian book? Or, what is the relationship of the Old Testament to the New Testament? Or, what is the principle of continuity in God's revelation and in God's act that may be the answer to the unity of the Testaments? Or, what is the unity of Holy Scripture?

The best general introduction to this kind of discussion about the nature of the Old Testament, especially its prophetic character, is Claus Westermann, editor, *Essays on Old Testament Interpretation*. The fifteen essays represent the range of thought in Old Testament today and the book is also enhanced by an excellent bibliography on the subject at the end of the book.

In the following we intend to give only in a summary

way the kinds of options that are being suggested today. In that this problem deeply involves the interpretation of the New Testament and the manner in which much of theology is written the list of opinions must not be reserved for Old Testament scholars alone. Such men as Bultmann, Barth, Moltmann, and Pannenberg have also written on this issue.

(1). *Repristination view.* "Repristination" means to take an opinion, a theory, or a position of some previous era of human history and to attempt to make it come alive again for the contemporary situation. It has the idea of correcting what was lacking in the earlier position and restating the position with the help of recent learning.

The most significant attempt to do this with reference to the prophetic interpretation of the Old Testament has been Wilhelm Visscher's *The Witness to Christ in the Old Testament* (2 vols.). This work is alleged to have had an important influence on Barth. In Barth's exegesis of Genesis 1 (in *Church Dogmatics,* III/1) he virtually goes back beyond even the historic Protestant view about the nature of prophecy to an allegorical interpretation of the text.

(2) *Educational view.* If a scholar does not believe in prophecy because that entails supernatural revelation and he cannot accept anything supernatural, and, if he nevertheless believes that the Old Testament must have some place in the Church, what place is that? If a scholar thinks this way he treats the Old Testament as an "educational" (propaedeutic) volume for getting the proper perspective of what the New Testament intends to say (Bultmann, Baumgartel, Hesse). Just how the Old Testament becomes instructional in the Church depends upon the theology of the Old Testament or Biblical scholar. To Bultmann the Old Testament is the record of man's spiritual existential failure. It is a record of the helplessness of the law to create "authentic existence." Hence the Old Testament gives a negative example of which the New Testament

gives the positive answer. Baumgartel thinks that the Old Testament teaches a concept of Lordship that was right in its intention but wrong in its formulation. Thus the New Testament teaches us the right concept of Lordship through Christ the Lord.

(3). *Promise view.* Zimmerli argues that the old notion of specific prediction with literal fulfillment in the New Testament is contrary to our modern knowledge of the Old Testament. What the Old Testament contains in its prophetic literature is a series of promises about how God will act in the future. It might be said that the prophetic elements of the Old Testament are *programmatic.* These elements indicate how God will act in the future. Hence in place of prediction and literal fulfilment we would have promise and realization. Jürgen Moltmann's *The Theology of Hope* is really a theology of promise. Moltmann expands the notion of promise and hope into an eschatological program for the interpretation of the total Scripture. All of God's revelations to man are of the nature of promises indicating how God intends to act in the future which in turn becomes the content of man's hope. Walter Capp in *The Future of Hope* makes the radical claim that a theology of hope calls for a whole new kind of human consciousness and therefore a whole rewriting of Christian theology.

(4). *Pattern view.* The Old Testament prophetic passages indicate to man the character of God's action. This is based on the idea that God's action is according to a pattern and is therefore capable of repetition. Hence what joins the Old and New Testament together is the concept of God's action which as a pattern may be repeated in history. Although each man states it his own way this is generally the kind of interpretation given the Old Testament by such men as von Rad, Eichrodt, and Pannenberg. In the case of Moltmann and Pannenberg the prophetic treatment of the Old Testament is really part of a larger view of the total nature of the divine action in history and of the divine revelation. Both men agree that the interpreter must work both backwards and forwards in view of the bodily resurrection of Christ.

BIBLIOGRAPHY

Bales, *New Testament Interpretations of Old Testament Prophecies.*

Davidson, *Old Testament Prophecy.*

Girdlestone, *The Grammar of Prophecy.*

Berry, *Premillennialism and Old Testament Prediction.*

Wace, *Prophecy: Jewish and Christian.*

Fairbairn, *Prophecy.*

————, *Fairbairn versus Fairbairn.*

A Catholic Commentary on the Holy Scripture.

Beecher, *The Prophets and the Promises.*

Johnson, *The Quotations of the New Testament from the Old.*

Feinberg, *Premillennialism or Amillennialism?* (second edition).

Wyngaarden, *The Future of the Kingdom in Prophecy and Fulfilment.*

Robertson, *Regnum Dei.*

Visscher, *The Witness of the Old Testament to Christ.*

Hebert, *The Throne of David.*

Briggs, *Biblical Study.*

Zenos, "Prophecy," *A New Standard Bible Dictionary*, p. 742.

Oehler, *Old Testament Theology.*

von Orelli, "Prophecy, Prophets," *The International Standard Bible Encyclopedia*, IV, 2459-66.

Meyrick, "Prophet," *Smith's Dictionary of the Bible*, III, 2590-2602.

Chafer, *The Science of Biblical Hermeneutics.*

Angus and Green, *Cyclopedic Handbook to the Bible.*

Murray, *Millennial Studies.*

Rutgers, *Premillennialism in America.*

Reese, *The Approaching Advent of Christ.*

Mauro, *God's Present Kingdom.*

Rall, *Modern Premillennialism and the Christian Hope.*

Snowden, *The Coming of the Lord.*

Allis, *Prophecy and the Church.*

Chapter XI

THE INTERPRETATION OF PARABLES

A. The Nature of Parables

The etymological meaning of the word *parable* is "a placing alongside of" for the purpose of comparison. It thus represents a method of illustration so that it could be said: "The kingdom of heaven is illustrated by the following situation." However, historical studies have revealed that the word is really not capable of simple definition, but has been used in many senses.[1] Besides the word *parabolē*, the word *paroimia* is used which means "a saying by the wayside, a proverb, a maxim." The use of *paroimia* is restricted to John's gospel.

Dodd's definition is that a parable "at its simplest . . . is a metaphor or simile drawn from nature or common life, arresting the hearer by its vividness or strangeness, and leaving the mind in sufficient doubt about its precise application to rouse it into active thought."[2] As such a parable differs from a *fable* in that it is neither trivial nor fantastic; from the *myth* in that the parable is not a creation of popular folklore; from the *allegory* which finds meaning at many points in the narrative; and from such *figures of speech* as simile or metaphor although in a qualified sense as Dodd has indicated the parable is a sort of metaphor or simile. At times too it is difficult to separate the parable from the allegory, especially in the longer parable where several elements have symbolic meaning.

Scholars differ widely in their count of the number of par-

[1] B. T. D. Smith, *The Parables of the Synoptic Gospels*, Chapters I and II.

[2] *The Parables of the Kingdom* (third edition), p. 16.

ables in the Gospels,[3] and this is due to the difficulty of deciding what is parabolic and what is not. Smith has indicated the different forms that parables may take, and also notes the types of introductions which usually preface parables.[4] The argument that the account of Lazarus and Dives is not a parable because it is not introduced as a parable is not valid because Oesterley has demonstrated that parables may be given with no typical introduction.[5] Generally scholars divide the parables into simple utterances, parables, and extended parables.[6] It is the extended parable which has similarities to the allegory.

There are about thirty parables usually treated in works on the parables. Luke has the most and John the least. The importance of the study of the parables is to be found in their sheer number representing a large part of the text of the Gospels, and thereby embodying considerable material of a didactic nature. They give us information as to the progress of the gospel in the world, the results of its propagation, about the end of the age, the dealings of God with the Jewish people and the Gentiles, and the nature of the kingdom of God. Any doctrine of the kingdom or eschatology which ignores a careful study of the parables cannot be adequate.

The intention of parabolic teaching is given by Christ in Matthew 13:11-17, Mark 4:10-12, and Luke 8:8-10. First, it is a method of teaching the *responsive* disciple. At the end of the first parable our Lord said, "He that hath ears to hear, let him hear" (Luke 8:8). When the disciples asked him why

---

[3] Moulton notes that by different countings scholars have suggested 79, 71, 59, 39, 37 and 33 parables. "Parables," *Dictionary of Christ and the Gospels*, II, 313. This is a most valuable article for the study of parables as is Nourse, "Parable," *Hastings Encyclopedia of Religion and Ethics*, IX, 628.

[4] Smith, *op. cit.*, p. 30 ff.

[5] Oesterley, *The Gospel Parables in the Light of Their Jewish Background*, p. 11.

[6] Dodd gives *Gleichnis*, *Parabel*, and *Novellen* (*op. cit.*, pp. 17-18), and cites Bultmann's division of *Bildwörter*, *Gleichnisse*, and *Parabel* (p. 18 fn.).

he said this and taught in parables our Lord answered that it was given unto the disciples to know the mysteries (disclosures) of the kingdom of God. Hence, parables were used by our Lord as instruments of his revelation to those who had ears to hear. Parables contain much that every Christian servant needs to know about the kingdom of God. Some parables teach him not to be depressed at the apparent failure of the gospel or the corruption of the gospel; others tell him not to be ambitious beyond which the gospel promises; and still others tell him not to be discouraged because the success of God is secure. Thus the parables stand as *sine qua non* material for intelligent Christian service.

The second intent of parabolic teaching was to hide the truth from the *unresponsive* and so aid in the hardening of their heart as they continuously rebelled against God. This is the special import of the citation from Isaiah 6. The truth taught in a parable is veiled and so is a test of a person's spiritual responsiveness, of whether he has the spiritual intention to follow through and learn its meaning.

The origin of parabolic teaching has been traced by Smith from Old Testament references, to rabbinical teaching, to New Testament usage.[7] The method was copiously used among the rabbis. The Greek word *parabolē* is equivalent to the Hebrew word *mashal*. One of the current rabbinic sayings was, "I will parable to thee a parable." Among the Greeks a parable stood for an argument from analogy.

There are four elements to a parable: (i) A parable is some commonly known *earthly* thing, event, custom, or possible occurrence. The emphasis is on the word *earthly*. Parables are about farming, marriages, kings, feasts, household relationships, business arrangements, or customs of the peoples. It is this concrete and pictorial grounding which makes them such remarkable instruments for instruction.

[7]Smith, *op. cit.*, p. 3 ff. Also, Oesterley, *op. cit.*, p. 3 ff. Cf. also the work of Feldman, *The Parables and Similes of the Rabbis.*

(ii). Beyond the earthly element is the spiritual lesson, or theological truth which the parable *intends* to teach.

(iii). This *earthly* element bears an *analogical* relationship to the spiritual element. It is this analogical relationship which gives the parable its illustrative, or argumentative force.

(iv). Because a parable has two levels of meaning every parable stands in need of interpretation. The actors, elements, and actions need to be identified. One of the tributes paid to Jülicher's famous work on the parables is that he freed the interpretation of parables from allegorization. Whenever any interpreter seeks an elaboration of meaning in a parable, and commences to find meaning in far more points than the parable can hope to make, that interpreter has returned to the reprehensible method of allegorizing the parables.

B. Rules for the Interpretation of Parables

A study of the literature of the parables reveals that the parables are not as easy to interpret as their simple nature would seem to indicate. We propose to discuss the interpretation of parables from the viewpoint of four principles: perspective, cultural, exegetical, and doctrinal.

(1). The *perspective principles* inform us that to adequately interpret the parables we need to understand them in their relationship to Christology and the kingdom of God.

One of the factors in which recent studies differ somewhat from older studies in the parables is that the recent studies indicate the *Christological nature* of parabolic teaching.[8] In these studies it is indicated that we have more than the *mashal* teaching of the rabbis, more than apt illustrations of moral or spiritual truths. In the Gospels it is the Christ who

---

[8] Cf. Hoskyns and Davey, *The Riddle of the New Testament*, p. 132, and, Wallace, "The Parables and the Preacher," *The Scottish Journal of Theology*, 2:13–28, March, 1949.

is teaching about *his* kingdom, and in some measure is re-flectively teaching truth about *himself*. In some parables Christ is the leading figure, or the parable has meaning only as related directly to Christ or his word. Thus in approach-ing any parable we must ask ourselves this: *how does this parable relate to Christ?* Are any of the persons in the parable Christ? Does the parable concern the word or teaching or mission of Christ? Only when we thus approach each parable Christologically do we obtain the correct perspective.

The second perspective principle is *the kingdom principle*. Christ came preaching a gospel of the kingdom and announc-ing that a kingdom was at hand. Many of the parables directly state that they are about the kingdom, and others not specifically stated cannot be divorced from the kingdom. Adequate interpretation of the parables must now be based upon an understanding of the kingdom of God and the rela-tionship of Jesus Christ and His gospel to that kingdom. This Hope stated when he wrote that "it must be borne in mind that all of [the parables] deal with one great subject, and one great subject only, namely, the kingdom of God." [9]

(i). First of all, *the kingdom has come*. In some sense it is in existence from Christ's first preaching, and men are enter-ing it. This is the kingdom in its *actualized* sense. It is entered by the new birth (John 3:3) and our Lord stated that the tax collectors and harlots were entering the kingdom (Matt. 21:31).[10] And whatever be the interpretation of Luke

[9] Hope, "The Interpretation of Christ's Parables," *Interpretation*, 6:303, July, 1952.

[10] Modern scholarship on purely lexical grounds has asserted that there is no difference between the kingdom of God and the kingdom of heaven. Concentration on these two terms has obscured the fact that there are *several* terms used interchangeably as a study of the harmony of the Gospels in the Greek will reveal. Cf. Oesterley, *op. cit.*, pp. 19-20; Dodd, *op. cit.*, p. 34; Berkhof, *The Kingdom of God*, p. 166; Ladd, *Crucial Questions about the Kingdom of God*, p. 106 f. For a stout defense of the dispensational interpretation cf. Feinberg, *Premillennialism or Amillennialism?* (second edition), p. 286 ff., and p. 297 ff.

17:20–21, the passage indicates that in some sense the kingdom is *here*.[11]

Being *here* the kingdom continues through this age. The parables of the kingdom were also *prophecies* of the kingdom. They describe the fortunes of the kingdom through the centuries. They tell of the sowing and the reaping of the word of the kingdom; they tell of the great net let down into the sea and not pulled in until the end of the age; they tell of the grain growing until it is ripe. There can be no clear understanding of many of the parables unless we understand the continuing character of the kingdom.

(ii). The kingdom is *eschatological* in character. There is a harvest at the end of the age. The final issues are not settled until the angels of God separate the true from the false. The rightful Heir of the kingdom must come in the power and the glory of his kingdom. Certainly the eschatological element looms large in any parable which mentions the end in the form of a harvest or separation. The parables of the talents (Matt. 25:14 ff.) and the virgins (Matt. 25:1 ff.) are certainly eschatological. This eschatological element is a real and necessary element in understanding the parables and the liberals who pruned it off obscured this depth of meaning in the parable.

In summary, the interpreter must keep in mind that the kingdom in some sense has come; it is continuing; and it will come, and with this in mind he must understand whether the parable under consideration is concerned with one or all of these aspects.

(2). *The cultural principles.* To understand the parables we need not only to see them from the standpoint of the

---

[11] Those holding that the expression *entos hymōn* means "within you" are Oesterley, *op. cit.*, p. 32 and Dodd, *op. cit.*, pp. 84-85, fn. 1. To the contrary is Fuller, *The Mission and Achievement of Jesus*, p. 28 ff.; Dinkler, *The Idea of History in Near East*, p. 176; Kümmel, *Verheissung und Erfüllung*, p. 27. I am indebted to Dr. Ladd of Fuller Seminary for these *per contra* references.

kingdom of God and Christology, but also from the cultural background. Our Lord lived in ancient Palestine amidst the Jewish people, and the parables are drawn from that cultural backdrop.

In general, the parables are drawn from material familiar to a poor, agricultural peasant. The manners, customs, and material culture exhibited in the parables amply substantiate this. Further, the parables were spoken in Aramaic and some helpful information can be gleaned by translating the parables back into Aramaic.[12]

Studies in the local color of the parables have turned up a rich store of information and one is tempted to say that one should never preach again on any parable until he has made himself familiar with this material. Jeremias' book, *The Parables of Jesus*, is filled with the local color which so clearly lights up the parables. *In the interpretation of every parable it is necessary to recover as much as possible the local color employed in it.*

For example, farmers sowed their fields and then plowed them up thus making the parable of the sower much clearer. Harvest, wedding, and wine were Jewish symbols of the end of the age. The fig tree is a symbol of the people of God. Lamps were put under baskets to extinguish them, hence to light a lamp and put it under a basket is to light it and immediately put it out. The lamb which strays from the fold lies down and will not move, so he must be carried back. Mustard trees grew from small seeds to trees eight to ten feet tall. One speck of leaven penetrated enough dough to feed 162 persons. What Jeremias is able to deduce about the life of the prodigal from knowledge of Jewish customs is remarkable.[13]

[12] Part of the value of the work of Jeremias (*op. cit.*) is that he has the requisite learning to make this retranslation, and his work is very valuable from this standpoint. It was the necessity of knowing the cultural background for the understanding of the parables which inspired Oesterley to write his work (*op. cit.*).

[13] Jeremias, *op. cit.*, pp. 103–104.

(3). *Exegetical principles.* We have tried to close in on the parables from two sides. Coming from theology we have noted the Christological and kingdom setting of the parables, and coming from background considerations we have noted the necessity of understanding the general cultural background of the parables and the specific matters of local color and customs which figure in each parable. We now come directly to the parable and consider the direct exegetical principles for the interpretation of parables.

(i). *Determine the one central truth the parable is attempting to teach.* This might be called the golden rule of parabolic‘ interpretation for practically all writers on the subject mention it with stress. "The typical parable presents one single point of comparison," writes Dodd. "The details are not intended to have independent significance." [14] Others have put the rule this way: *Don't make a parable walk on all fours.*

A parable is not like an allegory, for in the latter most of the elements of the narrative have meaning. To be sure, some parables are more elaborate than others and in this regard approach an allegory. But as a general or guiding rule, look for the one central thesis of the parable.

A parable is a truth carried in a vehicle. Therefore there is the inevitable presence of *accessories* which are necessary for the drapery of the parable, but are not part of the meaning. The danger in parabolic teaching at this point is to interpret as meaningful what is drapery.

(ii). *Determine how much of the parable is interpreted by the Lord Himself.* After reciting the parable of the Sower (Mat. 13:18 ff.) our Lord interprets it. After stating the parable of the enemy's sowing darnel among the wheat, our Lord interprets it later in the house. After setting forth the parable of the virgins he says, "Watch therefore, for ye know neither the day nor the hour wherein the Son of man cometh," (Matt. 25:13). In such instances we have the definite word of Christ concerning the meaning of the parable, which further conveys

[14] *Op. cit.*, p. 18.

to us the spirit of his teaching for help in parables that are not interpreted.[15]

(iii). *Determine whether there are any clues in the context concerning the parable's meaning.* The context may include what follows as well as what precedes. In Luke 15 occurs the triadic parable of the lost sheep, lost coin, and lost son. The interpretative context is Luke 15:1-2, "Then drew near unto him all the publicans and sinners for to hear him. And the Pharisees and scribes murmured saying 'This man receiveth sinners, and eateth with them.' " The parables that follow are a justification for eating with sinners and publicans. Therefore, the shepherd, the woman, and the father represent the attitude of love, forgiveness, and redemption in Christ; the lost sheep, lost coin, and lost son represent the publicans and sinners who gathered round our Lord.

The parable of the Tower and the King (Luke 14:25 ff.) is a parable of Christian service, not of salvation as indicated by the context (note v. 33, "He cannot be my disciple"). After giving the parable of the unjust steward Luke adds: "And the Pharisees also, who were covetous, heard all these things and derided him" (Luke 16:14). Therefore, the point of the parable must be taken as aimed at them.

(iv). *The comparative rule*—compare the parable with any possible Old Testament association, and with the parable as recited in one or more other of the Gospels. Both our Lord and his listeners were familiar with much of the content of the Old Testament. We must attune our thinking to be sensitive to possible Old Testament references in the parables.[16] Dodd [17] notes that such things as vineyards, fig trees, harvests, and feasts have Old Testament referents, and the Old Testament referent must be understood if we are to better understand the parable.

[15] Williams has written specifically on this point of noting how our Lord interpreted his own parables. "Jesus' Method of Interpreting Parables," *Review and Expositor*, 14:210-222, April, 1917.

[16] Cf. Wallace, *op. cit.*, p. 25.

[17] *Op. cit.*, p. 32.

Further, the interpreter must take a harmony of the Gospels in hand and study every version of each parable if it occurs in more than one Gospel. He must note concurrences and divergences, parallels and synonyms. The truest interpretation will arise out of such a comparative study.[18]

(4). *Doctrinal principles.* Any use of a parable for doctrinal purposes must observe historical sense. We ought not to read our theological debates back into the parables. Primary consideration should be given to what we judge to be the meaning which the immediate listeners garnered from the parable. There could well be more in the parable than was evident at that time but we must lay that bare with great care. We must not unceremoniously intrude into parabolic interpretation arguments about Calvinism, Arminianism, or millennialism.

Parables do teach doctrine, and the claim that they may not be used at all in doctrinal writing is improper. But in gleaning our doctrine from the parables we must be strict in our interpretation; we must check our results with the plain, evident teaching of our Lord, and with the rest of the New Testament.[19] Parables with proper cautions may be used to illustrate doctrine, illumine Christian experience, and to teach practical lessons.

The modern debates on the millennial question have frequently centered around the interpretation of some of the parables. In general, amillennialists and postmillennialists have interpreted certain parables optimistically whereas premillenarians and dispensationalists have interpreted the same parables pessimistically. For example, the growth of the mus-

---

[18] The thesis of Dodd (*op. cit.*) and Jeremias (*op. cit.*) is that the Church has elaborated and altered the parables. A summary of Jeremias' seven laws of transformation will be found on page 88 of his work. Needless to say this view does not reflect a substantial doctrine of inspiration by either Dodd or Jeremias.

[19] Dodd, *op. cit.*, p. 32. Wallace, *op. cit.*, p. 306. Kirk (*Lectures on the Parables*) gives more attention than most writers on parables to the matter of doctrinal teaching. Cf. pp. v–vi.

tard seed to a tree, and the permeation of the meal by the leaven is taken by the former to be a teaching of the powerful growth and spread of Christianity, and by the latter of the corruption of the professing Church. Further, some premillennial expositors interpret the pearl to be the Church, and the treasure, Israel, whereas previous interpreters took these parables as teaching how men found the Saviour.

With reference to the present status of affairs in parabolic interpretation the following may be said: (i) constant check must be made with students of rabbinics to see whether anything in their studies reveals beliefs about controversial matters in parabolic interpretation.[20] (ii) Convictions about the nature of the kingdom must certainly be built on a broader basis than two or three parables. The parables may be used to bolster millennial convictions, but the entire edifice cannot be made to rest on them. (iii) Millennial views must certainly contain the balance of optimism and pessimism as contained in the parables, as well as the teaching of the parables that the kingdom is established, is progressing, and is eschatological. A completely futuristic view of the kingdom (that in no sense does the kingdom now exist) and a completely spiritualized view of the kingdom (that the kingdom is solely the rule of God in the heart) are not true to the doctrinal teaching of the parables. The premillennialist must not be blind to the optimism of some parables, e.g., that the corn will ripen in the ear (i.e., God's purposes in this age *will be done*), nor can the postmillennialist be blind to the pessimism of other parables, e.g., the Enemy who sows darnel. Premillennialism does not require *ex hypothesi* that leaven means evil (though most premillennialists interpret it that way),[21] nor that the Hid Treasure is Israel, nor that the

---

[20]For example, with reference to leaven note the remarks of Findlay, *Jesus and His Parables*, p. 24; Smith, *op. cit.*, p. 121, and Oesterley, *op. cit.*, pp. 78-79.

[21]Oesterley notes that this parable really shocked the listeners, as to them leaven was uniformly associated with evil. Hence to compare the kingdom of God to leaven would be most improper. *Op. cit.*, p. 78.

Pearl is the Church. Millennial views are established on broader grounds than these.

BIBLIOGRAPHY

Angus and Green, *Cyclopedic Handbook to the Bible*, p. 220 ff.

Arndt, *The Parables of our Lord Interpreted and Illustrated.*

Bowie, "The Parables," *The Interpreter's Bible*, 7:165–175.

Barry, "Parables," *The Catholic Encyclopedia*, XI, 460–467.

Cadoux, *The Parables of Jesus, Their Art and Use.*

Dodd, *The Parables of the Kingdom* (third edition).

Findlay, *Jesus and His Parables.*

Godet, "Parables," *The New Schaff-Herzog Encyclopedia of Religious Knowledge*, III, 1739.

Habershon, *The Study of Parables.*

Hope, "The Interpretation of Christ's Parables," *Interpretation*, 6:301–307, July, 1952.

Horne, *Introduction to the Critical Study and Knowledge of the Holy Scriptures* (eighth edition), I, 366 ff.

Jeremias, *The Parables of Jesus.*

Jülicher, *Die Gleichnisreden Jesu* (1899–1910).

Kirk, *Lectures on the Parables.*

Manson (William), *Jesus the Messiah.*

Morgan, *The Parables and Metaphors of our Lord.*

Moule, "J. Jeremias 'The Parables of Jesus' and 'The Eucharistic Words of Jesus,'" *The Expository Times*, 66:46–50, November, 1954.

Moulton, "Parables," *Dictionary of Christ and the Gospels*, II, 313.

Nourse, "Parables," *Hastings Encyclopedia of Religion and Ethics*, IX, 628.

Oesterley, *The Gospel Parables in the Light of Their Jewish Background.*

Plumptre, "Parables," *Smith's Bible Dictionary*, III, 2327.

Schodde, "Parable," *The International Standard Bible Encyclopedia*, IV, 2243.

Smith (B.T.D.), *The Parables of the Synoptic Gospels.*

Cf. Allis, "The Parable of the Leaven," *The Evangelical Quarterly*, 19:254–273, October, 1947 for a thorough examination of the Old Testament usage of the word *leaven*.

Taylor, *The Parables of Our Savior*.

Terry, *Biblical Hermeneutics*, p. 188 ff.

Trench, *Notes on the Parables of Our Lord* (twelfth edition).

Wallace, "The Parables and the Preacher," *The Scottish Journal of Theology*, 2:13–28, March, 1949.

Westphal, "Some Notes on the Parables," *Crozer Quarterly*, 5:184–199, April, 1928.

Williams, "Jesus Method of Interpreting Parables," *Review and Expositor*, 14:210–222, April, 1917.

Zenos, "Parables," *A New Standard Bible Dictionary*, p. 697.

Feldman, *The Parables and Similes of the Rabbis*.

EPILOGUE

THE whole system of Conservative Protestant Christianity rests unreservedly on special revelation and the divine inspiration of Scripture. In that the message of God has meaning only when interpreted, it is ever incumbent upon the church to reflect and inquire if she has rightly interpreted the Word of God. A system of hermeneutics is crucial to our theology.

It has been the spirit of this work to endeavor to present a system of hermeneutics that would most faithfully uncover the native meaning of the Sacred Scripture. We have surveyed both the fields of general and special hermeneutics, and have given lists of many principles. Such lists are as good only as the training, intelligence, and ability of the interpreter, and the tools he uses. It is the solemn duty of every interpreter to see if these rules are correct and to equip himself with training and tools to do adequately the task of a faithful interpreter.

There is a prevailing danger to let differences in interpretation interrupt the unity of the Spirit. When differences are sharp, feelings are apt to run high. With foreboding storm clouds of oppression billowing on the distant horizon, it is well for conservative Protestantism to discover bases of fellowship rather than of divergence. If we stand together in the great truths of the Trinity, of Jesus Christ, and of Salvation, let us then work out our interpretative differences in the bounds of Christian love and endeavor to *preserve* the unity of the Spirit. A hermeneutical victory at the expense of Christian graciousness is hardly worth winning.

Finally, we all need a new sense of respect for Holy

Scripture. Believing it to be the veritable word of God, we must exercise all the human pains possible to keep from overlaying it with a gossamer pattern of our own spinning. In each of those cases where human error enters, divine truth is obscured. Let us then steer a straight course through the Holy Bible, neither turning to the left side of heresy nor to the right side of unbridled imagination.

Every interpreter, from the professional philologist to the Sunday school teacher, can well take to heart the following words of Barrows:

Foremost among the qualities that belong to the interpreter is *a supreme regard for truth.* . . . He will need a constant and vivid apprehension of the sacredness of all truth, more especially of scriptural truth, which God has revealed for the sanctification and salvation of men. "Sanctify them through thy truth: thy word is truth." These words of the Savior he will do well to ponder night and day, till they become a part of his spiritual life; and to remember always that, if such be the divine origin and high office of scriptural truth, God will not hold guiltless any who tamper with it in the interest of preconceived human opinions, thus substituting the folly of man for the wisdom of God.[1]

[1] *Companion to the Bible,* p. 522. Italics are his.

INDEX OF NAMES

Abrahams, 48 fn., 151
Alford, 13
Althaus, 147
Angus and Green, 13, 14
Aquinas, 40
Aristobulus, 26
Augustine, 34 ff., 104,
  theory of signs, 34 f.

Bacon, 101
Bales, 254
Barrows, 7, 15
Barth, 69, 85, 109, 110, 112, 138,
  144, 148, 161
Bauer, 128
Bengel, 61
Berkhof, 243
Bewer, 65
Broadus, 102, 198, 199
Brunner, 73, 99
Bultmann, 83 ff., 108, 109, 110,
  115

Calvin, 57 ff., 110, 116, 118
Capella, 149
Capp, 274
Chafer, 243
Clement, 31
Coburn, 135
Cocceius, 218
Collingwood, 90
Craven, 121
Crockett, 142

Danielou, 31 ff.
Davidson, 229, 244, 254, 255,
Deissmann, 94, 134
Dodd, 276, 283, 284
Dods, 12, 29

Eichrodt, 77

Ernesti, 59
Ezra, 46

Faber, 171
Fairbairn, 218fn., 249, 255
Farrar, 26, 49 f., 51
Feinberg, 258
Fosdick, 65, 66, 77, 102
Francke, 60
Fullerton, 30, 31

Gilbert, 48 fn., 50
Girdlestone, 132, 244, 247, 250,
  255
Glassius, 219
Goodwin, 143

Harnack, 67
Heidegger, 87 ff., 91
Hegel, 69, 109
Henderson, 17
Hillel, 46
Hodge, 173, 182
Hofmann, 79 ff.
Horne, 107, 121
Humphry, 39
Hutchinson, 218

Jeremias, 282
Jerome, 33 f.
Jewett, 222, 224
Johnson, 253

Kant, 69
Kierkegaard, 75, 78, 109
Kittel, 128, 134, 272
Kuyper, 131, 169

Leo XIII, 45
Lindsay, 98

Luther, 53 ff., 98, 109, 110, 116, 118

Maas, 212, 213
Marsh, 219
Moltmann, 274
Morris, 131

Newman, 41, 45, 106, 165
Niebuhr, 99

Oepke, 77
Origen, 31 f.

Parsons, 107, 110
Pelikan, 61 fn.
Philo, 27 f.
Piper, 66 fn., 80 ff.

Quintilian, 149

Richardson, 134
Riddle, 50 fn.
Roberts, 267
Robertson, A., 258, 271
Robertson, A. T., 17

Rowley, 15, 96, 107, 154

Sampey, 17
Schone, 130
Seisenberger, 100
Semler, 101
Shakespeare, 3
Smalley, 51, 52
Smith, 17
Smyth, 201
Spener, 60

Taylor, 179
Terry, 23, 220
Tillich, 100, 110, 115
Torm, 108, 225

Visscher, 273

Warfield, 138
White, 3
Wolfson, 26, 224

Young, 138

Zimmerli, 274

INDEX OF SCRIPTURE

GENESIS
  1—11   156
  3:15   251

EXODUS
  23:19   204
  24:17   143

LEVITICUS
  11:44-45   117

NUMBERS
  25:9   206

I SAMUEL
  13:1   206

II SAMUEL
  7:    252

I KINGS
  7:23   206
  17:1   251
  21:17 ff.   251

II CHRONICLES
  9:25   206

PSALMS
  16:    252
  22:    252

ISAIAH
  7:14-15   252
  7:16   252
  12:21   246
  53:    252
  60:    212

JEREMIAH
  3:12   250

  18:8, 10   250
  26:12-13   250

EZEKIEL
  18:30-32   250
  33:13-15   250

DANIEL
  11:    246

HOSEA
  7:8   143
  11:    246

OBADIAH
  10-14   246

JONAH
  3:4   250

NAHUM
  1:    212

HABAKKUK
  1:4   181
  1:5-6   253

ZECHARIAH
  1:1-6   250
  1:7-21   250
  5:5-11   251
  14:    244

MALACHI
  3:14   181

MATTHEW
  2:5-6   262
  2:15   230
  5:    207
  5:17   259

5:29, 30	189	7:16	164
5:41	134	7:17	164
5:48	118	12:1 ff.	191
6:10	183	13:23-23	156
6:30	156	21:18-19	192
7:28	164	21:25	143
13:11-17	277		
13:18 ff.	283	ACTS	
18:9	132	1:8	195
18:21	189	1:13	156
20:21	132	9:	207
21:	207	9:10-19	207
21:31	280	13:21	206
22:32, 43-44	262	13:37 ff.	248
25:1 ff.	156, 281	17:	156
25:13	283	18:9-10	193
25:14 ff.	281	22:	207
		22:12-16	207
MARK		ROMANS	
1:2	203	1—3	106
4:10-12	277	2:29	265
4:34	270	3:	141
6:18	183	4:	229
9:47	132	4:22-24	229
10:37	132	6:17	164
		7:	140
LUKE		8:1	183
1:2	195	8:4	183
2:36-38	106	10:18	262
4:21	259	15:4	262
6:	207		
8:8	277	I CORINTHIANS	
8:8-10	277	5:7	265
11:24	188	7:5	188
14:25	284	9:9	265
16:14	284	10:4	277
17:20-21	281	10:6, 11	262
		10:8	206
JOHN		12:13	206, 234
1:1, 14	167	15:	141
1:13	211	15:5	203
2:	207	15:29	105
2:6	156		
3:3	280	II CORINTHIANS	
3:7	113	2:6	176
5:	106	3:1	265
5:39	259	3:6	35
5:39-44	217	3:3-16	265
6:45	262	4:6	263, 265

GALATIANS
2:11	191
4:24	226
5:22-23	188
6:16	263

EPHESIANS
2:11	265
4:14	164
5:1	118
5:18	234
5:26	234

PHILIPPIANS
2:	141
3:3	265

COLOSSIANS
2:11	265
2:20	188
2:21	188

II THESSALONIANS
2:3	179

I TIMOTHY
2:9	189
3:2	197
5:17	196

II TIMOTHY
2:2	196
3:15	180
3:16	112, 129
3:15-17	96
3:16-17	164, 180, 185

HEBREWS
1:1-2	103
2:	140
2:13	230
3:1	263
4:4	263
5:7	134

5:11	203
6:4	263
8:9	265
9:	229
9:8-11, 23-24	217
9:28	249
10:	141, 229, 264
10:15-17	264
11:	229
11:3	212
11:6	263
12:20	262
12:22	263
13:10-12	266
13:13	266
13:14	266
13:15	266

JAMES
3:1	182

I PETER
1:6	117
1:10	234
1:10-12	249
1:11	267
2:24	106
2:25	234
5:1	196, 234
5:8	234

II PETER
1:6	117
1:10	203
1:20	269
3:	207
3:16	203

REVELATION
1:15	236
2:	194
3:	194
20:	141
22:18	193

INDEX OF TOPICS

Accommodation, 67, 99
  and liberalism, 67
Allegorical schools, 24 ff.
  Augustinian, 35
  Criticized, 29
  Greek, 24 f.
  Jewish, 25 f.
  Patristic, 28 f.
  Philonian, 27 f.
Allegory, 111
Amillennialism, 257 f.
Analogy of faith
  Augustine, 36
  Luther, 55 f.
Apocalypse and interpretation, 268 ff.

Biblical history, 154
Bibliography
  doctrinal, 183 f.
  exegetical, 19 ff.
  general, 161 f.
  historical, 92
  inerrancy and science, 214
  parables, 287 f.
  practical use of Bible, 200
  prophecy, 275
  typology, 240

Canon, 7
Catholicism, 38 ff.
  allegorism, 38 ff.
Christological principle
  Luther, 56
  neo-orthodoxy, 72
  prophecy, 267
Church, responsibility of interpretation, 181
Clarity of Scripture, 97
Commentaries, 18 f.
Context, 138

Contradictions, 205 ff., 213 f.
Critical principle, 84, 90
Cross reference, 140
Cults, 111
Culture and exegesis, 5, 149 ff., 189
  parables, 281 f.
  revelation, 211 f.

Demythological-existential principle, 87
Devotional schools, Chapter VII
  criticized, 62 f.
  modern emphasis, 62
  mystics, 60
  Spener and Francke, 60
Dialectical principle, 88
Divination, 194
Doctrine and parables, 285

Edification, 96
Education and the interpreter, 14 f.
Equipment of the interpreter, 16 ff.
Existential principle, 75

Fathers, 43
Figures of speech, 143
Form-criticism, 85

Geography, 153
Grammar, 136

Heilsgeschichtliche school, 79 ff.
Hermeneutic principle, 90
Hermeneutics
  defined, 10
  history of, Chapter II

need for, 1 f., 4 f.
New, 83 ff.
Protestant System, Chapters III, IV, V
Historical criticism, 9
Historical interpretation and liberalism, 68
Holy Spirit, 13
  illumination of, 18

Inerrancy, Chapter VIII
Inspiration, 93 ff.
  liberalism, 64
  neo-orthodoxy, 75 f.
Interpreter, qualifications, 12

Jewish literalism, 45 f.
Journals, expository, 17

Karaites, 46
Kingdom, 279 ff.

Language, 4 f.
  principle, 91
Latin Vulgate, 39
Law principle, 89
Letterism, 47, 49
Liberal interpretation, 63 ff., 174
Literal
  exegesis, 167
    Catholicism, 40
  interpretation, 119 ff.
  mold or genre, 142
  schools, 45 ff.
    Jewish, 45 f.
    Post Reformation, 59 f.
    Reformers, 51 f.
    Syrian, 48 f.
    Victorines, 51

Millennialism, 255 ff.
Mythological principle, 86
Mythology, 74

Neo-orthodoxy, 69 ff., 109, 165, 174

Numbers, 36, 235 ff.
  usage, 202
Parables, Chapter XI
Patristic exegesis, 31 ff.
Pattern view, 274
Perspective, 109
Phenomenal language, 210
Philological principle, 113 ff.
Philosophy and theology, 169
Pietism, 60, 111
Practical interpretation, Chapter VII
Preaching and interpretation, 195 ff.
Premillennialism, 255, 256
Progressive revelation, 101
Promises, 192 ff.
Promise view, 274
Proof texts, 175 f.
Prophecy, Chapter X
  fulfilment, 251
  terminology, 241 ff.
  typology, 258
Protestant Method of Hermeneutics, 97

Repristination view, 273
Revelation
  neo-orthodoxy, 70 f.

Science and interpretation, Chapter VIII
Scientific principle, 84
Scripture interprets Scripture, 104
Spiritual exegesis and Catholicism, 41 f.
Symbols, 233 ff.
Syrian school, 48 f.
System and theology, 172
Systematic theology, 108

Terminology, Confusion of, 241
Textual criticism, 8, 208 f.
  and theology, 183
Theological perspectives, 97 ff.

Translation, 5
Typology, Chapter IX
  allegorical interpretation, 221 ff.
  and prophecy, 258 ff.
  schools of, 218 ff.
Typological interpretation
  Origen, 33

Unity of Bible, 174 f.

Verbal inspiration, 126

Word study, 128 ff.